CATASTROPHIZING

CATASTROPHIZING

Materialism and the Making of Disaster

GERARD PASSANNANTE

The University of Chicago Press
CHICAGO & LONDON

The University of Chicago Press, Chicago 60637
The University of Chicago Press, Ltd., London
© 2019 by The University of Chicago
All rights reserved. No part of this book may be used or reproduced
in any manner whatsoever without written permission, except in the
case of brief quotations in critical articles and reviews. For more
information, contact the University of Chicago Press, 1427 East 60th
Street, Chicago, IL 60637.
Published 2019
Printed in the United States of America

28 27 26 25 24 23 22 21 20 19   1 2 3 4 5

ISBN-13: 978-0-226-61221-8 (cloth)
ISBN-13: 978-0-226-61235-5 (e-book)
DOI: https://doi.org/10.7208/chicago/9780226612355.001.0001

This publication is made possible in part from the Barr Ferree Foundation Fund
for Publications, Department of Art and Archaeology, Princeton University.

Library of Congress Cataloging-in-Publication Data
Names: Passannante, Gerard Paul, 1978– author.
Title: Catastrophizing : materialism and the making of disaster / Gerard Passannante.
Description: Chicago : The University of Chicago Press, 2019. | Includes bibliographical
    references and index.
Identifiers: LCCN 2018036448 | ISBN 9780226612218 (cloth : alk. paper) |
    ISBN 9780226612355 (ebook)
Subjects: LCSH: Catastrophizing. | Catastrophical, The. | Catastrophical, The, in art. |
    Catastrophical, The, in literature.
Classification: LCC BD375 .P37 2019 | DDC 146/.3—dc23
LC record available at https://lccn.loc.gov/2018036448

FOR DAVID CARROLL SIMON

CONTENTS

List of Illustrations *ix*

INTRODUCTION Catastrophizing: A Beginner's Guide 1
ONE Leonardo's Disasters 27
TWO Earthquakes of the Mind 79
THREE Shakespeare's Catastrophic "Anything" 114
FOUR The Earthquake and the Microscope 147
FIVE Disaster before the Sublime; or, Kant's Catastrophes 192
AFTERWORD Catastrophizing in the Age of Climate Change 236

Acknowledgments 245
Bibliography 249
Index 279

ILLUSTRATIONS

PLATES (FOLLOWING PAGE 86)

1. Leonardo da Vinci, "A deluge" (ca. 1517–18)
2. Leonardo da Vinci, "A tempest" (ca. 1517–18)
3. Leonardo da Vinci, "A tempest" (ca. 1517–18) (detail)
4. Leonardo da Vinci, "A deluge" (ca. 1517–18)
5. Leonardo da Vinci, "A deluge" (ca. 1517–18)

FIGURES

1. Leonardo da Vinci, "Fable, prophecy" (ca. 1500)   40
2. Hagop Sandaldjian, "Eternal Symbol (Mount Ararat)" (ca. 1986) 148
3. Athanasius Kircher, "System of Subterranean Fire" (1620)   151
4. Robert Hooke, "Ammonite fossils" (1705)   168
5. Anon., "Fürstellung des Erdbebens zu Lissabon" (1756)   215
6. After Jacques Philippe Le Bas, "Basilica de Santa Maria" (1755)   216
7. Johann Michael Roth, "Lisbon before and after" (1756)   218
8. Johan Henricus Giese, Tobacco box
   (late eighteenth century)   219

INTRODUCTION

Catastrophizing: A Beginner's Guide

Catastrophizing is at once something the mind does to itself and a thing that befalls it. It is a way of seeing and feeling beyond the world of the sensible. When I use the word "catastrophize" in this book, I am drawing upon the increasingly familiar sense of the word (a habit of leaping to the worst possible conclusion, of making something of nothing), but I am also seeking to recover the philosophical and affective history of the making of disaster in the early modern mind.[1] In these pages, "catastrophizing" refers to the imaginative and often involuntary creation of speculative disasters as an expression of and response to materialist philosophies and forms of explanation.

That the catastrophist, whose making of disaster can sometimes feel like superstition, and the materialist, whose reasoning aims to debunk superstitious thoughts, have something in common might at first seem counterintuitive. The best-known of the ancient proselytizers of materialism, Epicurus and Lucre-

---

1. The word "catastrophize" first makes its appearance in the modern lexicon of therapy and self-help in the early 1960s with the advent of cognitive behavioral therapy. See Ellis, *Reason and Emotion in Psychotherapy*, 71: "More specifically, he should perceive his own tendency to catastrophize about inevitable unfortunate situations—to tell himself: 'Oh, my Lord! How terrible this situation is; I positively cannot stand it!'" OED *Online*, s.v. "catastrophize, *v.*" Like me, Ellis is interested in an ancient inheritance, tracing his psychological theories back to philosophers such as Seneca and Epictetus. Ellis, *Reason and Emotion in Psychotherapy*, 64.

tius, advertise peace of mind, or *ataraxia*, as the primary benefit of their philosophy. To grasp the physics of atoms and the void, we are told, is to free oneself from the tyranny of superstition and fear that holds men in thrall to institutions—and to their own dark thoughts.[2] Stephen Greenblatt takes up this ancient prescription in *The Swerve: How the World Became Modern* (2011), which opens with the story of the author's mother, whose "obsessive fear" of dying prefaces his own discovery of Lucretius, poet and philosopher of emotional tranquility.[3] Yet the experience of materialist thought is never very far from the potentially frightening business of imagining ends or limits—what Andrea Nightingale has called "materialist eschatology."[4] Nor is it far from compulsion. As we will see, the making of catastrophe is both a vehicle by which materialism aims to represent the world and the most telling symptom of the malady it sometimes becomes.

Materialism is a way of knowing that carries the mind from the world of the sensible to the insensible, reaching for physical principles that render the notion of intention or divine agency unnecessary. It relies on the assumption that the mind might arrive at the hidden world of matter by means of its own devices—that is, by the joint effort of reason and sensory perception. Its paradigmatic form is atomism, which begins with our experience and bounds precipitously toward a basic unit or conceptual minimum.[5]

2. Epicurus defines pleasure, the chief end of his philosophy, as "the absence of pain in the body [*aponia*] and of trouble in the soul [*ataraxia*]." Epicurus, "Letter to Menoeceus," in Diogenes Laertius, *Lives* 10.131.

3. Greenblatt, *Swerve*, 5.

4. See Nightingale, "Night-Vision," 77: "The *eschata* can be completely physical. Lucretius, I suggest, offers a materialist eschatology: he depicts a journey beyond the human world into a 'distant,' nonhuman region constituted solely by material atoms and void."

5. While the tradition of Epicurean atomism embraces skepticism about the nature of particular causes (in an infinite universe a phenomenon may have any number of them), it is dogmatic about the atom and the void. See

When we talk about materialism in early modernity, we are usually talking about a school of philosophical thought—a system and a method. One is *initiated* into atomist thought—one *becomes* an Epicurean (and often not without difficulty). As we'll see, however, the mind's rush to the ground of experience need not always be a deliberate exercise. In moments, it may even elude conscious attention altogether, occurring seemingly on its own and as if by necessity.[6] Epicurus says that the atomic images or *simulacra* constantly streaming from bodies are "as quick as thought," which tells us something about both the speed of the particles traveling to our eyes and what it is like to think about them.[7] For some early moderns, I will argue, the experience of materialism did not involve the deliberate adoption of a philosophical paradigm or an intellectual commitment but was instead a reflexive style or habit of thought.

To speak of materialism in these terms is to consider its form as well as its content, and to look at the tradition in terms of what it does in addition to what it claims to do. It is to pay attention to the distinct shape of images and the feelings they elicit—and to understand the making of images itself as a form of argument.[8] It is finally to acknowledge the simple fact that

---

Epicurus's discussion in the *Letter to Herodotus* and *Letter to Pythocles* in Diogenes Laertius, *Lives* 10.78–79 and 10.86 respectively. See also Lucretius, *De rerum natura* 5.526–33 and 6.703–11. All references to Lucretius follow the Loeb edition unless otherwise noted.

6. In his nineteenth-century history of materialism, Friedrich Albert Lange hinted at the way the logic of atomism might present itself in the guise of a necessity: "For so long as men started at all from the external objects of the phenomenal world, this was *the only way* of explaining the enigmatical from the plain, the complex from the simple, and the unknown from the known." Lange, *History of Materialism*, 1:14 (emphasis mine).

7. Diogenes Laertius, *Lives* 10.48. See Deleuze, *Logic of Sense*, 269.

8. In *The Lucretian Renaissance*, I draw upon Arthur Lovejoy's concept of "metaphysical pathos" to describe the sympathetic response of some early modern readers to the poetry of Lucretius. Passannante, *Lucretian Renaissance*, 9. In a thought-provoking meditation on the influence of Empedocles in the Renaissance, Drew Daniel also takes up Lovejoy's concept to explore the image

we are not always in control of our thoughts and that they do not always (and often cannot) unfold as self-conscious reflections in our minds or in the margins of our books. In reading for style rather than philosophical commitment, we may begin to discern the influence and circulation of materialism across a much wider range of texts and practices—even in cases that suggest a fundamental misreading, ironizing, or explicit rejection of the tradition. We may begin to speak of an *atomism without atoms*—that is, the circulation of materialist patterns of thought beneath the threshold of conscious awareness.[9]

My focus in this book is what I call "catastrophic materialism," which is characterized by the following features: a reasoning from the sensible to the insensible, a precipitous shift or collapse of scale and perspective, a temporal compression of beginning and end, and an act of imaginative making that feels paradoxically like the evacuation of agency. One need not be an atomist to be imaginatively invested in (or captured by) the form of a materialist thought or image—even when one can't accept its principles or finds them hard to believe. Materialism's critical potential, I will argue, lies less in its ability to persuade anyone of its positive truth (e.g., the existence of atoms) than in the ways it foregrounds the production of seemingly necessary thoughts that occur without our conscious participation—that is, the way it stages catastrophe.

But in what senses can we call materialism "catastrophic"? In antiquity, earthquakes were commonly imagined in mythological terms, as the Giants and the Titans trying to escape from

---

and affect of materialism. See "The Empedoclean Renaissance." My argument also resonates with the work of Amanda Jo Goldstein, for whom the "materialist mode" of figuration was a "live possibility" for romantic era writers such as Blake, Goethe and Shelley. See Goldstein, *Sweet Science*, 31.

9. Catherine Keller has similarly described the pervasive way the script of biblical apocalypse has played out in our own collective unconscious: "It drifts in the subliminal margins, not really inaccessible to awareness but not accountable to it. Keller, *Apocalypse Now and Then*, 8.

their underground prisons—a reminder of their violent challenge to the gods. These losers of Olympian history were then linked to the materialists in the ancient cosmological polemics of Plato and Aristotle.[10] Picking up on this tradition, Lucretius might be said to have predicted his own extended dormancy when he spoke of those who "believe it right that, like the Giants, all they should suffer punishment for a monstrous crime, who with their reasoning shake the walls of the world [*qui ratione sua disturbent moenia mundi*], and would quench the shining light of the sun in heaven, tarnishing things immortal with mortal speech."[11] Here, reasoning itself assumes the force of a catastrophe—a theme to which we will return throughout this book.

Disaster presents the mind with an occasion for questioning its most fundamental ideas about the world (e.g., the providential order of things, God's justice) and for speculating about the nature of hidden causes. At the same time, the image of disaster is also a gateway into the insensible world, an instrument of thought that makes visible hidden natural processes, and a figure of the experience of the passage into the imperceptible.[12] The ancients understood that the very thought of disaster might induce a sudden sense of relativism, obscuring the

10. Plato, *Sophist* 246a-b; Aristotle, *De philosophia*, fr. 18, in *Fragmenta Selecta*, 85–86. See Reiche, "Myth and Magic in Cosmological Polemics"; Bignone, *L'Aristotele perduto e la formazione filosofica di Epicuro*, 2:79–81; Gale, *Myth and Poetry in Lucretius*, 44–45.

11. Lucretius, *De rerum natura* 5.117–21.

12. Daniel Tiffany draws our attention to the "iconography" of materialist thought, which he finds in lyric poetry's meditation on toys and weather. He explains: "Thus *all* atomistic phenomena, including the weather, are susceptible, in theory to mechanical explanation—and, by analogy, to the principle of the toy." Tiffany, *Toy Medium*, 106. As Tiffany notes, "the fact that we *make* a doll or a machine, and that we are *visited* by 'meteors,' makes a great deal of difference to our conception of material reality and to the premises of realism" (182). My concern is with the making of disaster as an experience of thought—one that feels as if it had "visited" us.

distinction between the big and the small, confounding the living and the dead, and transforming our normal perception of time by collapsing past, present, and future.[13] We experience the imagined catastrophes of materialism as if they were happening *now*. That this sounds like a doomsday prophecy is not a coincidence. The seemingly autonomous violence of the materialist image closely links it with the idea of prophetic vision. While Epicurus, for example, famously argues against the practices of prophecy and divination (not to mention poetry), he describes his own philosophy in oracular terms.[14] Lucretius says he will utter his atomic prophecies about the end of the world with more certainty than the Delphic oracle.[15] His fulfillment of that promise will depend not only on scientific theory but also on poetry—a poetry that compels assent with the emotional impact of prophecy and induces an almost religious experience of possession, what he describes as a "divine delight" (*divina voluptas*) and a kind of "shuddering" (*horror*).[16]

The primary vehicle of the materialist's *horror* is analogy. In his discussion of Lucretius, Gian Biago Conte has hinted that materialist analogies have a strange capacity to think *ahead* of us (or *for* us): "Analogy is the structured form of thought that knows."[17] Consider one very common materialist example: dust particles in a beam of sunlight. From the mere sight of these particles, we may divine nothing less than a hidden world of atoms. Lucretius explains: "So far as it goes, a small

13. As Peter Fenves has put it in another context, "The equal eye makes everything equivalent: such is the catastrophe pure and simple." Fenves, *Peculiar Fate*, 63.

14. Vatican Sayings 29, in Long and Sedley, *Hellenistic Philosophers*, 155; Diogenes Laertius, *Lives* 10.12. See Clay, *Lucretius and Epicurus*, 49.

15. See Lucretius, *De rerum natura* 5.110–13.

16. See Lucretius, *De rerum natura* 3.28–30.

17. Conte, *Genres and Readers*, 13.

thing [*parva . . . res*] may give an analogy of great things [*rerum magnarum*], and show the tracks [*vestigia*] of knowledge."[18] The poet's dust here provides "tracks" in two senses of the word *vestigia*—footprints and footsteps—and the image is at once forward and backward looking, conjuring up a sight of "first-beginnings" but also predicting the future, a time when all composite bodies will be reduced to collisions of dust and atoms. When he speaks of "great things," Lucretius glances to phenomena on a larger scale, but the plural noun also evokes the "minute particles" (*multa minuta*) he has just been describing.[19] The ambiguity captures the blur of the thought. By the click and whirl of the analogy, "small" things collectively become "great" and flood the imagination. In this case, "catastrophe" serves as a name for the sudden collapse of perspectives as thought outpaces our capacity to manage it.

An early modern reader might have come upon the image of dust in sunlight in any number of familiar sources, including the works of Aristotle, the writings of the church father Lactantius, and the medieval encyclopedia of Isidore of Seville, to name only a few.[20] As a physical example, the figure was nearly always at hand. Wherever one got one's dust, what is remarkable is how easily the argument of the analogy unfolds *as an image* prior to any movement of the mind toward approval or disapproval—unless we want to say that the contemplation of this image is itself a kind of unwitting affirmation. In this case, materialism is less a deliberate thought than an experience of mental vision. As we contemplate the flux of the image, that most banal (if mesmerizing) of household spectacles gives way to a tumultuous picture of particulate worlds coming together

18. Lucretius, *De rerum natura* 2.123–24.

19. Lucretius, *De rerum natura* 2.116.

20. Aristotle, *On the Soul* 404a; Lucretius, *De rerum natura* 2.112–24; Lactantius, *Works*, 22:15; and Isidore of Seville, *Etymologies*, 271.

and apart.[21] As Lactantius asks with this very analogy in mind, "What force [*vis*] of atoms had been so great that masses so incalculable should be collected from such minute elements?"[22] He no doubt means the question rhetorically, but the real "force" of atoms might be understood as the latent force of the *idea* of them.[23]

Lactantius's question calls to mind our more familiar sense of catastrophizing—how even the smallest or most inconsequential of things might set the mind into motion and also how precipitously such a frenzy might befall you. Who is invulnerable to such thoughts? In *De natura deorum*, Cicero suggests that not even the Epicurean gods enjoyed that privilege: "And yet I can't see how this happy god of yours is not to fear destruction, since he is subjected without a moment's respite to the buffeting and jostling of a horde of atoms that eternally assail him, while from his own person a ceaseless stream of images is given off. Your god is therefore neither happy nor eternal."[24] Instead of producing a state of *ataraxia*, the very idea of atoms produces the violent thought of an ending. Reversing the Epicurean imperative to be like the gods in their serenity, the gods themselves become catastrophizers.

21. As P. H. Schrijvers explains, what appears at first as an ordinary kind of analogy is revealed as itself "a manifestation of . . . the atomic processes and forces which it illustrates." Schrijvers, "Seeing the Invisible," 256.

22. Lactantius, *Works*, 22:15; *Opera omnia*, 27:86. Lactantius's example here is the philosopher Leucippus, who is said to have been the first Greek atomist and teacher of Democritus. On Lactantius's views on Epicureanism, see Hagendahl, *Latin Fathers and the Classics*, 48–52.

23. The word *vis* in this context echoes Lactantius's anxieties about the dangerous powers of rhetoric. As Hans Blumenberg explains, glossing the church father's words from another context, "The philosophers have at their disposal the incredible force of eloquence (*incredibilis vis eloquentiae*); a power that is 'pernicious and weighty for the disturbing of the truth.'" That something so "pernicious and weighty" could be so entirely insubstantial was cause for concern. Blumenberg, *Paradigms for a Metaphorology*, 37. See Lactantius, *De opificio dei*, in *Opera omnia*, 27:63; *Works*, 22:91.

24. Cicero, *De natura deorum* 1.41. Cf. Augustine, *Epistulae*, 34/2:693.

Historically, what I am calling the compulsion or reflex of catastrophic materialism has been described in many ways—as an illness or madness (caused, for example, by melancholy), a form of idolatry, a *furor* or an enthusiasm, a kind of vatic seeing, and a bad habit. Materialism, of course, was not the only philosophical tradition that threatened to seize control of the mind. In the *Republic*, Plato imagines the man who has escaped the cave being "compelled" to look at the light and being "drag[ged]" up a steep hill toward the truth.[25] Materialism was also not the only tradition that conjured up images of disaster. Lucretius himself describes skepticism about sense perception in decidedly catastrophic terms—as a shaking of the foundation.[26] One possible outcome of this book is that, by examining indirect forms of influence and compulsion in the history of materialism, it will also suggest new avenues of interpretation in other philosophical traditions—though this book can only hint at the bearing of the catastrophic on other histories.

With an eye on materialism in particular, my focus will be the reflexivity that often attends disastrous thinking—the way catastrophic materialism both employs coercive tropes and draws attention to the mind's making of such images. In staging and observing its own disasters, catastrophic materialism might even be said to contain within itself the possibility of a self-conscious philosophical anthropology. By pressing beyond the limits of sense perception in pursuit of adequate causal explanations over which the mind is supposed to establish dominion, materialist thought raises a distinctive set of questions about the mind's extravagant motion.

The word "catastrophe" refers technically to the ending or resolution of a dramatic plot (the dénouement). It begins to assume its modern sense through the reception of ancient

25. Plato, *Republic* 515e–516a.
26. See Lucretius, *De rerum natura* 4.507–8: "For not only would all reasoning come to ruin, but life itself would at once collapse, unless you make bold to believe the senses."

drama and an attention to the word's biblical usage in the six-teenth century.[27] As we'll see, this sense is further inflected by a renewed anxiety about materialist philosophy and an insistence on the meaningfulness of celestial signs that were said to portend the end of the world. Catastrophe (etymologically, κατά "down" + στρέφειν "to turn") is an end that we fashion and a thing we undergo. In this sense, the word might shed a light on another kind of "downturn." For Epicureans, we recall, the *clinamen* or swerve—the sudden turn of an atom from the vertical line of its descent through the abyss—is described as the physical guarantee of free will. This is one reason why the swerve has become an emblem of modernity. At the same time, this material aspect of our free will presents us with a paradox, for the swerve is also a figure of compulsion and involuntariness that reframes the question of what it means to be modern. In the place of an all-knowing deity, we generate the idea of the swerve and then feel its catastrophe as a logical necessity (a thing without which the system suddenly seems unthinkable).[28] Emerging seemingly out of nowhere, what amounts to the slightest deviation that one can imagine ("just so much as you might call a change in motion") is both the beginning of a world and a prophecy of its end.[29]

"STRANGE AND MONSTROUS FIGURES"

In his early essay, *Paradigms for a Metaphorology* (1960), Hans Blumenberg explains how metaphorology "aims to show with

27. See Schenk, "Historical Disaster Experiences," 20–23; Rosen, *Dislocating the End*, 6–11.
28. See Serres, *Birth of Physics*, 83: "The *clinamen* is the infinitesimal turbulence, first, *but it is also the passage from theory to practice*. And once again, without it, we understand nothing of what goes on." On Serres's reading of Lucretius, see Holmes, "Michel Serres's Non-Modern Lucretius."
29. Lucretius, *De rerum natura* 2.220.

what 'courage' the mind preempts itself in its images, and how its history is projected in the courage of its conjectures."[30] The mind reaches forward, as if on its own, responding with images to the theoretical questions it can neither answer nor ignore.[31] In his later work, *Shipwreck with Spectator*, Blumenberg traces the lives of one particular image, the Lucretian figure of the spectator looking upon others suffering at sea, "not because any man's troubles are a delectable joy, but because to perceive what ills you are free from yourself is pleasant."[32] For Lucretius, the image is of the Epicurean casting his gaze over those who do not yet know the truth of his philosophy. To live in a state of superstition and fear is to be *in* the disaster. For Blumenberg, the scene is also self-reflexive: "What the spectator enjoys is not the sublimity of the objects his theory opens up for him but his own self-consciousness, over against the whirl of atoms [*Atomwirbel*] out of which everything that he observes is constituted, including himself."[33] But if the philosopher is right to read this famous passage in *De rerum natura* as an allegory of the mind's encounter with itself, perhaps he is too quick to arrive at the safety and abstraction of the spectator, leaving the "whirl" in the background of thought.

In other words, Blumenberg directs our attention to the mind's victory over the violence of nature—what Kant would later call the sublime, himself drawing upon the affective lessons of Epicurus and Lucretius. As the mind comes to know that

30. Blumenberg, *Paradigms for a Metaphorology*, 4.

31. As Blumenberg explains, such figures, what he calls "absolute metaphors, "'answer' the supposedly naïve, in principle unanswerable questions whose relevance lies quite simply in the fact that they cannot be brushed aside, since we do not *pose* them ourselves but find them already *posed* in the ground of our existence." Blumenberg, *Paradigms for a Metaphorology*, 14.

32. Lucretius, *De rerum natura* 2.3–4. For Blumenberg's changing ideas about the uses of metaphorology, see Blumenberg, "Prospect for a Theory of Nonconceptuality," in *Shipwreck with Spectator*, 81–102.

33. Blumenberg, *Shipwreck with Spectator*, 26; *Schiffbruch mit Zuschauer*, 28.

even an earthquake is nothing in the great scheme of things, the thought of catastrophe is dedramatized (brought down to scale) and thus properly vanquished.[34] But catastrophizing does not always have such a clear ethical purpose or motive. As an involuntary reflex, it may not have a conscious motive at all. The history of catastrophizing teaches us that the experience of materialism is a highly contingent one—dependent on how (under what material and intellectual conditions) it unfolds.[35] Not everyone was vulnerable in the same way to the "whirl." Nor was its outcome always a state of serene abstraction or pleasure. As a thing that befalls us, catastrophizing reflects the contingency of thought itself.

Let us compare two examples from roughly the same moment in the seventeenth century, chronologically the middle of our story. Both make explicit the patterns of thought that characterize catastrophic materialism but suggest very different responses to it. Instructively, both direct us to mental reflex rather than considered and stable opinion. The first is from the English poet and philosopher Margaret Cavendish, who gives us an account of trying on Epicurean materialism for size— whereupon, she explains,

> the infinite Atoms made such a mist, that it quite blinded the perception of her mind; neither was she able to make a Vacuum as a receptacle for those Atoms, or a place which they might retire into; so that partly for the want of it, and of a good order and method, the confusion of those Atoms produced such strange and monstrous figures, as did more affright then delight her, and caused such a Chaos in her mind, as had almost dissolved it.[36]

34. See, for example, Lucretius's domesticating analogy at *De rerum natura* 6.546–51.
35. For the contingency of mood in the history of science and in literary studies, see, in general, Simon, *Light without Heat*.
36. Cavendish, *Blazing World*, 187.

Addressed to the culture of the new science, Cavendish's satire suggests that atomism does not free the mind from fiction (as it is supposed to do) but rather stuns and paralyzes the mind with fictions of its own. The disparity between small things such as atoms and the overwhelming feeling of catastrophe may feel like physical comedy, but it is only funny in retrospect. As Cavendish attests, barely escaping her dizzying encounter with atoms, sometimes merely entertaining an idea is enough to find oneself entranced and defeated by it.

Disaster lends expression to the feeling of necessity that the mind conjures up in the search for a conceptual ground. The mind suddenly generates and reacts to the disasters it has made as if they were substantial, testing its certainty against this feeling of danger, which appears to arise before there is time for conscious thought and as if it came from outside.[37] The "whirl" now moves into the foreground and briefly threatens to overwhelm the frame. In this case, however, the spectator of catastrophe awakens—not to the truth of atoms but to the mind's power to generate fictions in order to make contact with the imperceptible (to experience the imperceptible as an event of thought). For Cavendish, who tries on several different philosophical perspectives in the *Blazing World*, attention to the mind's creative powers authorizes her own sui generis philosophical fictions, suggesting a different kind of freedom.

In its precipitous evocation of disproportion and disorientation, Cavendish's encounter with the *Atomwirbel* calls to mind a more familiar mental earthquake—that of the philosopher and mathematician Blaise Pascal. Yet, unlike Cavendish, Pascal was seeking to *induce* a catastrophic response in his reader (and in himself), even giving us a set of instructions on how to work

---

37. Gian Biago Conte has described the compulsive force of this kind of image making as a "*Phantasia*," which "can then define a reality rendered almost objective in the moment that it appears (the clear evidence of what is imagined)." Conte, *Genres and Readers*, 17.

ourselves into a lather.[38] Here is one of them: "Let him [man] examine the most delicate things he knows. A mite with its miniscule body shows him incomparably more minute parts, legs with joints, veins in its legs, blood in its veins, humors in this blood, drops in the humors, vapors in these drops."[39] Pascal is closely following an atomist example. Without the advantage of a microscope, Lucretius had suggested a similar thought experiment: "Firstly, there are some living creatures so small that their third part cannot possibly be seen. What must you suppose one of their guts is like? the ball of the heart, or the eyes? the limbs and members? How small are they? What further of the first-beginnings which must compose the nature of their mind and spirit? Do you not see how fine and how minute they are?"[40] But whereas the Epicurean poet suddenly arrives at "the first-beginnings" of things, Pascal's journey is endless. As he writes of the observer of the "mite," "I want to make him see a new abyss in there."[41]

Pascal is both a catastrophizer and a student of catastrophizing, observing how little coaxing the mind needs once set into motion.[42] Simply to think of an insect's tiny parts is to gaze into the "abyss"—or, more precisely, into both of them: "Who-

38. As Matthew L. Jones argues, Pascal was responding to the lack of proper amazement in the face of nature's vastness, and an overconfidence in man's capacity to know: "New natural philosophies, using new forms of observation, had undermined traditional views of the natural world. In all but a few observers, these new philosophies had perversely failed to undermine the self-satisfaction and deceptive certainty accompanying those traditional views." Jones, *Good Life*, 138.

39. Pascal, *Pensées*, 60.

40. Lucretius, *De rerum natura* 4.116–22. On the frequent use of this image by seventeenth-century philosophers, including Pierre Gassendi, see Meinel, "Early Seventeenth-Century Atomism," 76.

41. Pascal, *Pensées*, 59.

42. In his study of the concept of the baroque, Christopher D. Johnson describes a number of "Baroque hyperbolist[s]," including Pascal, as "ever conscious of rhetorical precepts." Johnson, *Hyperboles*, 2. My interest extends to the involuntary staging of catastrophe by the imagination.

ever considers himself in this way will be afraid of himself, and, seeing himself supported by the size nature has given him between these two abysses of the infinite and nothingness, he will tremble [*tremblera*] at these marvels."[43] One nineteenth-century critic describes Pascal as a "melancholic" prone to "sudden and almost unaccountable disturbances of the intellectual atmosphere."[44] But in addition to reporting on his own bad weather, Pascal draws attention to the *process* by which the mind proceeds to such catastrophic ends. In this too he is following the example of the ancient materialists—and subjecting it to trial. Consider this fragment from the grandfather of atomism, Democritus, whom Pascal mentions dismissively in this context as one of those who "have claimed to know all things:"[45] "Whenever the bastard kind [of knowledge] is unable any longer to see what has become too small, or to hear or smell or taste or perceive it by touch, <one must have recourse to> another and finer [ἐπὶ λεπτότερον] <instrument>" (DK 68 B11).[46] Democritus here distinguishes "bastard" knowing (by means of the senses) from "genuine" knowing (by the rational mind), but the text breaks up just as he comes to explain how we move between them. The brackets indicate the place where the editor has attempted to supplement the passage. We can perhaps already hear a hint of compulsion in the phrase "one must have recourse to." In his interpretation of the fragment, Hermann Diels explains that "the genuine faculty takes over, since it possesses a more subtle tool for thought."[47]

Yet Pascal narrates the *failure* of the mind's attempt to

---

43. Pascal, *Pensées*, 59; *Pensées et opuscules*, 350.

44. Rogers, "Genius and Writings of Pascal," 214.

45. Pascal, *Pensées*, 60.

46. Sextus Empiricus, *Against the Logicians* 1.139. References to the testimony and fragments of Democritus follow Diels and Kranz, *Die Fragmente der Vorsokratiker*, in parentheses in the body of the text.

47. Diels and Kranz, *Die Fragmente der Vorsokratiker*, 2:141. Translated in Mann, *Hippocrates, On the Art of Medicine*, 27.

travel from the sensible to the insensible. Philosophers such as Democritus, he says, are absurd because they do not see that "the infinite number of things is so hidden from us that what is expressible in speech or thoughts is only an invisible trace of it."[48] Unlike Lucretius, for whom the miniscule bodies of insects unlock a world of fundamental particles, Pascal's mind does not—perhaps cannot—stop at the atom.[49] And this is the point: "We burn with desire to find firm ground and an ultimate secure base on which to build a tower reaching up to the infinite. But our whole foundation cracks, and the earth opens up into abysses [*mais tout notre fondement craque et la terre s'ouvre jusqu'aux abîmes*]."[50] That the imagined experience of catastrophe can both make sensible the insensible and describe the collapse of thought under its own weight might seem surprising, but this paradox organizes the Democritean tradition from within. Just as Pascal invokes the grandfather of atomism to highlight the absurd dogmatism of philosophers, he implicitly points us to a different aspect of the atomist's intellectual legacy. According to another fragment ascribed to Democritus, "In reality we know nothing; for truth is in the depths" (DK B117).[51]

Depending on how and where you read of the philosopher's "abyss" or "pit," these "depths" have at least two (seemingly contradictory) meanings. One is that we cannot know anything at all—that certain knowledge is impossible. This would make the atomist Democritus a kind of negative dogmatist. In

48. Pascal, *Pensées*, 60.

49. Johnson has put it nicely: "Reasoning by analogy can only go so far until it also becomes aporetic." Johnson, *Hyperboles*, 465.

50. Pascal, *Pensées*, 62; *Pensées et opuscules*, 354. In the same place, Pascal evokes the image of the Lucretian shipwreck: "We float on a vast ocean, ever uncertain and adrift, blown this way or that." On this connection, see Johnson, *Hyperboles*, 465.

51. Taylor, *Atomists*, 9.

the *Academica*, Cicero relates the philosopher's opinion "that truth is sunk in the depths, everything is subject to opinion and convention, with no place left for truth, and in a word that everything is shrouded in darkness" (DK 59 A95).[52] The second possible interpretation is more optimistic: truth lies in hidden things that can be known by reason through the senses—things such as atoms and the void. Democritus is said to have approved of the opinion that "appearances are a glimpse of the obscure" (DK 59 B21a), which hints at the possibility of a transition from perception to "genuine" knowledge.[53] The question is: Can we have any real knowledge of the imperceptible or not? The tension between the image of a bottomless pit and the fantasy of getting to the bottom of things has led one scholar to wonder whether we have forgotten a dialectical method in Democritus that makes sense of this apparent paradox.[54]

Whatever Democritus himself intended, the reception of this scattered tradition and the distortions it generated gave rise to a variety of interpretive and affective possibilities. To catastrophize, as Pascal suggests, may be to feel the pressures of the atomist and skeptic exerting themselves simultaneously. In Pascal's case, catastrophizing brings to the surface the strain of skepticism buried deep in Democritus's pit—a knowledge that both motivates the mind's reflexive action at the start and is its final destination. James I. Porter has raised a similar issue by arguing that the atom itself may have emerged in the an-

52. Taylor, *Atomists*, 146. Aristotle also gives us evidence for a skeptical Democritus in the *Metaphysics*: "Further, to many of the other animals the same things appear opposite from the way they appear to us, and to each individual things do not always seem the same, as far as the senses are concerned. So which of these is true or false is unclear; for this is no more true than that, but they are alike. This is why Democritus said that either nothing is true, or it is unclear to us" (DK 68 A112). Taylor, *Atomists*, 141.

53. Kirk, Raven, and Schofield, *Presocratic Philosophers*, 383. According to Sextus Empiricus, the thought is attributed to Anaxagoras.

54. Lee, *Epistemology after Protagoras*, 245–46.

cient imagination as a bulwark against the totalizing idea of nothing—a "fear of the abyss (*barathrum*)."[55]

This is not, however, to suggest that catastrophic materialism always ends with the revelation of groundlessness. Catastrophizing has many ends. The early modern period was a particularly fraught moment for the reception of materialism. The rupture of the Reformation generated controversy about the proper objects of human understanding and about man's place in the cosmic order—as did growing acceptance of Copernicanism and a revolution in science that revealed new frontiers of investigation with the help of innovative optical technologies and methodological protocols. Our two examples, Cavendish and Pascal, adumbrate a history of catastrophic materialism that reaches both backward and forward in time—one that connects an artist dreaming of a second great flood, an astrologer who predicts the end of the world on the basis of a starry conjunction, a poet who confronts death in the first signs of illness, and an Enlightenment philosopher who attempts to adapt the form of the materialist analogy to his own ends (to name only a few of the characters who populate this book). As we'll see, catastrophizing emerges repeatedly at the threshold between empirical and speculative forms of knowledge—as the very idea of the empirical was being reformulated and tested.

Sometimes, the event of mental catastrophe results in a state of tranquility grounded in knowledge of the natural world, as the Epicureans teach. Other times, catastrophic materialism serves as an instrument for further inquiry, illuminating the mind's powers and limitations. Still other times, it devolves into something like a bad habit or addiction, bringing us closer to our more familiar sense of the word "catastrophizing." In such cases, catastrophic materialism takes on a life of its own, rehearsing the same patterns of thought even when

55. Porter, "Lucretius and the Poetics of Void," 213.

philosophical questions of matter are very far from the mind's conscious concerns.

What I have called *atomism without atoms* describes the experience in which the action of the mind looks very much like the precipitous passage of the materialist from an insistence on the necessity of the atom to the idea of the world's destruction—but without the thought of atoms, the void, or any explicitly ontological question. The mental pattern itself has influence—and sometimes carries with it un- or barely acknowledged traces of philosophical materialism. Such habits of thought travel promiscuously in this period, taking hold even in professions of orthodox belief. They help us understand how and why a tradition that for much of the early modern period was considered absurd and easily dismissed was also considered dangerous. They also help us understand the structure of other kinds of eschatological thinking.

The detachment of philosophical style from philosophical principles, however, raises the question of why we should bother with materialism at all. My answer is both literary and historical. The early modern period provides us with a window into the processes by which the philosophical arguments of materialism become embedded in style. Consider, for example, the connection between what I am calling "catastrophizing" and Stanley Cavell's idiosyncratic conception of skepticism, which he describes as the misinterpretation of "a metaphysical finitude as an intellectual lack."[56] Cavell is thinking of the titans of Shakespearean tragedy, characters such as Lear and Othello, who explode with violence in response to very little—to the word "nothing," in one case (*Lear*, 1.1.88), and to "trifles light as air," such as Desdemona's handkerchief, in the other (*Othello*, 3.3.326).[57] As a beleaguered Othello falls into an

---

56. Cavell, *Disowning Knowledge*, 11.

57. All references to Shakespeare follow *The Norton Shakespeare*. Citations of *King Lear* follow the 1623 Folio version of the play.

epileptic fit, "tremb[ling]" upon contemplating the fatal object, he *becomes* the disaster: "It is not words that shakes me thus" (*Othello*, 4.1.39–40).[58] Where exactly this kind of disaster originates, however, Cavell does not say: "I do not command the learning to argue seriously on historical evidence that the shaking of the ground of human existence, in what philosophy calls skepticism, finds its way into Shakespeare's words."[59] In this book, I will show how this pattern of thought in Shakespeare, as in many other early modern authors, leads us back to a specific crossing of catastrophe, materialist philosophy, and hermeneutics. But to identify ancient and early modern materialisms as engines of "skepticism" is not to ascribe a cause to Shakespeare's "earthquakes." It is rather to understand how and why—for early modern thinkers no less than for late moderns, including Cavell himself—such disastrous habits of mind were closely linked to questions of ontology. In making sensible the insensible, I argue, catastrophizing also makes its materialist history felt.

REORIENTATIONS

In his essay on Heinrich von Kleist's story "The Earthquake in Chile," Werner Hamacher takes up the image of quaking in the long shadow of the Lisbon disaster of 1755—the earthquake that moved Kant from a distance and kept a young Goethe awake at night. For Hamacher, Kleist's story allegorizes the "quaking

58. The German physician and alchemist Paracelsus understood natural effects such as thunderstorms and earthquakes as corresponding to epilepsy when viewed through the lens of the microcosm-macrocosm analogy. See Temkin, *Falling Sickness*, 173–74.

59. Cavell, *Disowning Knowledge*, 4. As Cavell suggests, skepticism results (possibly though never precisely) from "the rise of the new science; the consequent and precedent attenuation or displacement of God; the attenuation of the concept of Divine Right; the preparation for the demand for political legitimation by individual consent" (21).

of presentation"—that is, how the narrative's conflict of positions "removes the ground upon which the unity of experience would rest."[60] He explains the fallout: "Under the impression exerted by the Lisbon earthquake, which touched the European mind in one of its more sensitive epochs, the metaphorics of ground and tremor completely lost their apparent innocence; they were no longer merely figures of speech."[61] But the idea that the events of Lisbon and their intellectual reception all of a sudden transformed the "metaphorics of ground and tremor" conceals a much longer and indeed stranger history.

In recent years, much invaluable research has been done on the transformations of Renaissance meteorology, the cultural and political meanings of catastrophe, and the rise of disaster science in subsequent centuries.[62] What has yet to receive scholarly attention is the way we have been *thinking* with disaster across historical periods. For the most part, we have been more interested in real disasters than imagined ones—that is to say, in the empirical study of disaster and the history of its interpretation. We have also perhaps been too quick to dismiss imaginative disasters in the history of philosophy—the way one might dismiss one's own irrational or absurd thoughts. In a late text, Kant will affirm this self-protective impulse by warning us against paying too much attention to "an inner history of the *involuntary* course of one's thoughts and feelings," citing Pascal's "terrifying and fearful" ideas.[63] Catastrophic materi-

60. Hamacher, *Premises*, 292.

61. Hamacher, *Premises*, 263. For the idea of the Lisbon earthquake as an intellectual and historical break, see Neiman, *Evil in Modern Thought*, 18–35; Huet, *Culture of Disaster*, 39–56.

62. On the transformation of ancient meteorology, see, for example, Martin, *Renaissance Meteorology*. For the political and religious contexts of interpreting disaster in the sixteenth and early seventeenth centuries, see Fulton, "Acts of God." For the changing idea of disaster as a political and literary concept in the eighteenth century and beyond, see Huet, *Culture of Disaster*. For the rise of earthquake science, see especially Coen, *Earthquake Observers*.

63. Kant, *Anthropology from a Pragmatic Point of View*, 22.

alism in particular has been easy to overlook because it often registers as a feeling or sensation rather than deliberate or logical thought, because as scholars we are still not used to thinking about the experience of philosophy as an embodied one, and because it's difficult to talk about the involuntariness of thought even if it is hard to deny.

Another obstacle has been the conflation of catastrophic materialism and the sublime. In *The Sublime in Antiquity*, Porter has recovered an expansive version of the sublime before and after Longinus: "The sublime pervades much of antiquity; it has simply been hiding in the light."[64] But if Porter has opened up the notion of the ancient sublime, for scholars working in later periods the connection between reason and disaster is usually tethered to Kant's much narrower concept, which humiliates the mind in order to stage its triumph over the immense and ungraspable. Kant explains: "We gladly call these objects [the violent spectacles of nature] sublime because they elevate the strength of our soul above its usual level, and allow us to discover within ourselves a capacity for resistance of quite another kind, which gives us the courage to measure ourselves against the apparent all-powerfulness of nature."[65] But, once again, like the pursuit of Epicurean *ataraxia*, such triumph is often an unpersuasive ending to the mind's metaphysical horror story.

So far I have attempted to describe the various features of catastrophic materialism; the remainder of this book is a testing of these initial thoughts. To recover this history is to see how and why the legacy of catastrophizing continues to haunt us and to rethink the critical value of materialism and the kinds of freedom it offers. Writing a book about disastrous thinking is a challenge, not least because the subject could potentially

---

64. Porter, *Sublime in Antiquity*, xviii.
65. Kant, *Critique of the Power of Judgment*, 144–45.

encompass a great number of other texts and topics. It inevitably leaves much out—and much to the imagination. While the events of actual disasters, for example, weave in and out of this story, they are not my primary focus. I've tried to be as clear as possible about what I mean and what I don't mean by the "making of disaster," foregrounding moments that involve the conjunction of catastrophe (especially *imagined* catastrophe) and materialist thought. Along the way, certain themes are privileged over others; the image of Democritus's pit, for example, appears throughout the book, as does the analogy of dust in sunlight. I treat materialism's fraught relationship to Christian eschatology in several key places, suggesting the way that imagining one kind of end can open the door to imagining others. The narrative moves roughly in chronological order, though I consciously refrain from telling a story of progress or the displacement of one mode of thinking by another. My interest is not how superstition or *religio* gave way to the triumph of reason, but rather how the disasters of materialism produced transferable patterns of thought—many of which still survive within our own critical practices.

A book is inherently a product of curation. The examples I've chosen provide a conceptual and historical density that allows me to open out from the specific case to a more general picture against which the reader can weigh the book's claims. My argument is cumulative, which means it takes shape as the parts unfold and in the relation of the parts to one another. My interest is in formal resemblances and echoes between examples that both collapse the time between them, allowing us, for instance, to discern an analogy between Leonardo da Vinci and Kant, and sharpen our sense of the historical distance that separates them. In my first book, *The Lucretian Renaissance* (2011), I began to explore the idea of an influence's "pervasiveness"—how we might perceive the mechanisms of influence beyond the most explicit kinds of textual allusion. In this book,

I further pursue this line of investigation, but shift my attention now to the experience of thought—to the question of our agency in thinking and the nature of our disavowals of agency. In an essay on Leonardo da Vinci, Paul Valéry writes: "The operations of the mind can serve our purpose of analysis only while they are moving, unresolved, still at the mercy of the moment."[66] As an act of thought "still at the mercy of the moment," catastrophizing requires attention to unconscious mechanisms of transmission if it is to be understood. To recover thought's "operations" in any historical moment demands a certain spirit of methodological experimentation and a willingness to take part in the work of imaginative reconstruction. To this end, this book seeks not only to illuminate a number of subterranean connections between seemingly distant people, projects, and places but also to elaborate a way of viewing and inhabiting the thought of the past that puts our own modes of catastrophic thinking into relief.

I begin with Leonardo da Vinci's lifelong preoccupation with the making of catastrophe—from his prophetic riddles to his late drawings of deluge—and what we might call his discovery of materialist style. In Leonardo we find an early modern thinker who wasn't particularly invested in the idea of the atom, but for whom catastrophizing was a way of testing an analogy that linked the sensible with the insensible—and of exploring the involuntary behavior of the mind. The image of disaster, I argue, emerges in Leonardo's work out of the problem of grasping those natural causes that lie beyond perception—to which he responds with analogies that assume a life of their own.

Moving to the late sixteenth and early seventeenth centuries, chapter 2 explores the mobility of materialism's catastrophic style. At the intersection of debates around astrology, speculative reason, and the end of the world, early modern

---

66. Valéry, "Introduction to the Method of Leonardo da Vinci," 9–10.

readers would discover the connection between materialism and prophecy on their own terms. Here I explore how Thomas Digges, the first English author to publicly endorse the Copernican theory, grasped for the image of an infinite universe in response to the lingering force of a materialist thought, and how John Donne's encounter with illness conjured up both the experience of catastrophic materialism and an apocalyptic response.

Chapter 3 considers the ways that materialist thought insinuated itself into the texture of early modern speech, sometimes by seemingly innocuous means. Here we find an alternative description of catastrophizing in one of the period's familiar sayings—*quidlibet ex quolibet*, or "whatever you like out of whatever you like"—a saying, I'll suggest, that opens up a new reading of Shakespeare. Tracing the meaning of this phrase back to its roots in ancient philosophy, I explore why the violent acts of speculation we see in tragedies such as *King Lear* and *The Winter's Tale* return us repeatedly to the interpretation (and misinterpretation) of the material world.

Chapter 4 shows how catastrophic materialism was reimagined and put to use during the scientific revolution. Here, I place the virtuoso Robert Hooke's well-known microscopic observations together with his lesser-known lectures on earthquakes. Under the lens and metaphor of the early modern microscope, I argue, speculation about the *history* of earthquakes provided yet another response to the lure of Democritus's pit.

The final chapter concerns the before and after of catastrophizing in Kant's philosophy. Beginning with his precritical meditation on the structure of the universe in 1755 (the year of the Lisbon earthquake) and following the thread of disaster through his later writings, I show how he converted the shudder of catastrophizing into the sublime. A brief afterword considers the various ways catastrophizing persists in contemporary ecocritical discourse, and makes a case for its continuing value. Here, I suggest that returning to the history of the mind's making of disaster might itself be a form of ecocritical attention, helping us to see what lies behind our own habits of catastrophic thinking—and to make sense of the imagined and very real disasters we face.

ONE

Leonardo's Disasters

In his 1958 book, *Leonardos Visionen*, Joseph Gantner read the portents of disaster in Leonardo da Vinci, finding catastrophe everywhere he looked—in the oblique finger of John the Baptist pointing upward into the void, in the rocky background landscape of the Mona Lisa, in the artist's infamous *non finito*, and in the apocalyptic turbulence of the late drawings of deluge now held at Windsor Castle, where disaster is admittedly less hard to find. Writing in the shadow of the Second World War (Gantner had fled Germany in 1933 to escape Nazi persecution), he imagined disaster as the red thread that led through the labyrinth of the artist's body of work.[1] Not everyone, however, saw the thread as clearly as he. In a 1959 review, Joachim Schumacher accused Gantner of confusing a "favorite approach to Leonardo with the essence of the actual Leonardo," echoing the objections of others that Gantner's account was deeply flawed.[2] "It may well be doubted," Schumacher wrote, "that Leonardo ever allowed any particular concept or subject of his formative fantasy to possess his mind to the extent that he ceased to be the master of his visions to become, in his most mature years, the mere follower and fanatic of his own early

1. See Sorensen, "Joseph Gantner."
2. Schumacher, "'Il non finito,'" 243. Even K. R. Eissler, in a psychoanalytic account of Leonardo where one might expect a certain sympathy, would "doubt whether Gantner adduc[ed] enough evidence to substantiate his own views." Eissler, *Leonardo da Vinci*, 301.

obsession with destruction."[3] But what would it mean to allow oneself to be possessed?

I want to begin by recuperating something of Gantner's insight: for Leonardo, catastrophes were not just objects of popular fear or scientific curiosity but images to think with. More specifically, I will argue that the artist's disasters are a point of entry into his materialism, the mere suggestion of which has been a cause of anxiety for his interpreters at least since Vasari accused him of thinking more about nature than about God.[4] But, again, materialism need not refer here to atomism or Epicurean philosophy.[5] Leonardo sometimes used the language of atoms to describe the nature of the elements, but he was not an atomist in any strict sense of that word. His materialism also cannot be explained entirely by his search for natural causes, though the value he placed on sensory experience and the identification of physical causes are good reasons to use the term. What I mean by Leonardo's materialism is rather a "cast of mind"—a style of knowing through which the mind tests its relation to what lies beyond the senses as it seeks out hidden causes and, in so doing, also tests its relation to itself.

I am adapting the phrase "cast of mind" from Michael Baxandall's seminal description of Leon Battista Alberti.[6] But whereas Baxandall writes of Alberti's sometimes "exasperated" desire for balance and analogical stability, I look instead to Leonardo's propensity to catastrophize, his mind reaching, as

3. Schumacher, "'Il non finito,'" 248.

4. See Müntz, *Leonardo da Vinci*, 2:32: "Doubts of Leonardo's orthodoxy are very old. As early as the middle of the sixteenth century, Vasari spoke of his 'capricci nel filosofar delle cose naturale,' adding that the author of the *Last Supper* 'had taken up such heretical notions that he really belonged to no religion, and, in short, that he laid more store by his quality as a philosopher than as a Christian.'" Vasari removed the passage in question in the second edition of the *Lives*.

5. For an argument for Leonardo's knowledge of and use of *De rerum natura*, see Beretta, "Leonardo and Lucretius."

6. See Baxandall, "Alberti's Cast of Mind."

if automatically, beyond the limits of the sensible by analogy.[7] My ambition here is not to discount the spiritual (particularly Augustinian) elements in Leonardo that Steven F. H. Stowell and others have described, but rather to suggest an alternative to be found in the artist's experience and representation of the mind when it is left to its own devices—or shakes lose from conscious control.[8]

The reflex of catastrophizing, I will argue, was for Leonardo an opportunity to observe the action of the mind when it approaches the imperceptible. The first part of the chapter concerns the discovery of disaster as a figure of thought by exploring Leonardo's "prophecies," or satirical riddles. It is in the context of these generic experiments that he begins to test a materialist style of thought, using the mind's rush to disaster or the worst as his laboratory. The second part reads the artist's representation of catastrophic wind and water as an expression of the mind's involuntariness—particularly the involuntariness of certain kinds of analogies. In the image of natural violence, Leonardo is taught to feel what lies beyond the realm of the senses as a dangerous confrontation. The chapter concludes by looking briefly to one of his contemporaries, Giambattista Pio, whose personal digressions in a humanist commentary shed another light on what it is like to be caught in the storm of catastrophic analogy.

PROPHECIES

"One shall be born from small beginnings which will rapidly become vast," Leonardo wrote of fire.[9] The imagination too was a highly combustible thing. At the turn of the sixteenth century, all it took was a few lines from an almanac to light

7. Baxandall, "Alberti's Cast of Mind," 30.
8. See Stowell, *Spiritual Language of Art*, 118–60.
9. Leonardo, *Notebooks*, ed. Richter, 2:360.

the match. When the prognostications of two German astrologers in 1499 were echoed and amplified in Italy shortly after, the vague predictions of an unspecified disturbance under the watery sign gave way to rumors of a second great flood that was to drown "nearly the entire world" in 1524.[10] The news was apparently so common that Machiavelli described it as the kind of small talk one heard in taverns.[11] Some took the prediction very seriously. Agostino Nifo tells us that a few men even built arks and fled to the tops of mountains in order to escape impending doom.[12]

If he had lived long enough to see the failure of these predictions, Leonardo would not have been surprised. Roughly between 1496 and 1500, he composed a series of "prophecies" (*profetie*), as he calls them in the notebooks—satirical riddles that manage at once to imitate and explode the kind of apocalyptic discourse that would gather momentum as the Italian wars raged on and Luther's Reformation reared its head in the not-so-distant background.[13] These riddles range in topic considerably. Leonardo gives us a taxonomy of them:

10. Pigghe, *Astrologiae defensio*, fol. 14ʳ; cited and discussed in Broecke, *Limits of Influence*, 83. The two German astrologers were Johannes Stöffler and Jacob Pflaum, who wrote of the fateful conjunction of Saturn and Jupiter in their 1499 *Almanach nova plurimis annis venturis inservientia*. In Italy, Luca Gaurico predicted a flood as early as 1501, echoing his predictions through 1524. For an overview of events leading up to 1524, see Thorndike, *History of Magic and Experimental Science*, 5:178–233. For the German and Italian contexts, see especially Zambelli, "Many Ends for the World."

11. Machiavelli, *Lettere*, 409. Discussed in Niccoli, *Prophecy and People*, 142.

12. Nifo, *De falsa diluvii prognosticatione*, sig. A1ᵛ. While noting the spirit of alarm among some of his contemporaries, Nifo himself "pointed out what seems not to have been realized by many at the time and by most subsequent writers on the controversy, who have represented the flood as predicted for the year 1524 itself, namely, that if this conjunction is like that which is said to have announced Noah's flood, its effects may not be felt for a century or so, in which case there is no cause for immediate alarm." Thorndike, *History of Magic and Experimental Science*, 5:193.

13. On the context of the prophecies and Leonardo's sometimes serious

First, of things relating to animals; secondly, of irrational creatures [*irrationali*]; thirdly of plants; fourthly of ceremonies;
fifthly of manners; sixthly of cases or edicts or quarrels; sev-
enthly of cases that are impossible in nature [paradoxes], as, for
instance, of those things which, the more is taken from them,
the more they grow. And reserve the great matters till the end,
and the small matters give at the beginning. And first show the
evils and then the punishment of philosophical things [*e mostra
prima i mali, e poi le punitioni delle cose filosofiche*].[14]

The groups of prophecies in the notebooks don't strictly ad-
here to these divisions. Moreover, what is a "great matter" and
what is a small one is sometimes hard to say. For E. H. Gombrich, the prophecies "belong to the most bizarre products of
[Leonardo's] ever-active mind. These are humorous inventions
in the same vein as his riddles and fables and some of them may
strike one at first as little better than schoolboy jokes."[15] Some
of them, indeed, are quite silly—even obscene. "Oh! how foul
a thing, that we should see the tongue of one animal in the
guts of another," he wrote of sausages.[16] Or this riddling pro-
nouncement: "In you, O cities of Africa, your children will be
seen quartered in their own houses by most cruel and rapa-
cious beasts of your own country."[17] The answer is "Cats that
eat Rats."[18] Other prophecies, however, seem less innocuous:
"Men will have such cruel maladies that they will tear their

---

sense of humor, see Vecce, "Leonardo e il gioco." For the dating of the riddles
ca. 1500, see Pedretti, *Literary Works of Leonardo da Vinci*, 2:278.

14. Leonardo, *Notebooks*, ed. Richter, 2:353.

15. Gombrich, "Leonardo and the Magicians," 61.

16. Leonardo, *Notebooks*, ed. Richter, 2:356.

17. Leonardo, *Notebooks*, ed. Richter, 2:354.

18. Leonardo once filled a page with drawings of cats (and a lion and a
dragon) playing, sleeping, moving, stalking, as if to dramatize how the most
domestic of creatures might appear, from another perspective, the most terrifying. A mouse sits precariously on the top left-hand corner of the page. Royal
Library, Windsor Castle, RL 12363.

flesh with their own nails."[19] The answer again is something familiar—an itch. But for anyone, like Leonardo, who lived through the devastating plague of 1485 in Milan, disaster was perhaps all too close at hand.[20]

We don't know what exactly Leonardo intended with his "prophecies."[21] He may have composed them to entertain the Milanese court—perhaps in a spirited competition with his good friend and fellow artist Donato Bramante, or his assistant Tommaso di Giovanni Masini, known as "Zoroastro" and sometimes called "Indovino," or "the prophet."[22] Perhaps he had in mind as his target Ambrogio Varesi da Rosate—the court astrologer who rose to prominence in Milan when he miraculously cured Ludovico Sforza of an illness.[23] In the *Treatise on Painting*, Leonardo bluntly condemns astrology as deceptive, writing sarcastically, "Let him who makes a living from fools by means of it forgive me."[24] While we know Leonardo carefully transcribed passages on animals from the medieval astrologer Cecco d'Ascoli's encyclopedic poem, he might have rolled his eyes at other verses, such as these on the effects of comets: "New, frightening and catastrophic / events can occur in the world when / the planet Saturn governs the weather. / Noblemen and kings, along with their / subjects and all other

19. Leonardo, *Notebooks*, ed. Richter, 2:367.

20. According to surviving records, 4,829 died from bubonic plague in Milan in 1485. Samuel Cohn describes the signs and symptoms of the plague in the period, including various skin disorders. See Cohn, *Cultures of Plague*, 20–21, 39–76.

21. For Edward MacCurdy, he "apparently created his own model" for the prophecies. Leonardo, *Leonardo da Vinci's Notebooks*, ed. MacCurdy, 35.

22. Nicholl, *Leonardo da Vinci*, 220.

23. On Leonardo's supposed dislike of Varesi, see Castelli, "Leonardo, i due Pico e la critica alla divinazione," 132, 157–58. See also Nanni, "Le 'disputationes' pichiane sull'astrologia e Leonardo." For astrology in Milan at this historical moment, see Azzolini, *Duke and the Stars*, 22–64.

24. Pedretti, *Literary Works of Leonardo da Vinci*, 2:119.

rational creatures, / shake with fear of uncontrolled violence" (lines 345–50).[25] In another riddle Leonardo jokes, "All the astrologers will be castrated, that is the cockerels [roosters]."[26]

One would not have had to go very far to hear prophets crying like roosters in public squares or to discover prognostications in cheaply printed pamphlets. Carlo Vecce cites Giuliano Dati's popular poem on a real Roman flood in 1495, *Del diluvio di Roma* (1496), as a key source for Leonardo's prophetic satire.[27] Here, the word *diluvio*, which traditionally refers to the biblical flood, blurs the line between a local disaster and a global event.[28] For Dati, the event was another telling sign of the world's approaching end.[29] If we glance slightly forward in time, Leonardo's prophecies resemble the carnivalesque rhymes that Ottavia Niccoli has documented—ballads, for example, in which astral conjunctions become "conjunctions of cheese and lasagna."[30] Like such texts, Leonardo's riddles translate the catastrophic into the stuff of the ordinary—though not always so deliciously.

Still, one might be forgiven for hearing his prophecies with dread. Leonardo even gives us a stage direction to this effect: "Tell it in a frenzy or crazy way, as if out of madness [*in forma di frenesia o farnetico | djnsanja dj ceruello*]."[31] As all good fortune-tellers know, such language derives its efficacy from its intensity, but also from its vagueness. The mind leaps to the worst, automatically generating something out of nothing. Even if

25. Ascoli, *Bitter Age*, 38.

26. Leonardo, *Notebooks*, ed. MacCurdy, 1101.

27. Vecce, "Leonardo e il gioco," 289–90.

28. On the increased usage of the word *diluvio* to refer to local floods (rather than the biblical one), see Niccoli, *Prophecy and People*, 143.

29. Ottavia Niccoli has suggested that with Dati, "prophecy entered into the repertory of the bench singers, the *cantambanchi*, hence into the patrimony of urban oral culture. It was to remain there." Niccoli, *Prophecy and People*, 15.

30. Niccoli, *Prophecy and People*, 158.

31. Pedretti, *Literary Works of Leonardo da Vinci*, 2:279.

you are already aware that you are hearing a riddle, you might nonetheless imagine the disaster in all its frightful immediacy, in spite of yourself. The relief of laughter can also be reflexive. Leonardo was an avid student of what he called *accidenti mentali*, or "mental events."[32] As he instructs the painter, "Consider those who laugh and those who cry; watch those who scream in anger and, by means of this, all that happens in our minds."[33] It was once reported that the artist told jokes so that he might study men in the act of laughing. Giovanni Paolo Lomazzo, the sixteenth-century Milanese artist, describes the scene of Leonardo cracking jokes in order to induce the desired response: "And after they had left, he retired to his room and there made a perfect drawing which moved those who looked at it to laughter, as if they had been moved by Leonardo's stories at the feast!"[34] We might understand the prophecies in a similar way—that is, as an opportunity to observe and study the figure of involuntariness, both the mind's sudden conjuration of the worst and an equally sudden deflation. The experience of involuntariness is the source of the riddles' comedy and also the key to their power.

Through the form of the riddle, Leonardo analyzes what imagining catastrophe *does* to thought—and what it makes possible conceptually. His materialist "cast of mind" emerges in and through seemingly innocuous examples, which offer leveling analogies between different species, images of otherwise invisible processes, and distortions of time, scale, and perspective.[35] I want to begin to explore some of these ideas by

32. Leonardo, *Libro di Pittura*, 2:259–60. See Bambach, *Leonardo da Vinci, Master Draftsman*, 327; Nicholl, *Leonardo da Vinci*, 9. For the argument that Leonardo composed a now-lost book on the embodied expression of emotions, see Kwakkelstein, "The Lost Book on 'moti mentali.'"
33. Leonardo, *On Painting*, 46–47.
34. Cited in Leonardo, *Notebooks*, ed. Wells, 286.
35. We might compare Leonardo's use of the prophetic riddle that stirs up

replaying the dramatic stroke of surprise in two of the more dire-sounding "prophecies" before slowing down to explain how their punch lines echo and ramify across the notebooks:

> These creatures will form many communities [*molti popoli*], which will hide themselves and their young ones and victuals in darks caverns, and they will feed themselves and their families in dark places for many months without any light, artificial or natural.

> And many others will be deprived of their store and their food, and will be cruelly submerged and drowned by folks devoid of reason [*giēte sanza ragione*]. Oh Justice of God! Why dost thou not wake and behold thy creatures thus ill used?[36]

These two riddles appear to be predicting some great calamity; the mind races. Once again, however, the solutions are quite ordinary. In the first instance, Leonardo is describing the mundane lives of ants; in the second, the fate of bees, which are sometimes drowned for their honey. There is a certain wit already in Leonardo's selection of these particular subjects, for the behavior of ants and bees was itself thought to be prognostic. Leonardo might have stumbled upon this idea in the poetry of Virgil or any number of familiar sources. From the medieval friar Albertus Magnus, for example, we learn that ants "foretell the weather since, before a storm, they gather together in their homes."[37] Bees likewise are described as "hav[ing] a natu-

---

catastrophic thoughts with the Anglo-Saxon riddle. For Daniel Tiffany, the latter raises questions of material substance by giving voice to inanimate objects. Leonardo, by contrast, stages the form of materialist thought in the catastrophic movement of the riddle. See Tiffany, *Infidel Poetics*, 34–44.

36. Leonardo, *Notebooks*, ed. Richter, 2:353–54.

37. Albertus Magnus, *On Animals*, 1:1749. Cf. Virgil, *Georgics* 4.379–80. Among his books, Leonardo possessed an epitome of Albertus Magnus's philosophy, the *Opus philosophie naturalis*, though its authorship was already being

ral knack for foretelling winter and its traits, as well as forecast-
ing rainstorms."[38] In Leonardo's hands, familiar acts of prognostication become doomsday prophecies.

Of course, one might find it easy to dismiss "prophecies"
such as these with a laugh or a groan. The diminishment of
human tragedy by comparing it to the comings and goings of
ants and bees is on its face ridiculous, calling to mind humanist
satire like Alberti's 1438 mock encomium on a fly, *Musca*, a text
that Leonardo may have consulted in his teacher Verrocchio's
workshop.[39] But, like Alberti, Leonardo was serious about his
play. After all, the way we "go to the ant" (as Solomon dic-
tates) and other insects for instruction was an important point
of contention for medieval and Renaissance commentators
on Aristotle, who had much to say about the lives of these
so-called irrational creatures ("irrationali," as Leonardo calls
them).[40] In glossing Aristotle's book on zoology, for example,
Albertus Magnus argued that "irrational animals" participate in
the perfection of man, though in a limited way:

> Thus the ant and the bee both build houses and fill them with
> their stores. But they do not bring back these stores in order
> that they might organically serve a society of other animals, be
> they of their own species or of different ones. For one swarm
> of bees or ants in no way serves another one the way the rich-

questioned in the Middle Ages. See Thorndike, "Some Thirteenth-Century
Classics."

38. Albertus Magnus, *On Animals*, 1:747. Cf. Virgil, *Georgics* 4.165–66.

39. "A printed Moscino" is listed among the books in Verrocchio's inventory upon his death. Nicholl, *Leonardo da Vinci*, 76–77. Evoking Lucian's ancient model, Alberti compares flies to men, praising, for instance, the insects'
sociable qualities, and observing with a grin that flies show religious devotion,
that is, by hanging around sacrificial altars. On Alberti's *Musca* and the tradition of mock encomia in the Renaissance, see Marsh, *Lucian and the Latins*,
148–80, esp. 159–61. See also Connor, *Fly*, 23–24.

40. "Go to the ant, thou sluggard: consider her ways, and be wise." Proverbs
6:6 KJV.

ness of the storehouses of humans serve each other as means of governing cities and nations.[41]

Such creatures create homes and "return to their dens and nests," but they do not "perceive of community as 'community' grasped in and of itself."[42] We are told that, unlike men, they are amoral and cannot show love, that they kill without mercy.[43] In Leonardo's prophecy on the bees, however, this is reversed. There, it is man who thoughtlessly (and cruelly) kills without mercy—who is "sanza ragione."[44]

Leonardo was quick to point out man's hypocrisy—and cruelty—particularly with regard to other creatures.[45] Riddles such as these also recall the language of medieval bestiaries, several of which we know he owned and studied carefully. The popular medieval bestiary *Fior di Virtù*, for example, makes bees the very illustration of justice in a passage that Leonardo copies out elsewhere in the notebooks, adding another layer of irony to the exclamation: "Oh Justice of God! Why dost thou not wake and behold thy creatures thus ill used?"[46] In suggesting that bees themselves are worthy of God's justice, Leonardo was also perhaps thinking of Virgil, who had said

41. Albertus Magnus, *On Animals*, 1:65. For Albertus Magnus's thoughts on the capacities of animals and their comparison to human capacities, see Guldentops, "Sagacity of Bees."

42. Albertus Magnus, *On Animals*, 1:771. Cf. Pliny, *Natural History* 11.12: "What men, I protest, can we rank in rationality with these insects, which unquestionably excel mankind in this, that they recognize only the common interest?"

43. Guldentops, "Sagacity of Bees," 287–88.

44. In the phrase "sanza ragione," we can perhaps hear an ironic echo of Ristoro d'Arezzo's astrological work, *Della composizione del mondo* (1282), which Leonardo consults elsewhere in the notebooks. According to Arezzo, Saturn "signifies fatigue, tribulation, anguish, lamentation, and folks without reason [*e la gente senza ragione*], less wise, and bestial on account of the use of animals." Arezzo, *Della composizione del mondo*, 88. See Iannucci, "Saturn in Dante," 58.

45. Kemp, *Marvellous Works*, 148.

46. See Leonardo, *Notebooks*, ed. Wells, 217.

in the *Georgics* that bees contain within them an infusion of the divine: "Led by such tokens and such instances, some have taught that the bees have received a share of the divine intelligence, and a draught of heavenly ether; for God, they saw, pervades all things, earth and sea's expanse and heaven's depth."[47] If anyone might have taken this idea seriously, it was Leonardo. In a well-known letter, the Florentine traveler Andrea Corsali would even compare "our Leonardo da Vinci" to the Hindus ("Guzzaratti"): men, he explains, who do not eat meat nor will allow anyone to do harm to "any living thing" (*alcuna cosa animate*), including insects.[48]

The other side of mistaking ants and bees for people is acknowledging the vulnerability of men. Harnessing the idea of disaster to alter our sense of scale and perspective, the riddles call to mind other moments of sudden relativism in ancient poetry—for example, when Virgil describes the fierce clash of bees in a field with the intensity of an epic battle only to put them again in their place: "These storms of passion, these savage conflicts, by the tossing of a little dust will be quelled and laid to rest."[49] As the commentator Servius noted, from the perspective of the bees, the dust prophesies a "future storm."[50]

This scene in Virgil raises a troubling question of identification. As L. P. Wilkinson has suggested, "Virgil does not say so, but the reader could hardly fail to reflect that if men can thus

47. Virgil, *Georgics* 4.219–22: "His quidam signis atque haec exempla secuti / esse apibus partem divinae mentis et haustus / aetherios dixere; deum namque ire per omnia, / terrasque tractusque maris caelumque profundum."

48. Beltrami, *Documenti e memorie*, 145: "Alcuni gentili chiamati Guzzarati non si cibano di cosa alcuna, che tenga sangue: nè fra essi loro consentano che si noccia ad alcuna cosa animate, come il nostro Leonardo da Vinci."

49. Virgil, *Georgics* 4.86–87: "hi motus animorum atque haec certamina tanta / pulveris exigui iactu compressa quiescent." Cf. Pliny, *Natural History* 11.58. Ascoli writes of the bees' avoidance of wind: "I say that sound causes motion in the air, which, to the bees, is a signal of disaster. They won't fly in the wind, as you know" (lines 4200–4202). Ascoli, *Bitter Age*, 233.

50. Servius, *In Vergilii carmina commentarii*, 4.87.

dispose of bees, Jupiter can thus dispose of men."[51] Leonardo's "prophecies" likewise make tiny creatures of us all. On the same leaf where we find the riddles concerning insects, for example, there is a draft of a fantastical story about a trip to Armenia that includes an account of Mount Taurus collapsing: a disaster imagined at our own scale.[52] Directly beside the scurrying of ants and drowning of bees are sketches of rocky crags and an ominously still body of water—the scene just moments before the collapse? In the foreground, one can make out "almost microscopic sail-boats" (fig. 1).[53] As Gombrich has observed, "It is hard to envisage how Leonardo might have integrated his satirical jest with his tale of ruin and destruction."[54] Reading across the page, we might understand this as the difficulty of attempting to make a home between seemingly incongruous scales and perspectives. Like a handful of dust scattered among a swarm of bees, even the joking evocation of disaster can unsettle our ordinary experience of scale and perspective.

This was not the first time such thoughts had crossed Leo-

51. Wilkinson, *Georgics of Virgil*, 102.
52. See Leonardo, *Notebooks*, ed. Richter, 2:389. Leonardo here mentions a "new prophet" (*novo profeta*) who had predicted the disaster, and one wonders, along with Gombrich, if he doesn't mean the scientific man who warned that cutting through the mountains would lead to inundation (a man-made disaster). Apparently, no one had listened to the "new prophet" (the scientific man), which at least preserves the idea that man might be able to avoid such disasters—at least in certain instances. Gombrich goes on to suggest that the artist might have been inspired by the accounts of Isidore of Seville and Sir John Mandeville to imagine the summit of Mount Taurus as a comet changing shape, an ominous portent that could be given a rational explanation and linked to the demystifying function of the riddling prophecies. Gombrich, "Leonardo and the Magicians," 85.
53. Pedretti, *Literary Works of Leonardo da Vinci*, 2:278.
54. Gombrich, "Leonardo and the Magicians," 85. Pedretti describes the prophecies nicely as a "contrapuntal motif" to the narrative of Mount Taurus and the drawing on the same page. Pedretti, *Literary Works of Leonardo da Vinci*, 2:278. For the methodological challenges and possibilities of reading between the lines of another Renaissance artist, see Barkan, *Michelangelo*.

FIGURE 1.   Leonardo da Vinci, "Fable, prophecy" (ca. 1500). Codex Atlanticus, fol. 393ᵛ. Photograph: © Veneranda Biblioteca Ambrosiana. Milano / De Agostini Picture Library.

nardo's mind. He was perpetually seeking out alternative perspectives—whether in picturing the topography of a landscape from above or the threat of an approaching storm from a distance or imagining the possibility of human flight. In Leonardo's hands, the riddles themselves become little engines of perspectival relativism, transforming the traditional notion of disaster as a punishment from God into something we make or imagine—that is to say, into a figure of thought.

Leonardo repeatedly comes back to the idea that disaster can precipitously alter one's view of the world. The strange leveling of ants and men in the face of catastrophe recalls another page of the notebooks where he describes the destructive power of a giant, whose bloody fall made the earth tremble "as with an earthquake":

From the violence of the shock he lay as stunned on the level ground. Suddenly the people, seeing him as one killed by a thunderbolt, turned back; like ants running wildly over the body of the fallen oak, so these rushing over his ample limbs. . . . Wherefore with a shake of his head he sends the men flying through the air just as hail does when driven by the fury of the winds. Many of these men were found to be dead; stamping with his feet.[55]

Leonardo sometimes likens the body of man to the world, but here humans are atomized: less like little worlds than rocks in a storm, or lice or ants scurrying. The giant is neither impersonal Nature nor a punishing God, but something in between. In comparing the giant to an earthquake, Leonardo draws attention to the way the mind sometimes fabricates such figures out of fear.[56] As man projects an anthropomorphized image

55. Leonardo, *Notebooks*, ed. Richter, 2:411.
56. The philosopher William James wrote after having experienced the San Francisco earthquake of 1906: "First, I personified the earthquake as a permanent individual entity. . . . It stole in behind my back, and once inside

onto the natural world in order to make it less alien, he himself becomes more like an animal or insect. In another draft,
Leonardo describes people seeking shelter from the monster
in caves much in the way he imagines the ants in the prophecy
above: "There remained not any place unless it were the tiny
holes and subterranean caverns where after the manner of crabs
and crickets and creatures like these you might find safety and a
means of escape. Oh, how many wretched mothers and fathers
were deprived of their children!"[57] On the same leaf, we come
upon a drawing of Leonardo's famous flying machine and a
brief note that recalls the myth of Daedalus: "And believe me
there is no man so brave but that, when the fiery eyes were
turned upon him, he would willingly have put on wings in
order to escape."[58] One might understand the comedic turn
of Leonardo's riddles as another wish to take flight from the
thought of catastrophe.

It's even harder to escape, however, when the catastrophe is
you. Leonardo repeatedly reminds us that *we* are the ones who
wreak havoc upon ourselves, upon other creatures, and upon
the earth. In the same manuscript that contains the riddles on
ants and bees, the lingering question of God's justice returns
with a stinging vengeance, reminding us just how destructive
we are:

> Animals will be seen on earth who will always be fighting
> against each other with the greatest loss and frequent deaths
> on each side. And there will be no end to their malignity; by
> their strong limbs we shall see a great portion of the trees of the

the room, had me all to itself, and could manifest itself convincingly. Animus
and intent were never more present in any human action, nor did any human
activity ever more definitely point back to a living agent as its source and origin." James, *Writings*, 1216.

57. Pedretti, *Literary Works of Leonardo da Vinci*, 2:308.

58. Pedretti, *Literary Works of Leonardo da Vinci*, 2:307. On the mythic and
technological fantasy of flight in Leonardo, see Maiorino, *Leonardo da Vinci*.

vast forests laid low throughout the universe; and, when they are filled with food the satisfaction of their desires will be to deal death and grief and labor and wars and fury to every living thing; and from their immoderate pride they will desire to rise towards heaven, but the too great weight of their limbs will keep them down. Nothing will remain on earth, or under the earth or in the waters which will not be persecuted, disturbed and spoiled, and those of one country removed into another. And their bodies will become the sepulture and means of transit of all they have killed. . . . O Earth! Why dost thou not open and engulf them in the fissures of thy vast abyss and caverns, and no longer display in the sight of heaven such a cruel and horrible monster.[59]

Lest anyone miss the point, this time Leonardo has given the solution first, writing impatiently just before this riddle and another: "O human foolishness, o crazy living! These two epithets must precede the proposition."[60] Leonardo notably does not appeal to God's sense of justice, as it is displayed in the biblical story of Korah's rebellion, but rather to the figure of Earth itself.[61] Here "heaven" is but a passive spectator. If a question about the nature of sin and punishment and a universe that is just and meaningfully organized arises again in this context, he does not attempt to answer it.[62]

59. Leonardo, *Notebooks*, ed. Richter, 2:364–65.
60. Pedretti, *Literary Works of Leonardo da Vinci*, 2:280.
61. Numbers 16 KJV: "But if the Lord make a new thing, and the earth open her mouth, and swallow them up, with all that appertain unto them, and they go down quick into the pit; then ye shall understand that these men have provoked the Lord." On Leonardo's views on nature, see Galluzzi, "Leonardo da Vinci's Concept of 'Nature.'"
62. Compare Leonardo's riddle here to Machiavelli's thoughts on the purgative function of disaster: "That these floods, plagues, and famines do in fact happen, I see no reason to doubt, both because we find all histories full of them, and recognize their effect in this oblivion of the past, and also because it is reasonable that such things should happen. For as when much superfluous

As Leonardo contemplates man, a new emotion emerges
from the background: disgust.[63] The language here recalls
several passages from Cecco's *Acerba*, such as this one: "Since
haughty men lay waste to the earth, / let them be subject to
plagues and warfare" (lines 1635–36).[64] While Leonardo might
not have had much interest in Cecco's astrological ideas, his
poem had much to offer in the way of "bitterness" (as its title
suggests). If the artist's prophecy on bees paints human cruelty
in miniature, here the threat of men who are "sanza ragione"
plays out in scenes of war and the violence of man's technological domination of the earth. The image of eating meat is
not only another nod to Leonardo's vegetarianism but a vision
of man glutted on the corpse of a ruined world. Several riddles
return to the theme of the body as sepulcher and to the disturbing idea that we become the things we eat as indeed they
become us—a literal breakdown of the distinction between
humans and animals.[65] "Every thing proceeds from every thing,
and every thing becomes every thing, and every thing can be

matter has gathered in simple bodies, nature makes repeated efforts to remove
and purge it away, thereby promoting the health of these bodies, so likewise
as regards that composite body the human race, when every province of the
world so teems with inhabitants that they can neither subsist where they are
nor remove elsewhere, every region being equally crowded and over-peopled,
and when human craft and wickedness have reached their highest pitch, it
must needs come about that the world will purge herself in one or another of
these three ways, to the end that men, becoming few and contrite, may amend
their lives and live with more convenience." Machiavelli, *Discourses*, 216.

63. Of the passage in question, among others, Vecce writes: "Forse in questi
testi Leonardo non gioca piú, il riso, come l'ironia, è molto amaro." Vecce,
"Leonardo e il gioco," 1:299.

64. Ascoli, *Bitter Age*, 96.

65. As Leonardo writes on "food which has been alive," "A large part of
the bodies which have had life will pass into the bodies of other animals, that
is the houses no longer inhabited will pass piecemeal through those which
are inhabited, ministering to their needs and bearing away with them what
is waste; that is to say, the life of man is made by things which he eats, and
these carry with them that part of man which is dead." Leonardo, *Notebooks*,

turned into every thing else," Leonardo wrote, paraphrasing Anaxagoras in his notebooks.[66]

The bitterness that sometimes accompanies the easy laughter of riddles such as this one might be said to conjure up the image of another pre-Socratic philosopher, namely Democritus, who was said to laugh perpetually at the foolishness of men.[67] Leonardo's friend Bramante once painted a double portrait of laughing Democritus and Heraclitus, the weeping philosopher: an image of the two men huddled around a globe of the earth.[68] The fresco was painted for the court poet Gasparo Visconti's Milanese palace, which Leonardo is thought have frequented.[69] In addition to being the grandfather of atomism, Democritus is sometimes said to have been the first philosopher to employ the microcosm/macrocosm analogy that was so dear to Leonardo, giving the simulacrum of the earth in Bramante's painting another significance.[70]

In his satirical dialogue *Momus*, Alberti recalls a conversation with Democritus in which a speaker claims that he can read the fate of the world in an onion that has been sliced

---

ed. Wells, 232. Here, as elsewhere in the notebooks, it is clear that book 15 of Ovid's *Metamorphoses* made an impression on Leonardo.

66. Leonardo, *Notebooks*, ed. Richter, 2:445. In a footnote to this entry Richter suggests that "Leonardo's notes on Anaxagoras are derived from Lucretius, *De rerum natura*, I, 830 ff." (29).

67. On the tradition of Democritus's laughter in antiquity, see Lutz, "Democritus and Heraclitus." On the darkness of Democritean laughter, see especially Simon, "Anatomy of Schadenfreude."

68. Lomazzo, *Trattato dell'arte della pittura*, 384. Pedretti has speculated that Bramante's Heraclitus may be a portrait of Leonardo, and the Democritus a self-portrait. Pedretti, "Sforza Sepulchre," 125.

69. Leonardo's list of books shows that he owned a collection of sonnets written by Visconti. As Kemp points out, Leonardo is probably the "butt of a humorously critical poem" by Visconti titled "Against a bad painter." Kemp, "Science and the Poetic Impulse," 197, 199.

70. Guthrie, *History of Greek Philosophy*, 2:471. On Leonardo's extensive use of the microcosm-macrocosm analogy and his understanding of its limits, see Kemp, *Marvellous Works*, 71–136, 313–14.

open: "Democritus said: 'Oh, what an amusing diviner you are! Where did you get this new kind of prophecy?'—'Right reason and you philosophers, who claim that the great world is an onion, led me to it,' I replied. 'You're doing something beautiful,' he said, 'seeking the fate of the great world in such a little sphere!' . . . Laughing heartily, [Democritus] said, 'So, O holiest of men, you are weeping for the ruin and destruction of the world!'"[71] Alberti here captures the coincidence of doomsday prophecy and the microcosm/macrocosm analogy in a joke. As everyone knows, when an onion is destroyed (i.e., cut up), tears follow. But for Democritus, the thought contained a certain truth—though not the one the speaker initially intended. The deflationary movement of the Democritean analogy reduces everything to the same material stuff, the world to its elements. As the ancient philosopher (and Leonardo) knew, such a shift in point of view might generate laughter.

As we've seen, the riddles' collapse of scale and perspective can raise moral and ethical questions. In some cases, they invite us to measure ourselves against the image of the natural world. We see this most clearly perhaps where Leonardo extends his prophetic style to ponder the physical workings of matter. Consider now these two riddles:

Something will fall from the sky which will transport a large part of Africa which lies under that sky towards Europe, and that of Europe towards Africa, and that of the Scythian countries will meet with tremendous revolutions.[72]

[Of the Rains, which by making the Rivers muddy, wash away the land.]

The greatest mountains, even those which are remote from the sea shore, will drive the sea from its place.

71. Alberti, *Momus*, 3.53.
72. Leonardo, *Notebooks*, ed. Richter, 2:358.

[This is by Rivers which carry the Earth they wash away from the Mountains and bear it to the Sea-shore; and where the Earth comes the sea must retire.][73]

The image of the catastrophic makes visible developments that are usually beneath our attention or simply beyond a human life span; it is as if the world were here represented in a time-lapse video. In the words of Valéry, "As though [Leonardo] found the metamorphoses of things too gradual when observed in a calm, he adores battles, tempests, the deluge."[74] Slow and imperceptible processes quicken so that they might be perceived. Leonardo invites the reader to picture these processes elsewhere—for example, where he describes the gradual rising of the sea from crumbling mountains: "In the end the mountains will be leveled by the waters, seeing that they wash away the earth which covers them and uncover their rocks, which begin to crumble and subdued alike by heat and frost are being continually changed into soil . . . and by reason of this ruin the waters rise in a swirling flood and form great seas."[75]

In riddles such as these, the mode of analogy resembles the epistemological procedure we see practically everywhere in the notebooks. One finds Leonardo frequently shifting between scales: for example, using sawdust in a turbulent stream to make its movements visible to the eye, which in turn leads his mind to the dynamic, curling forms of a hurricane.[76] In his projected book on water, Leonardo tells us he wishes to "describe all the shapes that water assumes, from its largest

73. Leonardo, *Notebooks*, ed. Richter, 2:366.

74. Valéry, "Introduction to the Method of Leonardo da Vinci," 33.

75. Leonardo, *Notebooks*, ed. Wells, 19.

76. Such examples are reminiscent of Homer's epic similes—as, for example, when Poseidon inundates Odysseus with wind and water and the waves are likened to straw: "As when a strong wind tosses a heap of straw that is dry, and some it scatters here, some there, just so the wave scattered the timbers of the raft." Homer, *Odyssey* 5.368–69.

to its smallest wave, and their causes."[77] Elsewhere, a sponge squeezed underwater illustrates why the "winds that make war upon the earth's surface descend from above."[78] These examples are like the prophecies in reverse.

Leonardo transforms the horror of prophecy into the stuff of the ordinary, but sometimes even his treatment of real disasters can seem bathetic. Kenneth Clark has noted, "The scientific care with which . . . appalling catastrophes are studied has an almost comic effect."[79] Which is to say, scientific attention brings disaster down to size. Here too Leonardo might have found sympathy with ancient models. Both Seneca and Lucretius, for example, were interested in the cognitive shift from the catastrophic to the quotidian. In his discussion of the causes of earthquakes, for example, Seneca invites the reader to understand the terrifying shaking of the ground in terms of an ordinary incident—the derailing of a wagon on the road:

> Whenever large loads are pulled through the streets <on a line> of several vehicles, and the wheels fall really heavily into potholes, you will feel the buildings shaking. Asclepiodotus reports that when a boulder broke off the side of a mountain and crashed down, nearby buildings collapsed in the tremor. The same can happen below the ground: some overhanging rock becomes detached and falls into a cavern below with great momentum and noise, and with greater violence the heavier it is or the further it falls; and thus the entire roof of the hollow depression is shaken.[80]

77. Leonardo, *Notebooks*, ed. Wells, 18.
78. Leonardo, *Notebooks*, ed. Wells, 42.
79. Clark, *Leonardo da Vinci*, 226.
80. Seneca, *Natural Questions* 6.22.1–2. As Loris Premuda has suggested, Leonardo may have become acquainted with the content of Seneca's *Natural Questions* while circulating in the intellectual environments of Milan, Venice, and Florence. Premuda, "Motivi senecani in Leonardo," 244. Cf. Lucretius, *De rerum natura* 6.543–51.

Here we have three events: a wagon passing by a building, the falling of a boulder from a mountain, and the trembling caused by an earthquake. All these events generate shaking, though at different scales, and all of them are equally ordinary from a cosmic perspective. We might even imagine Leonardo framing Seneca's analogy as a prophecy: "Houses will be moved by a sudden collapse." Sometimes the prophecies appear to function like this kind of domesticating analogy, "cooling" reason down, as Conte has described the cognitive effect of such analogies in Lucretius.[81] But if in moments the riddles unlock a cosmic perspective, they rarely (if ever) offer the same kind of consolation. Rather than console, they tend to raise more questions than they know how to answer. What is time in relation to movement? What is man in the space of the universe, in relation to other living creatures and to matter itself? How do we understand the notion of justice against a vision of indifferent nature — and, in moments it seems, an indifferent God? If Leonardo is drawing directly (or indirectly) upon an ancient model of domesticating analogy, he also observes the "unleashing of speculative energy" that this kind of analogy often entails — an energy that does not always seem entirely within his control.[82]

In the taxonomy I quoted above, Leonardo speaks somewhat ambiguously of the riddles "first show[ing] the evils and then the punishment of philosophical things." For his contemporaries, his use of the word "philosophical" might have pointed to the traditional divisions of logic, ethics, and metaphysics. Not surprisingly, the artist who celebrated experience had little patience for overreaching metaphysical speculations

81. Conte, *Genres and Readers*, 152n49: "It seems that his argumentative intention prevails over the emotional effects; the need to diminish the frightening phenomena makes the reasoning cool down in a comparison with banal and controllable experiences." Cited and discussed in Williams, *Cosmic Viewpoint*, 221–22. Williams finds a "like effect" in Seneca.

82. Williams, *Cosmic Viewpoint*, 222.

or the vain subtleties of Scholastic logic.[83] We've already seen how Leonardo treats questions of man's "virtue." But if the "prophecies" began for him as a parody of medieval Scholasticism, a satirical send-up of doomsday rhetoric, a trivial pastime for his own private amusement, or even a lesson in the hazards of "ordinary language," as Gombrich has suggested, they come to serve a more experimental function in the notebooks that may have surprised even the artist himself. [84] The sheer range of affect they produce—the laughter of Democritus, the silly and terrifying "furor" of the prophet, the terror of imminent disaster, the groan or delight of the answer, the barely disguised aggressiveness of some, the total banality of others—makes them not easily reducible to any one thing. Where one prophecy gives rise to another or activates other movements on the page, where the riddles echo and parody the artist's analytical moods in the notebooks, one can feel their electricity at work. Even as they are seemingly resolved, the questions they raise have a way of persisting. Perhaps part of the riddles' "punishment" is the unsettling feeling that might linger afterward. Like "the stroke in a bell [that] leaves its likeness behind it impressed as the sun in the eye or the scent in the air," as Leonardo observed in nature, so too did the "stroke" of the riddles leave an impression in that most vulnerable of media: the mind.[85]

83. The grammatical and logical ambiguities of the riddles, for example, recall the tradition of medieval *sophismata*, problem statements or puzzling propositions that were designed as exercises in reasoning. If Leonardo was parodying such forms, he was also mining their speculative and disruptive potential. In Leonardo's lifetime, the habit of mind characterized by *sophismata* was still very much in the air. The *Regulae solvendi sophismata* of the Englishman William of Heytesbury was printed in Pavia in 1481 and twice in Venice in the 1490s. As Paul Grendler observes, this was part of a wider trend. On the domination of English logic in Italian universities, see Grendler, *Universities of the Italian Renaissance*, 259. On the tradition of medieval *sophismata*, see Kretzmann, "Syncategoremata, exponibilia, sophismata."

84. Gombrich, "Leonardo and the Magicians," 65.

85. Leonardo, *Notebooks*, ed. Wells, 75.

Not all of the riddles, of course, lead to the sense of catastrophic relativism that I've aligned with materialist patterns of thought. But the strange mixture of serious ideas and throwaway lines generates a fertile context for the trial of thoughts that might not survive under the bright light of focused attention. The ambivalence of the prophecies suggests both a giddy embrace of a perspective that decenters man in the universe and a kind of nervous laughter.[86]

INSTRUCTIONS TO A PAINTER

In his book *The Film Sense*, originally published in English in 1942, the Soviet filmmaker Sergei Eisenstein quotes a passage from Leonardo's instructions to a painter on how to represent a deluge (part of the artist's projected book on painting). For Eisenstein, these instructions were an early example of audiovisual montage, the coordination of sound and image toward a heightened experience of perception. Here is an abbreviated excerpt from Leonardo's description that Eisenstein reproduces at greater length as an example of a "shooting script":

> Let the dark, gloomy air be seen beaten by the rush of opposing winds wreathed in perpetual rain mingled with hail, and bearing hither and thither a vast network of the torn branches of trees mixed together with an infinite number of leaves. . . . You should show how fragments of mountains, which have been already stripped bare by the rushing torrents, fall headlong into these very torrents and choke up the valleys. . . . Ah, how many might you have seen stopping their ears with their hands in order to shut out the loud uproar caused through the darkened air by the fury of the winds mingled together with the

86. For this point I am indebted again to Simon, who describes Democritean laughter as an affective response to contingency. See Simon, "Anatomy of Schadenfreude."

rain, the thunder of the heavens and the raging of the thunder-bolts! . . . Ah me, how many lamentations! How many in their terror flung themselves down from the rocks! . . . Others with frenzied acts were taking their own lives, in despair of ever being able to endure such anguish. . . . Already had hunger, the minister of death, taken away their life from the greater num-ber of the animals, when the dead bodies already becoming lighter began to rise from out the bottom of the deep waters, and emerged to the surface among the contending waves; and there lay beating one against another, and as balls puffed up with wind rebound back from the spot where they strike, these fell back and lay upon the other dead bodies.[87]

Michel Jeanneret has written: "The drift of the text is star-tling: As if intoxicated by his invented images of suffering, Leonardo accumulates scenes of horror until he forgets the limits of pictorial representation and slips from description to pure narration."[88] In the intoxication of the passage, the image flickers between temporalities—past, present, and the future tense of prophecy. Leonardo's source here is partly biblical, but he is also drawing on the accounts of Virgil and Ovid, contem-porary accounts of meteorological disaster, and the idea of the great flood to come in 1524.[89] The artist writes of the "cruel slaughter of the human race by the wrath of God" (*il crudele stratio fatto della umana spetie dall'ira di dio*) but evokes the "wrath of the gods" (*l'ira delli dei*) in the same breath.[90] In another

87. Eisenstein, *Film Sense*, 25–28. As an editor's note points out, Eisenstein's "broken arrangement of this passage represents [his] adaptation into script form" (*Film Sense*, 277).

88. Jeanneret, *Perpetual Motion*, 68.

89. Kemp, *Marvellous Works*, 319.

90. Leonardo, *Notebooks*, ed. Richter, 1:308. In a related passage, Leonardo describes the figures of Neptune and Aeolus arising in the storm: "Neptune will be seen in the midst of the water with his trident, and let Aeolus with his winds be shown entangling the trees floating uprooted, and whirling in the huge waves" (*Notebooks*, ed. Richter, 1:306).

place, he anticipates seventeenth-century philosophers such as Robert Hooke in questioning the singularity of the biblical flood.[91] As Martin Kemp points out, there is no ark to be found in Leonardo's description of the flood—only drowning animals and men, made visible in sporadic flashes of lightning.[92]

Leonardo observed a number of disasters firsthand. He may have experienced a particularly nasty storm in Vinci as a child—a storm Carlo Pedretti has suggested haunted Leonardo throughout his life.[93] In 1498, he traveled with Ludovico Sforza to Genoa to inspect the damage inflicted by a storm so strong that it broke the harbor wall.[94] The ekphrastic scene above is rendered not only with natural forces precisely observed but with the energy of human feeling. What Eisenstein calls "close-ups" have the effect of widening our experience of the disaster. Closing in on hands desperately clasping, or the slaughter of a child out of mercy, magnifies our sense of the storm's violence. Leonardo sets up this imagined drama of sympathy and attachment against the indifferent force of the storm, turning repeatedly to the image of animals and people jumbled together, clinging together for life, as if the distinction between them had already been dissolved. We might think back to the blurring effect of the prophecies. Here, bodies of all kinds are incorporated into the stuff of the storm like leaves.[95]

After the harrowing exercise in sympathetic absorption, however, Leonardo returns us to the practice of image making. What Eisenstein omits from the painter's instructions is the final gesture, a passage on how to render the movement of air visible: "Perhaps it will seem to you that you may reproach

91. Leonardo, *Notebooks*, ed. Richter, 2:208–9: "Here a doubt arises, and that is: whether the deluge, which happened at the time of Noah, was universal or not. And it would seem not, for the reasons now to be given."

92. Kemp, *Marvellous Works*, 69.

93. Pedretti, *Leonardo*, 9–24.

94. Leonardo, *Notebooks*, ed. Wells, 309.

95. See Jeanneret, *Perpetual Motion*, 57.

me with having represented the currents made through the air by the motion of the wind notwithstanding that the wind itself is not visible in the air. To this I must answer that it is not the motion of the wind but only the motion of the things carried along by it which is seen in the air."[96] This was a familiar preoccupation. Leonardo's notebooks are filled with studies of the effects of air on the flight of birds, observations of the flow of wind, images of water in motion.[97] On another page, Leonardo gives instructions on how to make visible the realm of the invisible: "In order to see the movement of wind and its swirling eddies, have a tube made out of a reed and put cotton well compressed at one end of it; and from the other end blow smoke through it. The smoke, coming out of the tube, will show how wind whirls about in the air."[98] From these turbulent forms, Leonardo draws an analogy to the "tremendous fury of the wind driven by the falling in of the hills on the caves within"—a catastrophe conjured out of thin air.[99]

As both physical example and analogy, the wind represented for Leonardo a problem of perceiving the imperceptible.[100] As Karl Jaspers once said, Leonardo "was convinced that everything could be made visible."[101] Like Alberti, who suggested painters pay special attention to the movement of air in garments, making sure to represent the proper direction of the wind, Leonardo gave a good deal of thought to the fluid dynamics of bodies—and to the kinds of analogies that rendered

96. Leonardo, *Notebooks*, ed. Richter, 1:309.

97. See Nova, *Book of the Wind*, 73–87. On the textual history of Leonardo's thoughts on wind and weather and their organization by later editors, see Farago, "Wind and Weather."

98. Leonardo, *On Painting*, 82. According to Pedretti, this note was probably dictated by Leonardo to Francesco Melzi.

99. Leonardo, *Notebooks*, ed. Richter, 1:312–13.

100. Nova, *Book of the Wind*, 86.

101. Jaspers, *Leonardo, Descartes, Max Weber*, 50.

their movements sensible.[102] One particular analogy returns with special fluency and force throughout the notebooks: "The movement of water within water proceeds like that of air within air."[103] Or as Leonardo describes it elsewhere, "The air moves like a river and carries the clouds with it; just as running water carries all the things that float upon it."[104] The analogy appears again when he turns to the flight of birds: "In order to give the true science of the flight of birds through the air you must first give the science of the winds, which we shall prove by the motion of the waters; and the understanding of this science, which can be studied through the senses, will serve as a ladder to arrive at the perception of flying things in the air and the wind."[105] Through this "ladder" of perception the artist was able to shift from the visible to the invisible. Here, analogy is a like an instrument; Leonardo is in control—not unlike the birds whose flight he seeks to understand and whose effortless navigation of the wind he describes elsewhere in mechanical terms. Just as the "imperceptible movement of the rudder" of a ship allows it to move "amid such a weight of water as presses on its every beam, and in the teeth of the impetuous winds which are enveloping its mighty sails," so too, he says, birds can navigate both above and below, strategically avoiding the "fury of the wind compressed in the hollows of the mountains" and

---

102. For Aby Warburg's seminal discussion of this topic, see "Sandro Botticelli's *Birth of Venus* and *Spring.*" On Leonardo's representation of fluid dynamics, see especially Gombrich, "Form of Movement in Water and Air." According to Pedretti, around 1510, roughly the same period as his drawings of the deluge, Leonardo "began to bring wind into his visions of landscapes as an element that produces the ever-changing sequence of bulging forms in the clouds ('gruppi') and affects the shape and colour of trees and vegetation." Pedretti, *Literary Works of Leonardo da Vinci*, 1:310. See also Viatte, *'Della figura che va contro il vento.'*

103. Leonardo, *Notebooks*, ed. Wells, 37.
104. Leonardo, *Notebooks*, ed. Wells, 86.
105. Leonardo, *Notebooks*, ed. Wells, 84.

the fate of being "dashed upon the cliffs and the high rocks and trees."[106] But even in the midst of this fantasy of avian mastery, the artist must acknowledge that birds can get swept up in "eddies and whirls" despite their best efforts to avoid them — just as the mind can get swept up in flight.[107]

In antiquity, the analogy between wind and water frequently took a catastrophic form. According to John F. Moffitt, for example, when Leonardo imagined his disastrous floods and storms, he may have been thinking of the following passage from the first book of *De rerum natura* where Lucretius gives us the analogy between wind and water in order to prove the existence of invisible bodies:

> First the mighty wind when stirred up beats upon the ocean and overwhelms huge ships and scatters the clouds, and at times sweeping over the plains with rapid hurricane strews them with great trees and flogs the topmost mountains with tree-crashing blasts: so furious and fierce its howling, so savage and threatening the wind's roar. Therefore undoubtedly there are unseen bodies of wind that sweep the sea, that sweep the earth, sweep the clouds of the sky also, beating them suddenly and catching them up in a hurricane; and they flow and deal devastation in the same way as water, which, soft as it is, suddenly rolls in overwelling stream when a great deluge of water from the high mountains swells the flood with torrents of rain, dashing together wreckage of forests and whole trees, nor can strong bridges withstand the sudden force of the coming water.[108]

106. Leonardo, *Notebooks*, ed. Wells, 94. On Leonardo's image of the navigation of birds in a storm, see Gombrich, "Form of Movement in Water and Air," 335–36.

107. Leonardo, *Notebooks*, ed. Wells, 94.

108. Lucretius, *De rerum natura* 1.271–86. See Moffitt, "Evidentia of Curling Waters and Whirling Winds," 29–30.

More than merely a source of catastrophic images, the poet's disaster might have suggested to Leonardo an instrument of speculation.[109] Leaping across the ladder of perception with Lucretius, we are led from a material body that can be seen (water) to an unseen motion that resembles water (wind) to a world beyond perception (atoms). If one can feel the wind, which is invisible but has body, one can imagine a world of invisible matter, also unseen but corporeal. For Lucretius, the movement across the threshold of the senses is imagined as a disaster, as if in reaching through the analogy from one realm to another we enter the storm — or the storm enters us. The experience of the imagined catastrophe as compulsive dramatizes the precipitous force of the analogy as an event that might precipitously befall the mind. This is perhaps what Valéry meant when he wrote of the "intoxication of analogy," which carries the mind's "actions to the limit of their tendency."[110]

Still, when Leonardo draws upon such images, we can hardly assume he is being an atomist or an Epicurean. Jaspers has it right: "Leonardo lived in no system, but used them all only as a means of expression."[111] While the artist, like his medieval sources, sometimes pondered the continuity, discontinuity, and divisibility of matter, the atom was decidedly too abstract (and too dogmatic) an idea for his empirical sensibilities.[112] This, however, would not necessarily stop the mind from testing such ideas on its own — particularly through images. Leonardo might have come upon his wind and water in Lucretius, but the analogy traveled in other ways, too — opening up a wider

109. Moffitt, "Evidentia of Curling Waters and Whirling Winds," 31.
110. Valéry, "Introduction to the Method of Leonardo da Vinci," 25.
111. Jaspers, *Leonardo, Descartes, Max Weber*, 36.
112. On Leonardo's attempt to reconcile "'discontinuity' with infinitely divisible 'continuity,'" for example, see Keele, *Leonardo da Vinci's Elements of the Science of Man*, 82. On the rich heterogeneity of materialist thought in the Middle Ages, see especially Robertson, "Medieval Materialism."

space for conjecture. Lucretius himself very likely derived some form of the analogy from the pseudo-Hippocratic author of *On Breaths*.[113] That text, along with Hippocrates's *Airs, Waters, Places*, was a source for scholars in the Renaissance concerned with pneumatic architecture, which stressed the circulation of air through buildings (a topic to which Leonardo himself had given serious thought in light of the plague in Milan).[114] It is possible that Leonardo knew of *On Breaths* from one of its Latin translators, the Greek scholar Janus Lascaris, who is one of the few witnesses to the artist's time at the French court when he was writing on and drawing the deluge.[115]

The author of *On Breaths* writes: "A breeze is a flowing and a current of air. When therefore much air flows violently, trees are torn up by the roots through the force of the wind, the sea swells into waves, and vessels of vast bulk are tossed about. Such then is the power that it has in these things, but it is invisible to sight, though visible to reason."[116] Notice the similar use of images—the wind, the sea, the ship—and the insistence on the figure of disaster at the edges of the unseen. Disaster dramatizes the force of the wind by intensifying the image, showing how something invisible can have real power. For this author, the subject of the analogy is not atoms but pneuma, a

---

113. See Phillips, "Lucretius and the (Hippocratic) *On Breaths*."

114. See Hardy, "'Study the warm winds and the cold.'" For Leonardo's thinking on the circulation of air and water in cities, see Kemp, *Marvellous Works*, 98.

115. In one of his epigrams, Lascaris claims to have seen the unfinished painting of Saint Anne that is now in the Louvre, comparing Leonardo to Apelles. Lascaris, *Epigrammata*, 114–15. On Leonardo and Lascaris, see Goukowsky, "Du nouveau sur Léonard de Vinci." On early translations of *On Breaths* (*De flatibus*), see Kibre, "Hippocrates Latinus," esp. 298–99; and Nelson, *Die Hippokratische Schrift "Peri physon,"* which includes the Renaissance translations of Francesco Filelfo and Lascaris.

116. Hippocrates, *Breaths* 3.6–11.

living breath that pervades the universe.[117] In the *Natural Questions*, Seneca too elaborates on the force of pneuma, which he describes in similar terms as the "tension" in the breath—one "that, when it is violently agitated and whips itself up, tears up trees and woods, seizes whole buildings, and smashes them high in the air. That stirs up the sea, which is naturally sluggish and still."[118] Giving us a sense of the persuasive force of disaster in arguments such as these, Seneca asks, "Who will deny that [breath] has tension when he sees the earth and its mountains being shaken, along with buildings and walls, large cities with their populations, and seas with their entire coastlines?"[119]

In reaching repeatedly for the speculative image of catastrophe at the threshold of the visible, Leonardo may have been thinking of any or all of these ancient sources. He was very much alive to the uncertainty of what lies beneath perception. "Nature is full of infinite causes that have never occurred in experience," he wrote in a note concerning optical illusions.[120] This uncertainty might also be the very thing that allows for (or compels) such catastrophic thoughts in the first place—the mind reflexively seeking to understand what it can't perceive through the senses.

The action of an analogy that makes sensible the insensible was a persistent source of fascination for Leonardo—and one he returns to in different ways throughout the notebooks. "The air which successively surrounds the moveable thing that is moving through it makes divers movements in itself," he writes in another place. "This is seen in the atoms that are found in

117. For the idea of pneuma in the Hippocratic corpus, see Langholf, "L'air (pneuma) et les maladies."

118. Seneca, *Natural Questions* 2.6.4.

119. Seneca, *Natural Questions* 2.8.

120. Leonardo, *Notebooks*, ed. Wells, 8. See Pedretti, *Literary Works of Leonardo da Vinci*, 2:237. This passage caught the interest of Freud in *Leonardo da Vinci and a Memory of His Childhood*, 100.

the sphere of the sun when they penetrate through some window into a dark place."[121] Citing Isidore of Seville's encyclopedia as the source for the image, Kemp argues that "there is no evidence that Leonardo ever seriously considered adopting the basic tenets of classical 'atomism.'"[122] But Leonardo need not have "adopt[ed]" the principles of atomism to have been affected by its analogies. Nor would deriving the image from Isidore (as opposed to Lucretius) shield him from learning that the sight of dust in sunlight might transport the mind from "atoms," as in small things, to even smaller particulate matter.[123]

Elsewhere, we watch Leonardo replay the turbulence of a different set of ancient analogies, tracing the movement from the idea of the unseen to what lies below. In this case, the experience of analogy leads him from the violence of the invisible wind to the subterranean world. The passage begins in medias res:

Like a whirling wind scouring through a sandy and hollow valley which with speeding course drives into its vortex everything that opposes its furious course . . .

Not otherwise does the northern blast whirl round its tempestuous progress . . .

Nor does the tempestuous sea roar so loud, when the northern blast dashes it in foaming waves between Scylla and Charybdis; nor Stromboli nor Mount Etna when their pent-up sulphurous flames send and burst open the mountain fulminating stones

121. Leonardo, *Notebooks*, ed. MacCurdy, 543.
122. Kemp, *Marvellous Works*, 300. For the argument that Leonardo's source was Lucretius, see Beretta, "Leonardo and Lucretius," 362.
123. As Isidore explains, "[Atoms] are said to fly through the void of the entire world in unceasing motion and to be carried here and there like the finest dust motes that may be seen pouring in through the window in the sun's rays." Isidore of Seville, *Etymologies*, 271.

and earth mingled together in the issuing flames. Nor when
Mount Etna's inflamed caverns vomiting the ill-restrained element and thrusting it back to its own region, driving before it
whatever obstacle withstands its impetuous rage . . . [124]

The artist is describing the force of the wind, and his interest
is arguably as scientific as it is literary. We see him here investi-
gating a style of analogy rather than simply making an analogy.
Written by a young Leonardo entranced by Ovid's vision of
perpetual change, the passage draws heavily from the poet's
account of Boreas's rape of Orithyia, which imagines the wind
god tearing through the world, shaking the sea, grappling with
his brothers. As Boreas says, "I struggle with them so fiercely
that the mid-heavens thunder with our meeting and fires leap
bursting out of the hollow clouds."[125] Anticipating Leonardo's
own turn to volcanoes, Boreas shifts his attention to the
"vaulted hollows of the earth"—her "lowest caverns"—and to
a subterranean rumbling that scares the "whole world."[126] Ovid
himself was following (and remythologizing) Lucretius's scientific account of wind, thunder, and lightning in book 6 of *De
rerum natura*, where the poet makes an analogy between winds
trapped in clouds and "caverns reared with vaulted roofs, which
when a tempest arises the winds fill."[127] The image of lightning
escaping recalls the eruption of a volcano—the winds "rolling

124. Leonardo, *Notebooks*, ed. Wells, 246–47.

125. Ovid, *Metamorphoses* 6.694–96. Leonardo's inventory of books lists a
1497 prose translation of Ovid. See Reti, *Library of Leonardo da Vinci*. According to Gerolamo Calvi, Leonardo displays a debt to Ovid in another passage
dated around 1480 that concerns the destructive nature of time. Calvi, *I manoscritti di Leonardo da Vinci*, 51.

126. Ovid, *Metamorphoses* 6.697–99. Aristotle speculated that the fire of volcanoes is generated by the friction of the wind confined in tight spaces in
the earth, "for when the air is broken up into small particles, percussion then
causes it to catch fire." Aristotle, *Meteorologica* 367a. Cf. Albertus Magnus, *Liber
de causis proprietatum elementorum*, 114–15.

127. Lucretius, *De rerum natura* 6.195–97.

together the seeds of fire . . . and send[ing] the flame rushing about the hollow furnaces within, until they have shattered the cloud and flashed forth coruscating."[128] As Leonardo channels these ancient sources directly and indirectly, the image (and sound) of catastrophe seems to outrun his ability to write it down.

In passages such as this one, we see Leonardo staging catastrophic analogies and getting caught up. At moments, however, he also steps back to observe them working, with a certain curiosity, as if he were observing the workings of a machine. This dialectic of absorption and detachment runs throughout the notebooks, with the artist experiencing the involuntary and then generating a kind of critical distance in its wake. Slightly further down the page after the magma of the volcano (and the mind) settles, a description of a rocky cavern begins to take shape.[129] As an exercise in catastrophic analogy gives over to the demands of allegory, Leonardo unfolds another scene of discovery:

> And drawn on by my eager desire, anxious to see a great multitude of varied and strange shapes made by formative nature, having wandered for some distance among overhanging rocks, I came to the entrance of a great cavern. . . . And repeatedly bending first one way and then another, to see whether I could discern anything inside, from this I was prevented by the deep darkness within. And after remaining there for a time, suddenly there arose within me two emotions, fear and desire—

128. Lucretius, *De rerum natura* 6.200–203. On the next ordered page of the manuscript following the description of ferocious winds, Leonardo writes the heading "Example of Lightning in Clouds." Leonardo, *Notebooks*, ed. Richter, 2:309. Cf. Lucretius's description of volcanoes at 6.680–93.

129. This early literary description anticipates Leonardo's later studies of the earth and the geological landscapes of the *Virgin of the Rocks* and the *Mona Lisa*. See Smith, "Observations on the Mona Lisa Landscape."

fear of the threatening dark cavern, desire to see whether there might be any marvelous thing therein."[130]

The volcanic force of the images above transforms into the inner pull of curiosity. Out of the rapid sequence of analogies that point to a world of hidden causes, the image of the underground becomes manifest.

What lies beneath the ground has long been a figure for what lies beneath perception. Albertus Magnus is often credited with creating the first experimental model—a volcano made of a brass vase and two stoppers to demonstrate how eruptions work by means of heat and pressure.[131] "For it is [the task] of natural science," he writes in *De Mineralibus*, "not simply to accept what we are told but to inquire into the causes of natural things."[132] The pseudo-Virgilian *De Aetna*, which Leonardo's contemporary Pietro Bembo draws upon in his own account of a journey to the volcano, captures a similar spirit of discovery.[133] Putting aside the "fictions poets tell" and seeking natural causes in their place, the ancient poet of *De Aetna* speculates on the nature of invisible winds, which "whirl in eddying storm and roll from the abyss":

> Oftentimes you may look out on vast cavities and tracts of land cut off ruinously and plunged into thick darkness; 'tis far-flung chaos and unending debris. Moreover, do you see how in for-

130. Leonardo, *Notebooks*, ed. Wells, 247.

131. Albertus Magnus, *Meteororum*, in *Opera omnia*, vol. 4, 3.2.17. On Albert's natural philosophy, see Weisheipl, *Albertus Magnus and the Sciences*.

132. Albertus Magnus, *Book of Minerals*, 69.

133. On the transmission of the *Aetna* and the *Appendix Vergiliana*, see Reeve, "Textual Tradition of *Aetna*, *Ciris*, and *Catalepton*." For Pietro Bembo's treatise, which was published by Aldus in 1496, see Bembo, *Lyric Poetry, Etna*, vii–xxi. As translator Mary P. Chatfield observes, "Although the attribution of *Aetna* to Virgil began to be doubted as early as Donatus's fourth-century life of the poet, Bembo seems to have believed the poem authentic" (xxin9).

ests there are lairs and caves of widely receding space which
have dug far down their deep-sunk coverts? Undiscovered is
the route of such working: only within there is an outflow. . . .
These [caves] will furnish true proofs of a depth unknown to
us. Let but your mind guide you to a grasp of cunning research:
from things manifest gather faith in the unseen.[134]

Like Leonardo's cavern, this cave is both literal and figurative.[135]
It is at once the result of violent natural events, for which it is a
kind of evidence (in Leonardo's words, the "varied and strange
shapes made by formative nature"), and a figurative threshold
between a world perceived and what lies below the senses.[136]
As Democritus said, "Truth is in the depths."[137]

But while Leonardo understood there were limits to man's
knowledge, he was not one to lament the bottomlessness

134. Pseudo-Virgil, *Aetna*, lines 210–11, 137–45 (emphasis mine). James I.
Porter writes: "Much of the sublimity of the *Aetna* derives from the same
shiver of awe that runs through Lucretius' poem in the face of the same realization as the *Aetna* poet conveys—namely, that the world is an uncertain
place and substance, that it is not what it seems, that the ground on which we
stand is as hollow as the sky above . . . and just as abyssal too." Porter, *Sublime
in Antiquity*, 508.

135. Nicholl ingeniously connects the cave passage to Leonardo's scenic design for Angelo Poliziano's *Orfeo*. Nicholl, *Leonardo da Vinci*, 164–65.

136. Leonardo, *Notebooks*, ed. Wells, 247.

137. Leonardo could easily have found a version of this Democritean fragment in any number of sources, including Diogenes Laertius's *Lives* (he also
owned a translation of this text) or Isidore's medieval encyclopedia. See,
again, Laertius, *Lives* 9.72.10. Isidore writes on the same theme: "The Aca-
demics . . . believe that everything is doubtful, but, just as it must be said
that many things are doubtful and hidden, which God has wished to be beyond the intelligence of humans, nevertheless there are many things that can
be grasped by the senses and understood by reason. The philosopher Arcesi-
laus of Cyrene founded this school; his follower was Democritus, who said
that truth lies hidden, as if in a well so deep that it has no bottom." Isidore of
Seville, *Etymologies*, 179.

of the pit.[138] The romantic image of the explorer descending into the cavern might even be understood as an early version of the Renaissance topos of Time rescuing Truth from the pit, though here it is the artist doing the rescuing.[139] Indeed, what Seneca once said of the pre-Socratic philosophers might be said here of Leonardo: "It took great courage to prize open nature's hiding places, and, not content with her outward appearance, to look inside, and to immerse oneself in the secrets of the gods."[140] Then again, it was not only with excitement that Leonardo peered into the gaping maw of the cavern, but also with "fear." Just as he attempts to refashion the involuntary experience of the catastrophic analogy as a heroic scene of discovery, the passage suddenly breaks off. Among several notes on the opposite side of the page, Leonardo's mind notably turns to the end of the world: "Then the earth will be forced to close with the element of fire and its surface will be burnt to cinders, and this will be the end of all terrestrial nature."[141]

The idea of disaster as a figure of the insensible world allows us to see Leonardo's description of the deluge with new eyes. In this description, it is not only the element of chaos nor the imagined violence of the composition that links Leonardo to a materialist perspective, but rather what I've been describing as the experience of analogy itself.[142] Leonardo invites us

138. Valéry puts it nicely: "An abyss would make [Leonardo] think of a bridge." Valéry, "Note and Digression," 79.

139. On the history of this iconography in the Renaissance, see Saxl, "Veritas Filia Temporis."

140. Seneca, *Natural Questions* 6.5.2.

141. Leonardo, *Notebooks*, ed. Wells, 17.

142. It is on this point that I want to distinguish what I am proposing here about Leonardo from the work of other scholars who have detected materialist influences in artists both contemporary with Leonardo and after him. Stephen J. Campbell, for example, makes a compelling case for the presence of Lucretius in Giorgione's *Tempest*. See Campbell, "Giorgione's 'Tempest.'" In his reading of Tintoretto's *The Conversion of St. Paul*, Jonathan Goldberg de-

(and his ideal painter) to inhabit the middle space of the figure. Whereas the ancient analogies that concern wind and water all describe a simple landscape of naked force devoid of people, Leonardo asks us to think of the image of suffering in the unfolding of the analogy, raising a question about how we can and should encounter his imagined painting. As Claire Farago points out, Leonardo's "idea that painting is created by 'discourse' but viewed at one time like eternal, divine 'essences' is central to his defense of painting."[143] But if seeing things at one glance is associated with the angelic and divine, the challenge of viewing suffering with detachment in this scene of deluge is a reminder that such vision does not come easily to us here on earth, not even to Leonardo.

Where the rapid change in scale and perspective frames this problem of detachment, disaster embodies the transitional space of thought tacking between the sensible and the insensible. In this regard, the artist's description of the flood is perhaps closer in affective impact to Lucretius's arresting account of the Athenian plague than to the spare economy of the wind and water analogy. In the slow motion of death-bringing waves, it is almost as if the artist is bringing the uncanny temporality of plague to bear upon the deluge, feeling his way through it as a figure of thought. What may at first seem like a didactic

---

scribes the composition as a "jumble of bodies" and a "vectoring of energies" reflective of "Lucretian questions of materiality." Goldberg, *Seeds of Things*, 25. In my reading of Leonardo, materialism is less indebted to Lucretius specifically than to a style of catastrophic thinking he discovers and tests through a practice of analogy making.

143. Farago, *Leonardo da Vinci's "Paragone,"* 327. See, for example, Leonardo, *Notebooks*, ed. Wells, 185. See also Stowell, *Spiritual Language of Art*, 150–60. Thomas Aquinas had used the idea of seeing things at one glance to distinguish human discursive reason from angelic intelligence, citing the authority of Augustine (in *De Trinitate* 14.3): "In heaven *our thoughts will not be fleeting, going and returning from one thing to another, but we shall behold all our knowledge at the same time by one glance.*" Aquinas, *Basic Writings*, 1:540; cited in Farago, *Leonardo da Vinci's "Paragone,"* 327.

description for a projected painting or even genre of painting becomes a meditation on the violence of the kind of thought that automatically reduces everything to matter and the laws of matter. If the ancient materialist position is one that "objectifies all experience in a resolutely scientific, calculating, and ultimately nonphilosophic (unthinking) manner," as John T. Hamilton has characterized it in another context, Leonardo may be said to have given a rare expression to the lived experience of this kind of unthinking thought.[144]

Leonardo once said that while the poet deals primarily in moral things, the painter is a student of natural philosophy.[145] In a passage celebrating "the divinity which belongs to the science of painting," he writes of the divinity of art "transmut-[ing] the painter's mind into a likeness of the divine mind," turning to the creation of images of violent rivers descending from mountains, great floods, the fury of the sea.[146] The idea that the painter is a "lord of all types of people and things" takes on special meaning in the context of envisioning the misery caused by catastrophe. Unlike God, however, the artist exists in time, and the experience of the imagined catastrophe is inescapably temporal, rooted in the body. In his instructions on how to paint a deluge, we see the artist qua philosopher posing this question of "creation" again to himself, which also means encountering the involuntariness of his own imagination. If in one instance the artist teaches with a godlike detachment, in another he pictures the extreme agony of men, reflecting on the power of thought itself. Consider Leonardo's description of the compulsive course of a river:

144. Hamilton, *Security*, 263.

145. Leonardo, *Notebooks*, ed. Wells, 185: "Truly painting is a science, the true-born child of nature, for painting is born of nature, but to be more correct we should call it the grandchild of nature; since all visible things were brought forth by nature and these her children have given birth to painting."

146. Leonardo, *Treatise on Painting*, 280; cited and discussed in Gombrich, "Leonardo and the Magicians," 71.

Against the irreparable inundation caused by swollen and proud rivers no resource of human foresight can avail. For in a succession of raging and seething waves gnawing and tearing away high banks, growing turbid with the earth from ploughed fields, destroying the houses therein and uprooting the tall trees, it carries these as its prey down to the sea which is its lair, bearing along with it men, trees, animals, houses, and lands, sweeping away every dike and every kind of barrier, bearing along the light things, and devastating and destroying those of weight, creating big landslips out of small fissures, filling up with floods the low valleys, and rushing headlong with destructive and inexorable mass of waters. What a need there is of flight for whoso is near![147]

The image resonates with Machiavelli's famous description of Fortune as a river that "inundates plains, uproots trees, ruins buildings, and rips up the earth from one place to deposit it in another."[148] Leonardo imagines the river as a ravenous beast hunting its prey, but this fiction of intention only underlines nature's indifference. The flood is an encounter between organic life and the dead matter out of which all living things are made up and into which they must finally resolve. Leonardo's description of the flood's compulsive course is a vision of necessity.

"Oh! marvellous, O stupendous necessity," Leonardo writes in another place, "by thy laws thou dost compel [*costrigni*] every effect to be the direct result of its cause, by the shortest path."[149] The idea of necessity was central to Leonardo's thinking. One could also say, however, that disaster was central to his idea of necessity. As Paolo Galluzzi has observed, "While

147. Leonardo, *Notebooks*, ed. Wells, 26.

148. Machiavelli, *Prince*, 363. For a speculative account of Leonardo's possible collaboration with Machiavelli on a failed project to redirect the Arno River around Pisa, see Masters, *Fortune Is a River*.

149. Leonardo, *Notebooks*, ed. Richter, 1:19.

there are several examples of how Leonardo contrasts a good and provident nature with a fierce, merciless humanity, much more numerous are the texts in which nature appears forced to obey the strict laws imposed on her; laws that do not provide for any privileged treatment of mankind. Nature is, in fact, indifferent to the fate of her own creatures, man included."[150] If disaster makes sensible the insensible, it was also an affective experience of what is "irrevocable" about nature's laws, painful but necessary and thus also a source of pleasure. In other words, catastrophe represents the place in Leonardo's thought where the idea of nature's "marvellous necessity" collides with the self-generated compulsion of catastrophizing, which is the mind's attempt to confer necessity upon its thoughts—that is, to *feel* them as necessary. It is this affective structure (rather than a commitment to the principles of atomism) that most strongly links Leonardo to the materialists.

In the English preface to *The Film Sense* (1942), which was not incorporated into the book on account of the war, Eisenstein describes art as "the most sensitive seismograph," and states that the "tragic impasse of it in the last years reflected only the degree of tension into which the world has been plunged by its lacerating contradictions."[151] Calling to mind the "slaughter" that took place "on an unprecedented scale," he writes: "Neither the paradoxicality of what is happening, neither the scale of what has already happened, nor the perspective of what awaits the world to experience—can be grasped by a single consciousness."[152] After the war, Eisenstein would publish *Nonindifferent Nature: Film and the Structure of Things* (1948), in which this preface was partly reproduced, elaborating the "pathos formula" he recognized in Leonardo's deluge.[153] In following this

150. Galluzzi, "Leonardo da Vinci's Concept of 'Nature,'" 14.

151. Eisenstein, *Nonindifferent Nature*, 289.

152. Eisenstein, *Nonindifferent Nature*, 290.

153. The phrase "pathos formula" recalls the work of Aby Warburg, although, as Antonio Somaini has suggested, the fact that both Warburg and

"prescription," as he called it, the viewer would arrive at the desired state of "being beside oneself"—an ecstasy by which he or she could experience the universal processes of nature itself.[154] For Eisenstein, this state was inherently dynamic, a continuous "leap" from quality to quality through the "ever-heightening intensity of the emotional content."[155] The "pathos formula" allows the artist who seeks an elusive unity in a world of chaos to draw formal connections across fields of inquiry—from the study of "changing geological eras and historical epochs and succeeding social systems" to the "cosmos and history" to the "practical application of the atom, which is now so much obsessing the imagination of nations after the destructive action of the atom bombs dropped on Japan."[156] In the involuntary throes of induced ecstasy, Eisenstein reminds us, "we are not dealing with God, but with the principles of those laws by which the Universe, Nature, etc. exist and function—that is, by which the manifestations of matter function."[157]

THE ART OF LOSING

Near the end of his life, while living in France at the court of Francis I, Leonardo composed a series of eleven drawings, now held at Windsor Castle: images that depict a violent, swirling flux of a storm sweeping up walls and trees, and entire towns viewed from a distance and consumed in an orgy of natural

Eisenstein use the term is perhaps only a surprising coincidence. Somaini, *Ejzenštejn*, 25. Nevertheless, a comparison to Warburg is illuminating. Robert Buch has described Warburg's notion of the *Pathosformel* thus: "In keeping with the characteristic polarities of the category, Warburg's term encompasses the tension between the appeal to a certain affective excess and the need to get this affective overload under control, precisely by casting it into a form, by fixating this intense vitality in an image." Buch, *Pathos of the Real*, 21.

154. Eisenstein, *Nonindifferent Nature*, 28.
155. Eisenstein, *Nonindifferent Nature*, 38.
156. Eisenstein, *Nonindifferent Nature*, 159.
157. Eisenstein, *Nonindifferent Nature*, 174.

forces.[158] Eisenstein perhaps encountered the drawings himself at Windsor, where he mentions having seen Leonardo's notebooks.[159] Scholars have understood these drawings in various ways. Edgar Wind once speculated (rather oddly) that the pictures were designs for elaborate mechanical fountains destined for court entertainments.[160] Pedretti has read them as fragments of the artist's early memory of a disastrous storm.[161] Others have seen in them the artist's own anxious vision of the second global flood that captured the imaginations of contemporary prophets and astrologers and gave Dürer nightmares.[162]

The drawings themselves contain multiple perspectives. Between the frames of this series (in their very challenge to seriality), Leonardo reminds us of the contingency of thought's experiment—the fleeting intensities of the mind's absorption and the fragility of detachment. Many of the drawings are rendered in black chalk, which Alessandro Nova has suggested

158. For individual descriptions of Leonardo's deluge sketches, see Pedretti, *Drawings and Miscellaneous Papers*. See also Clark, *Leonardo da Vinci*, 221–28; Jeanneret, *Perpetual Motion*, 50–70.

159. Eisenstein, *Beyond the Stars*, 675.

160. Wind, "Mathematics and Sensibility," 706: "It has been asked why Leonardo would, in such an exact form, study phenomena scientifically which in nature would presumably not occur; and why, in designing them, as it were, on paper he made these extremely careful calculations. My own suspicion is that whereas naturally such a deluge is a fantasy, at the same time it is related to fantasies of a more realistic kind, and that as Leonardo was really a designer for festivals, he may have also been a designer for water arts."

161. See, again, Pedretti, *Leonardo*, 9–24. Clark has also taken a turn as analyst, inquiring of the late sketches of deluge: "Through what strange inhibition did Leonardo attempt to hide from himself the true motive of these drawings? . . . Was it a kind of reserve which prevented him from betraying his innermost feelings in words, even though they were expressed in line? For these drawings come from the depths of Leonardo's soul." Clark tellingly footnotes this passage with a nod to Freud. Clark, *Leonardo da Vinci*, 226.

162. On the evening of June 7–8, 1525, Albrecht Dürer recorded his terrifying dream of a great flood with an accompanying watercolor image known as his *Dream Vision* (Vienna, Kunsthistorisches Museum, W. 944). See Rosenthal, "Dürer's Dream of 1525."

captures "the quality of expanding perception in time, since the eye needs to focus in order to distinguish the uncertain outlines of objects and to reconstruct what the graphic medium leaves unexpressed."[163] Their relatively small size, which one inevitably forgets while examining them, gives this sense of expansion a spatial dimension in addition to a temporal one. We watch Leonardo turning the idea of disaster around in his mind much as he did human anatomy, though here this change in perspective is psychological as well as physical. In one drawing (pl. 1), for example, we see from an aerial view the faint indication of a town in the moment of being suddenly swept up by a storm. Details emerge, though indistinctly. There are no men or women, but we grasp the windows of their houses; we see the outline of human structures, homes instantly demolished as if they were made of a child's building blocks. Like the word *diluvio*, the disaster shuttles between the local and global, threatening to fill the imagination.

In another drawing (pl. 2), barely visible gods emerge from the shapes of clouds, terrifying the tiny figures below. The gods become visible in the great tumult as if in brief flashes of lightning (pl. 3). The specter of the oncoming deluge appears to arise from the upper right-hand corner of the drawing. Across an ambiguous passage of unused space, the figures below appear as if they had already suffered the blow. In the collapse of the present and future that is the visual equivalent of prophecy, we are invited to see divinity in the clouds through their terrified eyes. *Timor facit deos*, fear creates gods.

Nearly obscured in another drawing (pl. 4)—a vision of collapsing "blocks"—is a technical note on how to represent the effect of transparency in a storm (the barely visible text itself enacting the effect the artist is describing): "Of rain. You will show the degrees of falling rain at various distances and of varying degrees of obscurity, and let the darkest part be closest to the middle of its thickness." Here, the artist steps back again, suspending thought between the actions of the mind and the hand. He is talking again to his imagined student and to himself. As the flood moves toward us and flows out of the picture, Leonardo sets into motion a spatial play of surface and depth. We stand in the direct line of the flood, though we now see as the artist sees—through the picture.

One final sketch (pl. 5) depicts what remains of several trees being torn from their roots, though it's not clear from what perspective. We encounter this view seemingly from both head-on and above, an illusion that evokes a sense of movement. The tree having been rendered by Leonardo with care, we feel it being torn away as the representational gives way to the geometry of the storm, another imminent loss of scale and perspective. In lieu of the suffering bodies of the verbal description, we have the struggle of a tree, and the challenge here is *not* to see our own suffering in it. The image moves in and out of an anthropomorphic perspective.

With these drawings in mind, I want to end by turning briefly to one of Leonardo's learned contemporaries who was also exploring what it meant to inhabit the catastrophe of materialist thought and feeling. Around the same time Leonardo was conjuring up the deluge in France, the Bolognese humanist Giambattista Pio was feeling his own way through the disasters of materialism. Amid the learned notes of his 1511 edition of *De rerum natura* (the first printed Renaissance commentary on the poem), Pio scattered personal "digressions."[164] He begins the first excursus by recounting a recent apparition in the

164. On Pio's commentary in general, see Raimondi, "Il primo commento umanistico a Lucrezio"; Del Nero, "G. B. Pio fra grammatica e filosofia"; Dionisotti, "Giovan Battista Pio e Mario Equicola"; Longo, *Savoir de la nature et poésie des choses*, 38–41; Palmer, *Reading Lucretius in the Renaissance*, 155–62. In his digressions, Pio was following the example of his teacher, Filippo Beroaldo. On the uses of Beroaldo's digressions, see especially Casella, "Il metodo dei commentatori umanistici esemplato sul Beroaldo"; Krautter, *Philologische*

"salty fields" of Bologna: the spectacle of two "giants" fight-
ing that was witnessed, he says, by almost "all of Italy."[165] The
note comes in the context of Lucretius describing the way that
men falsely see images in the clouds—making of them what
they will. In the case of the giants, it was a matter of finding signs and portents of future disasters. The note proceeds
to document the misfortunes that *did* follow soon after: the
earthquakes Pio experienced in 1505; the death of his teacher,
Filippo Beroaldo, and his father the same year; and the papal
capture of Bologna (another kind of disaster for his patrons, the
Bentivoglio family). It was as if the giants were, in fact, a sign.
But even as he recounts this narrative, he appears detached and
skeptical. Recent history is narrated as a flow of events rather
than as the effects of a divine plan—a flow that moves in and
out of scales, personal and public, micro and macro. Alongside Lucretius's critique of people who superstitiously see what
they want in the clouds, Pio seems to be offering his own skeptical critique of those who imagine in the recent earthquakes
a vision of God's punishing hand and, in the arrival of a usurp-
ing pope, an end to their troubles. In the case of this particular digression, the commentator seems to have found a way
to make the poet's detachment his own—to find distance and
even pleasure in times of disaster.[166]

But capturing the *afflatus* or spirit of a poet who declared
the soul mortal, and was said to have committed suicide, was
not always so easy.[167] The accidental quality of Pio's notes in the

Methode und humanistische Existenz, 40–52; Gaisser, *Fortunes of Apuleius and the
"Golden Ass*," 197–242.

165. Lucretius, *De rerum natura*, ed. Pio, fol. 123ᵛ.

166. At the end of this first digression, Pio writes of the sweetness of diverting one's attention with history. Lucretius, *De rerum natura*, ed. Pio, fol. 123ᵛ.

167. A good commentator, Beroaldo insisted, was like a Platonic rhap-
sode—inspired by a *poeticus afflatus* that allowed him to participate in the mysteries of the text as he carefully penetrated into their hidden recesses. Bero-

commentary—their occasional nature—conveys the shifting feeling of the mind's encounter with a materialist perspective and the resistance it can generate. The weight of Pio's digressions is perhaps most deeply felt in a digression on the death of his mother. Her memory arises as he is reading the sixth book of *De rerum natura* where Lucretius is explaining the nature of volcanic eruptions. The passage begins with more general instructions to the Epicurean initiate who is learning to see the universe from a cosmic perspective:

> In considering these matters you must cast your view wide and deep, and survey all quarters far abroad, that you may remember how profound is the sum of things, and see how very small a part, how infinitesimal a fraction the whole universe is to one sky—not so large a part as one man is of the whole earth. If you should keep this steadily before your mind, comprehend it clearly, see it clearly, you would cease to wonder at many things.[168]

The question is, how "steadily" can one hold this unsettling idea before the mind—an idea that is both brought on by the image of disaster and itself productive of catastrophic thoughts? What follows is the familiar analogy between microcosm and macrocosm, which the ancient poet invokes to explain that, like the body, the earth too is subject to violent upheavals:

> For is there any of us who feels wonder, if someone has got into his limbs a fever that gathers with burning heat, or any other pain from disease throughout his body? For the foot suddenly swells, a sharp aching often seizes the teeth, or invades the eyes

aldo, *Commentarii in Propertium*, fol. A2ʳ. See Beroaldo, *Annotationes Centum*, 7–9.

168. Lucretius, *De rerum natura* 6.647–54.

themselves, the accursed fire appears creeping over the body and burning each part it takes hold on, and crawls over the limbs, assuredly because there are seeds of many things, and this earth and sky produce enough noxious disease that from it may grow forth an immeasurable quantity of disease.[169]

Here, Lucretius turns our attention to the experience of the human body. The analogy serves a specific point, allowing the poet to refer to large-scale effects. "In this way therefore," he writes, "we must believe that a supply of all things is brought up from the infinite to the whole heaven and earth, enough to enable the earth on a sudden to quake and move, the swift whirlwind to scour over land and sea, Etna's fires to overflow, the heaven to burst in a blaze."[170] The thought doesn't stop there. What begins as a discrete analogy between the microcosm and macrocosm carries the mind still further. It is not only that man himself is minuscule in relation to the earth but also that "all with earth and sea and sky thrown in are nothing to all the sum of the whole universe."[171]

It is at this point in his commentary that Pio brings us to another kind of remembering—to a scene of dying and a figure of the suffering body that resists the imperative to go "wide and deep, and survey all quarters far abroad." This is what he says:

It was because of such a disease that my mother Helena, of sacred memory, ended her days. At the risk of making any omissions let me say that no woman has ever been more pious, unassuming, devout, or more deserving to be included in the ancient rolls of married women. When she was alive it was a

169. Lucretius, *De rerum natura* 6.655–64.
170. Lucretius, *De rerum natura* 6.665–69.
171. Lucretius, *De rerum natura* 6.678–79.

delight to be alive; since she died every day I have spent has been gloomy and mournful.[172]

As Pio knew well, the philosophy of Epicurus and Lucretius generally advocates an abstinence from excessive emotion and, as some readers in the Renaissance complained, from any emotion at all.[173] Like Leonardo's instructions to a painter, Pio's digression on his mother unlocks an unexpected place for feeling in materialist thought—one that deepens and inflects the undercurrent of melancholy in Lucretius's poem.[174] What Lucretius minimizes here (a single human being in the space of the universe) is precisely what has stayed with Pio as he moves across the dizzying scale of the analogy and back again. At the threshold between the microcosm and the macrocosm, the commentator interrupts the precipitous and violent shift of the mind to catastrophe as an image of the insensible. In light of the memory of one woman, the figure of disaster gains another kind of affective force, pointing not only to hidden processes but also to a surplus of emotion that can feel like an eruption. The memory of a mother quietly opposes the cosmic force of analogy. In the end, it's not clear if Pio has cultivated a

172. Lucretius, *De rerum natura*, ed. Pio, fol. 202ʳ (my translation). Pio goes on to credit his mother, who provided his teachers with special incentives to educate him well, for his considerable reputation in oratory.

173. In Bartolomeo Scala's *Dialogus de Consolatione* (1463), for example, Scala's patron Cosimo de' Medici describes the limitations of Epicurean philosophy on matters of sorrow, loss, and suffering—limitations that render the philosophy useless. Written on the occasion of the death of Cosimo's son, the text understands the Epicurean position as untenable—impossibly cold and inhuman. Scala, *Essays and Dialogues*, 104–5. On mourning and humanism in the Quattrocento, see King, *Death of the Child Valerio Marcello*.

174. Marsilio Ficino writes of "melancholic genius" (*ingenium melancholicum*) with regard to Lucretius. Ficino, *Platonic Theology*, 4:308–9. In this case, to capture the *afflatus* of the poet, as Beroaldo had suggested, was ironically to be captured by the poet's melancholy.

reading of Lucretius that exposes an underlying tension within the poem or whether the relation he develops is ultimately one of resistance or failed identification. As in Leonardo's images and descriptions of storm and flood, it is perhaps merely in making room for ambivalence that his catastrophic digressions are most powerful.

TWO

Earthquakes of the Mind

In "The Intentional Fallacy," W. K. Wimsatt and Monroe Beardsley turned to a line in John Donne's "A Valediction: Forbidding Mourning" (ca. 1611) in order to make a point about the limits of reading historical context into poetry: "Moving of th' earth brings harms and fears: / Men reckon what it did, and meant" (9–10). For Wimsatt and Beardsley, there was no "reckon[ing]" required: the meaning of the lines was only too obvious. But for the critic with whom they were sparring— a man with the inauspicious name Charles Coffin—the poet was evoking no ordinary earthquake, but the moving earth of the Copernican hypothesis.[1] It was this claim (and others like it) that rubbed Wimsatt and Beardsley the wrong way. "To make the geocentric and heliocentric antithesis the core of the metaphor," they wrote, "is to disregard the English language."[2] When William Empson joined the fray with his essay "Donne the Space Man," he would take them to task. Once again, the earthquake that shook the "Valediction" was central to the debate. For Empson, the earthquake represented both a terrestrial event and the circulation of the earth around the sun, but more than that, it conveyed the *experience* of disruption: "The effect of giving the phrase both meanings is to say: 'And also the sudden introduction of the idea that there may be life on

1. Coffin, *John Donne and the New Philosophy*, 97–98.
2. Wimsatt and Beardsley, *Verbal Icon*, 14. See Graff, *Professing Literature*, 191–92.

other planets has affected the Churches like an earthquake.'"[3]
"If you dislike my claiming to know so much," he explains,
preempting the objections of critics, "I have to answer that I
think it absurd, and very harmful, to have a critical theory, like
Mr. Wimsatt's, that a reader must not try to follow an author's
mind."[4]

In this chapter, I will "try to follow . . . the mind[s]" of
several early modern authors for whom the encounter with
materialist thought was a catastrophe—and to watch them
attempt to keep track of their own minds' movements. I am
interested in how the image of disaster lent expression to the
violence of the speculative imagination—and in the perception of materialism as an unwanted thought that might all of a
sudden deprive the mind of its faculties. Donne's little earthquake brings us back to a moment when the patterns of catastrophic materialism emerged in conversations about the possibility of worlds beyond our own, the imminent end of the
world, and the counterintuitive proposition that the earth is
rotating around the sun.

The first part of the chapter looks at the anxieties around
catastrophic materialism in the context of astronomical debate
in the sixteenth century—from Philipp Melanchthon's answer
to "Epicurean" doubters of astrology to Thomas Digges's attempt to prove the Copernican hypothesis and his own precipitous leap to the idea of an infinite universe. The image of
disaster emerges here at the threshold between empirical and
speculative forms of knowledge—as the very notion of the
empirical is being tested and transformed under new and, for
some, unsettling pressures. The second part explores how this
catastrophic style echoed and amplified in the expanding and
contracting spaces of Donne's imagination. Donne appears

3. Empson, *Essays on Renaissance Literature*, 123.
4. Empson, *Essays on Renaissance Literature*, 124.

here not only as a master of catastrophic metaphor, as Empson hints, but as a catastrophizer himself—a man who saw in the new science not only the possibility for literary and imaginative freedom but also the threat of compulsive thought. In each case, catastrophic materialism is taken up even as the claims of philosophical materialism are denied—*especially* as they are denied.

DIGGES'S LEAP

In Giordano Bruno's *Expulsion of the Triumphant Beast* (1584), the king of the gods wrings his hands, worrying about whether the heavens really were unchangeable: "Ah, Venus, Venus! Do you think that what humans imagine about us is true, that he among us who is old is always old, that he who is young is always young, that he who is a boy is always a boy, and thus we eternally continue as we were when first taken into heaven . . . ?"[5] In 1572, nearly half a century after the great flood that never came, a nova entered the sphere of fixed stars.[6] Earthquakes happen, comets and meteors come and go portending various dooms, but the great firmament of stars was not supposed to change. Even the gods apparently were unsettled by the thought of it. The phenomenon in question was what we now call a "supernova"—the final explosion of a dying star. Mounting skepticism about Aristotelian and Scholastic thought was coming again to a head, or rather to a point. This particular nova, a comet in 1577, and an earthquake in 1580 all contributed to the eschatological mood of the decade. To many

5. Bruno, *Expulsion of the Triumphant Beast*, 98.

6. Lynn Thorndike gives a broad overview of the intellectual response to the new star in his monumental study, *A History of Magic and Experimental Science*, 6:67–98. See Hellman, *Comet of 1577* and "Gradual Abandonment of the Aristotelian Universe"; Weichenhan, *"Ergo perit coelum"*; and Westman, *Copernican Question*, 230–43.

it seemed—once again—that the world was on the verge of ending.[7]

The Englishman Thomas Digges's first attempt to read the nova was filtered through the lens of astrology and prognostication, though he hesitated to say too much on this front. He wrote to his patron, William Cecil, Lord Burghley, on December 11, 1572: "I have waded as far as ancient grounds of Astrology and authors' precepts of approved credit will bear me to sift out the unknown influence of this new star or comet, which is like to be no less vehement than rare." He may not have known exactly what the nova was, but he was relatively sure that "calamity is to be expected."[8]

By 1573, however, Digges's uncertainty about the status of the phenomenon had cleared up entirely. The "magnificent and splendid title" of his treatise says it all, capturing the rush of a newfound confidence.[9] Here it is in full: *Mathematical Wings or Ladders, by which the Remotest Theaters of the Visible Heavens are Ascended and All the Planetary Paths are Explored by New and Unheard of Methods. And so the Immense Distance and Magnitude of this Portentous Star, this Unexpected Tremulous Fire in the Northern World, and forthwith its Awe-Inspiring Place, may be found; and so also may*

7. In a poem that was published alongside the printed version of Michael Maestlin's observations, for example, Nicodemus Frischlin cried apocalypse, citing scripture to lay out the unmistakable context of this most rare and miraculous event. See Frischlin, *Consideratio novae stellae.* Tycho Brahe, who is credited with the most accurate observations of the nova, included talk of both human and natural disasters in his treatment of the phenomenon. Brahe, *De nova,* sig. D4ʳ. As Robert Westman has pointed out, however, Tycho was "unusually restrained in making eschatological interpretations" and was critical of the abuses of astrology. See Westman, *Copernican Question,* 252.

8. Digges, Letter of Thomas Digges to Lord Burghley, December 11, 1572.

9. The phrase "magnificent and splendid title" is Tycho Brahe's, but, in his estimation, the contents did not quite live up. Brahe, *Astronomiae instauratae progymnasmata,* 1:653. For Brahe's criticisms of Digges, see Granada, "Tycho Brahe's Anti-Copernican Campaign."

God's Astonishing and Frightening Presence be displayed and known most clearly.[10]

In flying high on mathematical "wings," Digges was drawing from deep Platonic wells.[11] As he wrote, "Whoever wears the Platonic—to use a more accurate expression—Mathematical wings and heads upwards into the ethereal realm, leaving behind entirely the elemental regions, will see that [the nova] is much further away than the place of the comets."[12] At the same time, Digges was signaling a sympathy with the Protestant reformer Philip Melanchthon, whose words would prove infectious.[13] In the following passage, Melanchthon explains what it means to have "wings":

The souls whose wings [*alae*] have fallen off wander about on the ground and desire impure pleasures from earthly things, and they do not behold that most beautiful light of heavenly things. Even if Plato thinks of the wings as heroic impulses of the minds [*heroicos impetus ingeniorum*], it is nevertheless not these impulses alone that lift up the minds, but the arts are also needed by which these impulses are raised up. Consequently, the wings of the human mind are arithmetic and geometry. If someone

10. The Latin title of Digges's treatise reads: *Alae seu scalae mathematicae, quibus visibilium remotissima coelorum theatra conscendi et planetarum omnium itinera nouis et inauditis methodis explorari, tum huius portentosi syderis in mundi boreali plaga insolito fulgore coruscantis, distantia et magnitudo immensa, situsque protinus tremendus indagari, Deique stupendum ostentum, terricolis expositum cognosci liquidissime possit.* I am borrowing Westman's translation from *Copernican Question*, 268.

11. Digges was, in fact, following the example of Copernicus and his expositor Rheticus, who, as Robert Westman explains, "reinvent Plato and the Pythagoreans as 'the greatest mathematicians of that divine age.'" Westman, *Copernican Question*, 101.

12. Digges, *Alae*, sig. A1ᵛ; cited and translated in Goulding, "Wings (or Stairs) to the Heavens," 48.

13. On Thomas Digges's use of Melanchthon, see Tredwell, "Melanchthon Circle's English Epicycle"; Hooykaas, "Thomas Digges' Puritanism."

endowed with an intellect that is not mean attached these to himself, he would easily enter heaven and would wander freely in the heavenly company, and enjoy that light and wisdom.[14]

Emending Plato's example, Melanchthon advocates for some combination of *furor* (an involuntary flight of the mind) and a deliberate application of reason and "art." The practices of arithmetic and geometry are called to supplement the mind's "heroic impulses"—lest they go astray. As it turns out, Melanchthon had good reason not to leave the mind to its own devices. Digges did too.

At stake in the appearance of the nova was the idea that the meaningfulness of the world was legible to man—that miraculous signs and portents might be interpreted. If the nova was not a divine miracle portending a most welcome apocalypse (a sign from God to be read), one particularly worrisome alternative was that it was a strictly natural phenomenon that had appeared by chance. Such a thought might shake the very idea of providence itself—a consequence either too dangerous to consider or too absurd, or *both*. In a draft of his treatise on the nova, the German astronomer Michael Maestlin would quickly dismiss the thought out of hand as a thing no sane person would say ("nemo sanus dixerit").[15] But even if one couldn't *say* such a thing, one might very well *think* it.

To understand Digges's response to the nova, it is worth spending some time with the thought of Melanchthon, who, long beforehand, was making a case against those who denied the meaningfulness of celestial signs. For him, an "Epicurean" was anyone who undermined belief in God's providence—particularly philosophers such as Pico della Mirandola, who in his massive (and massively influential) treatise against as-

14. Melanchthon, *Orations on Philosophy and Education*, 94; *Opera omnia*, 11: 288. On this passage, see Methuen, "Role of the Heavens," 393–94; Pumfrey, "'Your astronomers and ours differ exceedingly,'" 45n51.

15. Granada, "Michael Maestlin and the New Star of 1572," 113.

trology doubted the efficacy and significance of the stars.[16] Railing against the "Epicureans," Melanchthon would suggest just how easy it was to slip into the kind of *furor* that one should rather avoid. The materialist image of random scattering was particularly vivid:

> All who are sound in mind understand that these things are most in accordance with nature, and not those Cyclopic ideas, which the Epicureans defend wildly [*furenter*], namely that all things are brought together fortuitously from atoms, that all things are moved and joined without order and without a guiding mind, and that continually other worlds and other species come into being. It is not only [a sign of] wisdom to oppose such madness [*furoribus*], but also outstanding virtue that is pleasing to God, and for which rewards are given by God. The falsehood of the Epicureans can be clearly refuted and their madness [*rabies*], too, by greater steadfastness of the mind [*maiore animi constantia*]. At the same time, the conviction of providence needs to be assiduously [*diligentissime*] strengthened in the mind by observation of the most beautiful order in nature, and the parts of nature are to be contemplated often, as well as the construction of the parts of the body, and experience reflecting the teaching on the use of remedies. Just as men often carelessly attract to themselves [*sibi accersunt*] deadly danger by a slight mistake [*levi errato*], so, on the other hand, the

16. See Kusukawa, *Transformation of Natural Philosophy*, 128–29. Melanchthon is combining the idea that Epicurus had rejected divination and astrology with the ancient philosopher's impious reputation. See Melanchthon, *Orations on Philosophy and Education*, 94: "As is proper, your ears and your souls shrink from the absurdities of Epicurus, who derides astronomy." On the Epicurean rejection of divination, see, for example, Cicero, *On Divination* 1.3.5 and 1.39.87; Diogenes Laertius, *Lives* 10.135. As Pico put it sarcastically, even the Epicureans wouldn't stoop to believe in the vulgar nonsense of the astrologers. Mirandola, *Disputationes adversus astrologiam divinatricem*, 48, 527–28. For the trials of astrology in the wake of Pico, see Broecke, *Limits of Influence*; and Westman, *Copernican Question*.

wise physician often disperses deadly dangers by wholly common remedies.[17]

This passage links the opinion of the Epicureans directly with
the idea of multiple worlds—a proposition that Digges himself will later confront when he imagines the earth as a star.
Melanchthon here gives us a sense of what it was like to have a
materialist thought, which he describes as a kind of bad *furor*—
a delusion of the mind that might suddenly come upon you
like a change in the weather. The idea of "attract[ing] to oneself" or summoning danger suggests that a person might do
this in spite of herself (by a kind of inclination rather than a
choice). For Melanchthon, a "slight mistake" might give way
to a "deadly danger": the very definition of catastrophizing in
our colloquial sense.

In the context of discussing Epicureanism and madness in
a treatise celebrating the art of medicine, Melanchthon no
doubt had one particular example in mind: the madness of
Lucretius. As the story goes, the Epicurean poet drank a love
philter administered by his wife, went insane, and wrote his
poem between bouts of insanity.[18] In his *Platonic Theology*, Marsilio Ficino had used Lucretius as an example of one of those
who had been seized by a divine frenzy.[19] Later in the same
text, however, Ficino will warn of the *perils* of Lucretian madness. There is, he suggests, a fine line between poetic *furor* and
melancholy, one that should be carefully observed:

17. Melanchthon, *Orations on Philosophy and Education*, 94; *Opera omnia*, 11:
809–10.
18. See Jerome's continuation of the Eusebian chronicle in Eusebius,
Eusebii Pamphili Chronici canones, 231: "Titus Lucretius poeta nascitur. Qui postea amatorio poculo in furorem versus, cum aliquot libros per intervalla insaniae conscripsisset, quos postea Cicero emendavit, propia se manu interfecit
anno aetatis XLIIII." On the reception of the life of Lucretius, see Canfora,
Vita di Lucrezio; Holford-Strevens, "*Horror vacui* in Lucretian Biography";
Palmer, *Reading Lucretius in the Renaissance*, 97–191.
19. Ficino, *Platonic Theology*, 4:126–27.

PLATE 1. Leonardo da Vinci, "A deluge" (ca. 1517–18). Black chalk, 16.3 x 21.0 cm. Windsor Leoni Volume (12378). Photograph: Royal Collection Trust / © Her Majesty Queen Elizabeth II 2018.

PLATE 2. Leonardo da Vinci, "A tempest" (ca. 1517–18). Black chalk, pen and ink and wash with touches of white heightening, 27.0 x 40.8 cm. Windsor Leoni Volume (12376). Photograph: Royal Collection Trust / © Her Majesty Queen Elizabeth II 2018.

PLATE 3. Leonardo da Vinci, "A tempest" (ca. 1517–18) (detail).

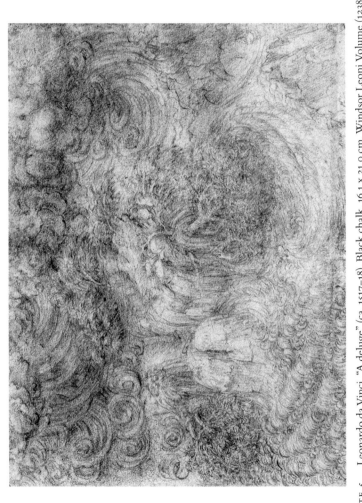

PLATE 5. Leonardo da Vinci, "A deluge" (ca. 1517–18). Black chalk, 16.1 x 21.0 cm. Windsor Leoni Volume (12386). Photograph: Royal Collection Trust / © Her Majesty Queen Elizabeth II 2018.

For the rest, we must remember not to put full trust in that opinion or affection which results either from a melancholic bent [*ingenium melancholicum*], one sick and contrary in a way to life, or from an inappropriate and harmful position of the stars that both perverts the human temperament and brings with it a weakness with regard not only to our confidence in life but also to the governance of human affairs. Hence impious men are for the most part either extremely idle as Epicurus was said to be, or profligate like Aristippus, or mad as was their follower Lucretius. When his madness [*insania*] was roused on account of his black bile, Lucretius first tried to slaughter his soul verbally in the third book of his *On the Nature of Things*; then slaughtered his body with a sword.[20]

For Ficino, Lucretius does not write his poem *between* moments of insanity but in the very grip of it. Instead of a love philter, Ficino points to black bile. He names "melancholic genius" and the stars as causes of such distortions of mind. According to Melanchthon, one remedy for the dangerous delusions of the Epicureans was to be found in astronomy and mathematics — disciplines that Epicurus had argued against. These "arts" were man's Platonic "wings," which might allow him to rise above his baser desires — and his doubts.[21]

It is against this backdrop of Epicurean thought and the mystery of the stars that we can begin to see the term "catastrophe" come into its modern usage. In 1531, Melanchthon witnessed his first comet (Halley's), which he predicted would bring about καταστροφή, or "catastrophe."[22] This sense of the word as a figure of impending doom or an ending derives from

20. Ficino, *Platonic Theology*, 4:308–9.

21. On the question of Melanchthon's Neoplatonism, see Frank, "Melanchthon and the Tradition of Neoplatonism."

22. Philipp Melanchthon to Joachim Camerarius, November 2, 1531. Melanchthon, *Opera omnia*, 2:551–52. See Kusukawa, *Transformation of Natural Philosophy*, 124–26.

ancient drama and its commentary tradition as well as biblical usage (Peter uses the word to describe the destruction of Sodom and Gomorrah).[23] Melanchthon himself was well aware of the word's uses in dramatic theory, having written a commentary on Terence in which he explains the principles of comedic structure in the preface.[24] His friend Erasmus too had discoursed on this meaning of the term in the *Adagia*, explaining how a technical word could be "diverted to another use": "We call the outcome of anything, in proverbial language, the *catastrophe* or *dénouement*."[25]

This expanded sense of "catastrophe" loomed large for Melanchthon, for whom the idea was closely tied to refuting the Epicurean opinion that the world was created by chance and that astrology could tell us nothing about the providential order of things. The same month that he cast his eyes on the comet and reached for the word "catastrophe," he would write a preface to Sacrobosco's *De Sphaera* celebrating the uses of astrology and astronomy and denouncing as Epicureans and atheists those who would not acknowledge the meaningfulness of celestial signs:[26]

> For this reason—if astronomy corroborates the belief about God in the minds of men—we have to consider that Plato said not only learnedly, but also piously that eyes are given to us

23. According to Donatus, "*Catastrophe* is the unravelling of the story, through which the outcome is demonstrated." Donatus, "On Comedy," 308. See 2 Peter 2:6 KJV: "And turning the cities of Sodom and Gomorrah into ashes condemned them with an overthrow [καταστροφῇ], making them an ensample unto those that after should live ungodly."

24. Melanchthon, *Opera omnia*, 19:694.

25. Erasmus, *Adages Ii1 to Iv100*, 177–78. As Gerrit Jasper Schenk has suggested, "it was no accident" that in the wake of the 1524 flood scare, Melanchthon, "a friend of Erasmus, took up the Greek word for a politico-religious upheaval that he expected in 1531." Schenk, *Historical Disaster Experiences*, 21.

26. Kusukawa, *Transformation of Natural Philosophy*, 126–27.

because of astronomy. For they are certainly given to us chiefly for the reason that they may be our guides for searching for some knowledge of God. Only those among the philosophers [i.e., the Epicureans] who spurned astronomy were professedly ungodly [*atheoi*]; having done away with providence, they also removed the immortality of our souls. If they had reached this knowledge, they would have perceived the manifest traces of God in nature, and, having noticed them, they would have been forced to acknowledge [*coacti essent fateri*] that the universe is made and governed by a mind.[27]

The term "catastrophe" provided Melanchthon with another way of talking about the legibility of the "manifest traces of God in nature"—the portentous signs that would compel the "ungodly" to acknowledge that the world was more than some fortuitous collisions of atoms.

It's not difficult to see the appeal of Melanchthon's winged words for Digges, a Protestant mathematician looking to make sense of celestial signs in the wake of an entirely unprecedented one like the nova of 1572. The thought that the nova was a product of chance might befall a person with the kind of bad *furor* Melanchthon warned against—the disastrous end of a "slight mistake."[28] As Katherine A. Tredwell has shown, Digges and other English writers were particularly attuned to the passages from Melanchthon that emphasized providence and wrestled with the godless.[29] In the *Alae*, Digges would use the last passage above to frame his own mathematical and as-

27. Melanchthon, *Orations on Philosophy and Education*, 106–7.
28. As Melanchthon suggests elsewhere, such an effect might come upon one by doubt about religion—or from bad theology: "And since no Furies torture the mind more violently than this doubt about religion, finally all of religion is cast aside in hatred, and their minds become impious and Epicurean." Melanchthon, *Orations on Philosophy and Education*, 128.
29. Tredwell, "Melanchthon Circle's English Epicycle," 29.

tronomical project, reproducing Melanchthon's words almost verbatim.[30] Speaking now in unison, Digges and Melanchthon would argue that the "ungodly" (both past and present) *needed* to be compelled—and that the science of the stars, properly conceived, would be the very thing to vanquish any doubts about the orderliness of the universe.[31] By the flickering light of the nova, Melanchthon's prophetic words took on even greater relevance if only because the new star (if indeed wrongly construed) might actually suggest a vision of chance and infinite worlds proliferating in infinite space—a scattering of stars like dust. As the generic insult "Epicurean" met this specific crisis of interpretation, the hint to respond to the wicked atheists with mathematical "wings" became an imperative.

Although Melanchthon had found value in Copernicus for the accuracy of his observations, he stuck firmly to old mental habits, keeping the Ptolemaic picture intact.[32] Decades later, Digges would take Melanchthon's ideas to new places, suggesting that Copernicus's hypothesis might actually be instrumental to the understanding of God's providential order. As Robert Goulding has shown, Digges—along with his "mathematical father," John Dee—had already been working on reforming astronomical practice by refining the use of parallax to mea-

30. The corresponding passage may be found in Thomas Digges, *Alae*, sig. A1ᵛ. Thomas's father, Leonard Digges, had also begun his almanac with an echo of the German reformer railing against the wicked "Epicurei Theologi" who put no stock in the stars. Digges, *Prognostication euerlastinge*, sig. A1ʳ.

31. Methuen points out: "For Melanchthon . . . it is precisely astronomy's capability to interpret the natural world and to decode the motions of the heavens that gives it its value, for in doing so it is able to show the will of God. Astronomy can only do this because of the order and harmony in the celestial region it describes. These have been ordained by God; by unlocking the motions of the planets and stars for human understanding, astronomy is able to give an insight into God's intended order for the world." Methuen, "Role of the Heavens," 394.

32. See Kusukawa, *Transformation of Natural Philosophy*, 171–73.

sure the distance between heavenly bodies.[33] The occasion of the nova prompted Digges and Dee to publish their findings "somewhat prematurely."[34] Proving the Copernican theory suddenly seemed possible—and urgent.

Melanchthon's heavy hand can be felt shaping Digges's wish to compel the impious through mathematical proofs, to shore up belief through the observation of God's providential order as reflected in the natural world. We see this clearly, for example, at the end of the treatise where Digges describes the earth as a "dark and obscure *Terrestrial Star*, where, wandering as strangers, we lead, in a short space of time, a life harassed by varied fortunes [*vitam variis exagitatam casibus*]."[35] This melancholic image no doubt points to the vanity of the changeable world and, as Miguel A. Granada suggests, to the idea of the soul as alien to the body, awaiting its transcendence in heaven.[36] But the same image might also suggest a materialist picture of the world. Melanchthon had already suggested as much: "Since violence often rules, and there are many sudden and unforeseen changes, the Epicureans believe that human affairs are moved by chance, and that each can obtain as much as he is worth in power."[37] As if responding to this thought, Digges follows up the image of "varied fortunes" by returning again implicitly to the reformer's screed against the Epicureans, reminding us that God created our eyes for the contemplation of the heavens. Here, Melanchthon's imperative to guard assiduously against "deadly danger" translates into the assiduous work of empirical observation. Bolstered by a Pla-

33. Goulding, "Wings (or Stairs) to the Heavens"; Digges, *Alae*, sig. A2^r.

34. Goulding, "Wings (or Stairs) to the Heavens," 42.

35. Digges, *Alae*, sig. L2^v; cited and translated in Johnson and Larkey, "Thomas Digges," 111.

36. Granada, "Thomas Digges, Giordano Bruno y el Desarrollo del Copernicanismo en Inglaterra," 15.

37. Melanchthon, *Orations on Philosophy and Education*, 176.

tonic and eschatological impetus, Digges exhorts astronomers everywhere not to let this most rare occasion slip through their fingers.[38] By God's visible works, he says, we may conjecture about the nature of invisible things.[39] All he needs are some more accurate observations to prove that the nova is a portent, that the world is meaningfully organized and legible, and that our eyes are made for viewing the heavens—that, or the end of the world. Digges concludes the treatise with a vision of Christ's return and the Apocalypse.[40]

In passages such as this one, we may begin to notice a tension between the careful method of the mathematician, who will wait for observations before jumping to conclusions, and the demands of the eschatological imagination, which feels the future in the instant. As Digges imagines the opportunity slipping through his fingers, the pulse of his treatise quickens, and the language and feeling of prognostication and prophecy rise again to the surface. This is the end of the treatise, after all—the place where one might expect a more intense rhetoric, and Digges had largely restrained himself up until this point.[41] But it would be a mistake to understand this as mere rhetoric. The claim that the phenomenon was a "new star" did not actually require any reference to Copernicus, but for Digges, at least, the consummation of Copernicus's theory in scientific fact would appear to *guarantee* the meaningfulness of the

38. Digges, *Alae*, sigs. L3ʳ.

39. Digges, *Alae*, sigs. L2ᵛ–L3ʳ. Digges is here invoking the words of Paul in Romans 1:20 KJV: "For the invisible things of him from the creation of the world are clearly seen, being understood by the things that are made, even his eternal power and Godhead."

40. Digges, *Alae*, sigs. L3ʳ⁻ᵛ. This eschatological note is echoed in an anonymous letter on the nova, which Pumfrey convincingly attributes to Digges. Pumfrey, "'Your astronomers and ours differ exceedingly,'" 47. On the relationship between astrology and astronomy in the sixteenth century, see, again, Westman, *Copernican Question*.

41. Granada, "Thomas Digges, Giordano Bruno y el Desarrollo del Copernicanismo en Inglaterra," 12.

"portentous" sign. In proving the theory, he believed, he could pressure the impious Epicureans (and perhaps his own wandering thoughts) into submission. With Melanchthon and Dee just visible in the background, Digges reminds us that it's not always easy to separate the wish for empirical data from a desire for metaphysics.

By the time Digges had published the *Alae*, however, the nova had already begun to fade.[42] By 1574 it had disappeared entirely, never to return. The question of its status would not be confirmed by a Copernican proof, and Digges would have to hang up his wings—for now, at least. When he came back to the question of Copernicus's theory several years later, he would add a more *visceral* inducement to belief—one that would effectivly silence any thoughts of contingency and scattered stars. A sudden collapse of scale and perspective would do the trick.

In the *Perfit Description* (1576), which is appended to an edition of his father's almanac, Digges returns to the matter of Copernicus's world system—suggesting that Copernicus himself "meant not as some have fondly accused him, to deliver these grounds of the Earth's mobility only as Mathematical principles, feigned & not as Philosophical truly averred."[43] It is here, in the midst of his translation and reframing of the

42. To explain this phenomenon, the Englishman presents two incompatible possibilities. One was that the star would disappear and then return. On the strength of this theory, Digges hoped he could use annual parallax to establish the movement of the earth as certain, which would prove the Copernican hypothesis conclusively. The second possibility was that the nova itself was receding from earth. In fact, Dee had been developing just such a theory, arguing that the star was moving in a straight line upward, which required that the distance of the star from the earth far exceed the traditional size of the universe. See Goulding, "Wings (or Stairs) to the Heavens," 51.

43. Digges, *Perfit Description of the Caelestiall Orbes*, sig. M1^{r-v}. Digges is here referring to Osiander's 1543 preface to Copernicus, which suggested that the system described in the book was not necessarily true and, worse, that no astronomer could be certain. In 1609, Kepler would call Osiander's preface a

Copernican text, that he bounds suddenly to the idea of the sphere of the fixed stars expanding without limit, an image of a Christian infinity:[44]

> But that *Orbis magnus*, being as is before declared, but as a point in respect of the immensity of that immoveable heaven, we may easily consider what little portion of God's frame our Elementary corruptible world is, but never sufficiently of that fixed Orb garnished with lights innumerable and reaching up in Spherical altitude without end. . . . And this may well be thought of us to be the glorious court of the great God, whose unsearchable works invisible, we partly by these his visible, conjecture; to whose infinite power and majesty, such an infinite place, surmounting all other both in quantity and quality, only is convenient.[45]

Copernicus himself had touched upon the question of infinity, but left the answer finally "to the philosophers."[46] Already in Ptolemy, Digges could have read that "the earth has, to the senses, the ratio of a point to the distance of the sphere of the so-called fixed stars."[47] Anyone interested in Platonism would have also been familiar with sources such as Boethius's *Consolation of Philosophy*, wherein Lady Philosophy instructs the reader in the vanity of earthly things: "Consider this: by astronomical demonstrations that the compass of the whole earth compared

---

"fabula absurdissima." Cited and discussed in Blumenberg, *Genesis of the Copernican World*, 298.

44. Westman has urged attention to the format of the *Perfit Description*, pointing out the son's juxtaposition of a partial English translation of *De revolutionibus* with the father's traditionally geocentric, astrological prognostication, a conjunction that argues for the central importance of astrological prognostication as the primary context in which Copernicus's ideas continued to be considered. Westman, *Copernican Question*, 272.

45. Digges, *Perfit Description*, sig. N4ʳ.

46. Copernicus, *On the Revolutions of Heavenly Spheres*, 14.

47. Ptolemy, *Almagest*, 43.

to the scope of heaven is no bigger than a pin's point, which is as much as to say that, if it be conferred with the greatness of the celestial sphere, it hath no bigness at all."[48] But Digges takes the thought a step further. His language of "conjecture" directly echoes the language at the end of the *Alae*, though now the idea of infinity takes the place of the double fantasy of proving Copernicus's theory and imagining the end of the world.[49]

In their seminal 1934 article on the *Perfit Description*, Francis R. Johnson and Sanford V. Larkey argue that Digges's conjecture about infinity was the product of scientific investigation and reasoning, making the English astronomer the proper forerunner of the scientific outlook that is usually associated with Galileo. While reminding us that one can never really know how insights come about, they insist that the idea of

48. Boethius, *Consolation of Philosophy* 2.7. In the *Dream of Scipio*, the final book of *De re publica*, Cicero describes the earth as a "point" in a vast heaven: "From here the earth appeared so small that I was ashamed of our empire which is, so to speak, but a point on its surface." Cicero, *Scipio's Dream*, 72. Likewise, Macrobius's commentary on Cicero's text contains the idea. Macrobius, *Commentary on the "Dream of Scipio,"* 153–54.

49. In imagining that God's "unsearchable works invisible, we partly by these visible, conjecture," Digges might have found another precedent in the infinitist and Christian Neoplatonist Nicholas of Cusa, whose 1514 *Opera* is listed among the books in Dee's famous library (Roberts and Watson, *John Dee's Library Catalogue*, no. 89). In *De Docta Ignorantia*, in a section titled "Mathematics assists us very greatly in apprehending various divine [truths]," Cusa writes, "All our wisest and most divine teachers agree that visible things are truly images of invisible things and that from created things the Creator can be knowably seen as in a mirror and a symbolism." He cites several examples of philosophers such as Pythagoras and thinkers such as Augustine and Boethius who used mathematics to divine ends. Soon afterward Cusa writes of the uses of mathematics for dispelling the impious opinions of the Epicureans: "And to speak more concisely, if you wish: was not the opinion of the Epicureans about atoms and the void—an opinion which denies God and is at variance with all truth—destroyed by the Pythagoreans and the Peripatetics only through mathematical demonstration?" Cusa, *Complete Philosophical and Theological Treatises*, 18–19.

infinity followed directly from observation and calculation (rather than from metaphysics). They even picture a scene of the English astronomer peering through an early telescope (or "proportional glasses"), insisting, "No one was more eager than [Digges] to try to verify [the Copernican hypothesis] by observation and experiment."[50]

But just as Copernicus's theory was not necessary to prove the new star was above the region of fixed stars, it was not necessary for Digges to imagine an infinite universe to make room for the nova. He might have simply expanded the outer sphere and left it at that. What we might call the *compulsion* of Digges's leap of (infinite) imagination brings us back to Melanchthon's observations on the dangers of materialist thought and the power of certain thoughts (even passing ones) to possess the mind.

Gabriel Harvey reports that Digges knew at least part of Palingenius's familiar school text, *The Zodiake of Life*, "bie hart, & takes mutch delight to repeat it often."[51] Along with the writings of Melanchthon, this encyclopedic poem had captured Digges's imagination. In the twelfth section, "Pisces," Palingenius describes the sphere of God's influence as being without limit, for "no kinde of thing may God conclude, / nor limits him assigne, / Nor propre force doth once restrayne / the Maiestie deuine."[52] But this was not all. In Palingenius's

50. Johnson and Larkey, "Thomas Digges," 113. In the preface to the post-humously published *Pantometria* (1571), a book on the geometrical principles of surveying, Thomas writes of his father's use of "proportional glasses," which allowed him to view objects at a distance. Digges, *Pantometria*, sig. Aiii^v. Scholars have debated to what extent this device can be understood as the first telescope. See Dupré, "William Bourne's Invention."

51. Smith, *Gabriel Harvey's Marginalia*, 161; cited in Johnson and Larkey, "Thomas Digges," 103. On Digges's use of Palingenius, see Granada, "Thomas Digges, Giordano Bruno y el Desarrollo del Copernicanismo en Inglaterra," 14–15.

52. Palingenius, *Zodiake of Life*, sig. uui^r. I am following Barnaby Googe's 1565 translation.

verses, we also learn the origin of Digges's image of the "dark and obscure *Terrestrial Star*" and understand in retrospect that he has been making reference to it all along.[53] At the start of his translation of Copernicus and exposition of infinity in the *Perfit Description*, Digges cites three passages from the poem. Two *affirm* the ontological hierarchy that separates the world of death (the earth) from the immutable world above the moon, but one betrays a latent materialist trace:

> Singula nonnulli credunt quo'q; sydera posse
> Dici Orbes, TERRAM'q appellant sydus opacû
> Cui minimus Divûm præsit &C.[54]

> [But some have thought that euery starre a world we well
>   may call,
> The earth they count a darkned starre, where as the least
>   of all
> The God[s] doth reign.][55]

Here, the capital letters of "TERRAM" register the unexpected strength of the analogy between the new star and the earth. The analogy seems to have *already* proliferated outward ("euery starre a world").[56] Johnson notes that Digges "makes a special point of Palingenius' allusion to the early ideas of Anaxagoras and Democritus that every star was a world . . . calling attention to some of the startling implications of the new theory by means of the adroit use of a quotation from an author known and admired by nearly all of Digges's fellow countrymen."[57] As I mention above, Digges quotes two other passages from Palin-

53. Granada, "Thomas Digges, Giordano Bruno y el Desarrollo del Copernicanismo en Inglaterra," 18.
54. Digges, *Perfit Description*, sig. M2[r].
55. Palingenius, *Zodiake of Life*, sig. Yi[r].
56. Johnson and Larkey, "Thomas Digges," 102.
57. Johnson, "Thomas Digges and the Infinity of the Universe," 185.

genius's poem that maintain the traditional distinction between the realms of god and man — an idea that assumes visual
form in the diagram included in the text. As Alexandre Koyré
argued long ago, Digges's notion of infinity with its hierarchies
intact was quite distinct from the infinity of Giordano Bruno,
who posited a homogenous infinity of worlds by remaking the
theories of Lucretius and Nicholas of Cusa.[58] "Thomas Digges,"
he wrote, "puts his stars into a theological heaven; not into an
astronomical sky."[59]

This is not to say, however, that Digges wasn't *reacting* to
a materialist idea, indeed much as Melanchthon was before
him — specifically to the thought "that all things are brought
together fortuitously from atoms, that all things are moved and
joined without order and without a guiding mind, and that
continually other worlds and other species come into being."
Thus while it has been argued that Digges included the more
traditional passages from Palingenius "as a concession to the
believers in the old cosmology, in order to disarm opposition
to the idea present in the last of the quotations," there is another possibility.[60] What I am suggesting is that Digges's turn
to the idea of infinity was, among other things, an attempt to
integrate into his system an unwanted thought — to transform
the reflexive violence of a bad *furor* into an occasion for Christian wonder.[61]

58. See Granada, "Kepler and Bruno" and "Giordano Bruno y la eternidad del mundo."

59. Koyré, *From the Closed World to the Infinite Universe*, 38.

60. Johnson and Larkey, "Thomas Digges," 102.

61. We can observe a similar strategy at work nearly a century later in the
writings of Henry More, the Platonic philosopher and poet who is credited
with having composed the first English poem on infinity, *Democritus Platonissans* (1646) (its very title denoting the synthesis of materialist and Platonic
perspectives). Writing in the wake of Galileo and Descartes at the beginning
of the English Civil War, the Cambridge Platonist was also attempting to
counter the melancholic influence of materialism and other "Fooleries much

Slightly later, Francis Bacon would make explicit what was at stake in the notion of infinity and multiple worlds, asking, "Whether the world or universe compose altogether one globe, with a centre; or whether the particular globes of earth and stars be scattered dispersedly each on its own roots, without any system or common centre?" In answering this question, the "school" of Democritus and Epicurus springs immediately to mind: "For when Democritus had set down matter or seeds as infinite in quantity and finite in attributes and power . . . he was driven by the very force of this opinion [*vi ipsa illius opinionis adductus est*] to constitute multiform worlds, subject to birth and death, some well ordered, others badly put together, even essays of worlds and vacant spaces between."[62] As if assuming a life of its own, the force (*vi*) of Democritus's ideas about the nature of atoms leads him to conclude that there are infinite worlds. The passage recalls Lactantius's reflection on the dangerous force (*vis*) of materialist thoughts: "What force [*vis*] of atoms had been so great that masses so incalculable should be collected from such minute elements?"[63] Lactantius, as we know, was discussing the materialist analogy of dust ranging in sunlight. Bacon gives us another image of "scattering" when he writes, "the effect of this opinion [that the earth was one of the stars]" is that planets and stars "are scattered and suspended through that immense expanse which we behold above us . . . like so many islands in an immense sea."[64] Bacon includes in this "school" of thought the English Copernican William

---

derogatory to the Truth." "We cannot imagine any thing of our own Being," More wrote of those who would deny the soul's extension, "and if we doe, are prone to fall into despair, or contempt of our selves, by fancying our selves such unconsiderable Motes of the Sun." More, *Immortality of the soul*, 342.

62. Bacon, *Works*, 10:419; 7:299.

63. Lactantius, *Works*, 22:15; *Opera omnia*, 27:86; discussed in the introduction.

64. Bacon, *Works*, 10:420.

Gilbert, who endorsed the idea of infinity after Digges, "and all those (except Copernicus) who believed that the earth was a planet and moveable, and as it were one of the stars."[65]

If we want to understand what drove Digges to the idea of infinity, we might look to the structure of the specific kind of analogy, like dust in sunlight, that starts small and suddenly fills the imagination. Digges was attempting to override the catastrophic thought of materialism with an overwhelming idea of his own. With the force of a doomsday prophet, he would wrest infinity away from the Epicureans. His leap to infinity mimics the form of catastrophic materialism as it seeks to refute the principles of philosophical materialism. If he still couldn't prove the truth of the Copernican hypothesis (and thus the meaning of the nova) by empirical means, he could nonetheless make himself feel it. In lieu of imagining the end of the world, he would conjure up another imaginative catastrophe to take its place—one that would capture and repurpose the sudden violence of a materialist analogy, redirect the force of an eschatological vision, and stand in for empirical proof where there wasn't any. This begins to explain the uncanny power of the image of Digges's "dark star," which carries over from the context of the *Alae* and continues to exert its subtle influence—much, we might say, like the nova itself.

As Bacon had implied, the sudden bounding of the mind to infinity was perhaps less a reassuring answer to the threat of materialism than an expression of it. Recalling the new star of 1572 and reflecting on the appearance of another nova in 1604, Johannes Kepler would argue that men who used infinity to explain such events "immediately, and as if inspired (by some kind of enthusiasm), conceive and develop in the walls of their heads a certain opinion about the arrangement of the world." The words "inspiration" and "enthusiasm" reflect the kind of

65. Bacon, *Works*, 10:420.

automatic thinking that sometimes seems to happen *to* us. In
this context, the phrase "walls of their heads" reads as a joke because infinity, by definition, has no boundaries, and yet the idea
of endlessness fills and possesses the imagination. Kepler describes the precipitous action of the mind, the trancelike intention of those who violently attract everything into the orbit of
their thoughts: "Once they have embraced [a certain opinion],
they stick to it and they drag in by their hair [anything that
serves their point]."[66] It is really *they* who are being dragged.

Kepler's examples are Gilbert, who argued for infinity
after Digges in his treatise on the magnet (which might have
suggested another image of "dragging"), and Bruno: both
are "Pythagoreans" who misused the authority of Copernicus.[67] But this critique also extended to other philosophical sects, most notably the "Epicureans," who attributed new
stars to "the accidental wanderings of atoms" (*fortuitis atomorum
oberrationibus*).[68] Like Digges, Kepler was following the example
of Melanchthon closely on Epicurean matters. As Patrick J.
Boner explains, for Kepler too an Epicurean was "any individual who accepted the concurrence of infinite possibilities as
the source of origin of the new luminary. . . . In such a system,
he lamented, 'infinite chaos' stemming from 'blind and reck-
less motion' produced the new star as randomly as it did any-

66. Kepler, *Gesammelte Werke*, 1:251–52; cited and discussed in Westman,
Copernican Question, 400. Translation adapted from Koyré, *From the Closed
World to the Infinite Universe*, 59.

67. Westman has argued that Kepler's discussion of infinity is a response
to his friend (and one of Bruno's patrons) Johannes Matthias Wacker von
Wackenfels. Westman, *Copernican Question*, 400. See also Granada, "Kepler
and Bruno," 471–75.

68. Kepler, *Gesammelte Werke*, 1:283; cited and translated in Boner, "Kepler v.
the Epicureans," 207. Bruno, who cites Epicurus and Lucretius frequently in
his discussion of infinity, comes again to mind. Westman, *Copernican Question*,
606n20.

thing else."[69] Kepler called this a "most abominable idolatry" (*idolum . . . detestabilissimum*), hinting at the way a seeming absurdity might possess the imagination.[70] An absurdity wouldn't be "most abominable" if it weren't also dangerous.

At the same time, the astronomer wants to demonstrate just how easily such an idea might be dismissed. As he says, believing that the new star was a product of infinite possibilities (i.e., of chance) was no better than writing letters on playing cards and shuffling them to see if any meaning might be made: "So I gave up my cards to the Epicurean eternity, to be carried away into infinity."[71] But the thought wasn't so easily dispatched. The image of infinite possibilities and chance haunted Digges even as he attempted to reimagine infinity in Christian terms. It haunted Kepler as well. By the time Robert Burton composed the preface to *The Anatomy of Melancholy* in 1621, Copernicanism, infinity, and materialism had converged again. Here, Burton assures his readers that though he calls himself "Democritus, Jr." he will not be discussing "some prodigious tenet, or paradox of the earth's motion, of infinite worlds, *in infinito vacuo, ex fortuita atomorum collisione*, in an infinite waste, so caused by an accidental collision of motes in the sun."[72] The notion of infinity turns back again to the analogy that begins

69. Boner, "Kepler v. the Epicureans," 207; Kepler, *Gesammelte Werke*, 1:284.

70. Kepler, *Gesammelte Werke*, 1:284; cited and translated in Boner, "Kepler v. the Epicureans," 209–11.

71. Kepler, *Gesammelte Werke*, 1:285; translated in Brewster, *Martyrs of Science*, 177. In the same place, Kepler gives the example of his wife tossing a salad. Cf. Cicero, *De natura deorum* 2.93–94: "I cannot understand why he who considers it possible for this to have occurred should not also think that, if a countless number of copies of the one-and-twenty letters of the alphabet, made of gold or what you will, were thrown together into some receptacle and then shaken out on to the ground, it would be possible that they should produce the *Annals* of Ennius, all ready for the reader. I doubt whether chance could possibly succeed in producing even a single verse!"

72. Burton, *Anatomy of Melancholy*, 1:1.

small and suddenly occupies the imagination—that is, to that most uncanny figure of catastrophizing.

DONNE'S LITTLE EARTHQUAKES

From the world of early modern astrology and astronomy, we can begin to trace the catastrophic pattern we find in Digges across a range of texts where the mind's movement from the sensible to the insensible results in a radical shift in scale and perspective. In *Devotions upon Emergent Occasions* (1624), John Donne took the lessons of catastrophizing to heart, making disaster out of the first signs of an oncoming illness:

> O multiplied misery! we die, and cannot enjoy death, because wee die in this torment of sicknes; we are tormented with sick-nes, & cannot stay till the torment come, but pre-apprehensions and presages, prophesy those torments, which induce that *death* before either come; and our *dissolution* is conceived in these *first changes, quickned* in the *sicknes* it selfe, and *borne* in *death*, which beares date from these first changes. Is this the honour which Man hath by being a *little world*, That he hath these *earthquakes* in him selfe, sodaine shakings; these *lightnings*, sodaine flashes; these *thunders*, sodaine noises; these *Eclypses*, sodain offusca-tions, & darknings of his senses; these *blazing stars*, sodaine fiery exhalations; these *rivers of blood*, sudden red waters?[73]

This passage gives us a portrait of Donne quite different from the one painted by his biographer, Izaak Walton, who tells us that the disease "continued long, and threatened him with death, which he dreaded not."[74] It is precisely dread, in the

---

73. Donne, *Devotions upon Emergent Occasions*, 7–8.

74. Walton, *The lives of Dr. John Donne, Sir Henry Wotton, Mr. Richard Hooker, Mr. George Herbert*, 49.

sense of helpless foreknowledge, that Donne is evoking here. To encounter this passage in the original 1624 edition is to feel the claustrophobia of the thought: the small format of the devotional book frames an intimate nightmare. Ramie Targoff describes it nicely: "Modest physical symptoms become ecological disasters in Donne's imaginative landscape."[75] While the idea of man as a "little world" and the images of biblical apocalypse would have been familiar to most early modern readers, the precipitousness of the mind's assault on the body is what is surprising, merging with the force of the imagined illness.[76] Donne gets ahead of himself: "[The fever] doth not only *melt* him, but *Calcine* him, reduce him to *Atomes*, and to *ashes*; not to *water*, but to *lime*. And how quickly? Sooner than thou canst receive an answer, sooner than thou canst conceive the question."[77] Donne might have been shaking from the fever—or beginning to—but thought produces its own tremors, which are arguably even worse. It is as if thinking the end were enough to bring it about. At least there are "no bad surprises": this is Eve Kosofsky Sedgwick's gloss of the self-defeating (for Donne, self-annihilating) desire of the "paranoid" reader.[78]

Donne's sudden eruption of fear can be called materialist, but not because he has adopted the philosophy of Epicureanism (the panic he describes is precisely opposed to the goal of that philosophy). Nor is it simply a matter of his mentioning "atoms." His materialism also comes through in his catastrophic style—the sudden leap from the "little" to the body instantly dissolved in the mind, the movement from the sensible to the insensible, and a seeming loss of agency. Once again we see how casually such thoughts might begin. The mere passage of an image or idea through the mind can sometimes be

75. Targoff, *John Donne*, 139.
76. John Carey has described the experience as the "appalled fantasy about bodies turning, with lightning speed, to fluid." Carey, *John Donne*, 175.
77. Donne, *Devotions upon Emergent Occasions*, 11.
78. Sedgwick, *Touching Feeling*, 130.

enough to overtake it. A thought might even seem expendable or absurd in the moment, but in the next it might seize hold of you—as in the case of a mental fever.

In narrating this earthquake of the mind, Donne was describing his own experience, but we can find a parallel in Michel de Montaigne, who recounts the acute pain of a kidney stone in the essay "Of Diversion" and rehearses a very similar pattern of thought: "Finding myself in this plight, I considered by what slight causes and objects [*legeres causes et objects*] my imagination fostered in me the regret for life; out of what atoms [*quels atomes*] the gravity and difficulty of this dislodgment from life built itself up in my soul."[79] Figuratively a small "atom" (and literally made of them), the stone transports his mind to the worst. The pain it causes is simultaneously a figure and provocation of the reflexive action of the imagination bounding from the small to the monstrous.[80] Here, the word "atom" might seem like just another metaphor in the fast-flowing stream of the essays, but the word assumes an outsized significance in the light of a seemingly unrelated reflection on materialism just a few moments before.[81] "We scarcely look at things in gross and alone," he writes; "it is the minute and superficial circumstances and notions that strike us, and the empty husks that peel off from the things."[82] Montaigne has just quoted a passage from Lucretius on grasshoppers shedding their skins to illustrate the idea that images "peel off from the

79. Montaigne, *Complete Works*, 636; *Les essais*, 837.

80. As Hugo Friedrich explains, "[Montaigne] knew to what a great extent life consists in adhering to the small things; when they founder, it is already the great death." Friedrich, *Montaigne*, 285. See also Sedley, "Irony and the Vacuum," 293.

81. For Montaigne, the figure of atoms could signify the direst of thoughts or nothing at all. On the latter, see, for example, Montaigne, *Complete Works*, 618; *Les essais*, 814. On Montaigne's engagement with Epicurean philosophy, see MacPhail, "Montaigne's New Epicureanism"; Passannante, *Lucretian Renaissance*, 104–19.

82. Montaigne, *Complete Works*, 635.

things." In *De rerum natura*, the image of molting grasshoppers is used elsewhere to represent the *simulacra* of atoms that are constantly shedding from material bodies—the subtle "things" that make perception possible.[83] In this casual movement from the "rinds" that "peel off" to the terrifying grip of thoughts that proceed from the onset of physical pain, Montaigne hints that even an ordinary act of perception is enough to produce a sudden seizure of the mind. "It is not only fevers, the potions, and the great accidents that upset our judgment," he says in another place in the *Essays*; "the slightest things in the world whirl it around."[84]

Donne himself was no stranger to being whirled about. In "The First Anniversary," he recalls the appearance of new stars in the sky, describing the thoughts that followed from them like an earthquake in heaven:

> We think the heavens enjoy their spherical,
> Their round proportion embracing all,
> But yet their various and perplexèd course,
> Observed in divers ages, doth enforce
> Men to find out so many eccentric parts,
> Such divers downright lines, such overthwarts,
> As disproportion that pure form. It tears
> The firmament in eight and forty shares,
> And in those constellations there arise
> New stars, and old do vanish from our eyes,
> As though heav'n suffered earthquakes, peace or war,
> When new towers rise and old demolished are.
> (lines 251–62)

---

83. Montaigne is quoting Lucretius, *De rerum natura* 5.803: "Folliculos ut nunc teretes aestate cicadae / Linquant" (As now in summer the cicadas leave behind / Their filmy shells) (*Complete Works*, 635; *Les essais*, 836).

84. Montaigne, *Complete Works*, 424.

When the new stars come into focus, they confirm the catastrophe. The coming and going of stars is not only like a succession of earthquakes; it is also like the rising and falling of towers in times of peace and war. Donne transforms our sense of the movement of history by calling to mind several different time scales at once. This is the poem's second allusion to the new stars. Earlier it describes this mental earthquake on another scale: "And freely men confess that this world's spent, / When in the Planets, and the firmament / They seek so many new; they see that this / Is crumbled out again to his Atomis" (lines 209–12).[85] These lines are often cited by literary and intellectual historians to second the poet's claim that the "new Philosophy" had destroyed a former idea of the world, leaving it "in pieces, all cohaerence gone" (lines 205, 213).[86] In the passage I quoted from the beginning of the *Devotions*, Donne calls to mind an old microcosm-macrocosm analogy (the body as a "little world"), but here the analogy itself appears to be "crumbled out" under the pressure of thought.

As we've come to see, catastrophic materialism can transform even the most stable and stabilizing of analogies. We might recall that the atomist Democritus is sometimes said to have been the first philosopher to use the term "microcosm," arguing that everything was made of the same invisible stuff.[87] As George Perrigo Conger pointed out long ago, "It is easy to construct microcosmic theories in an atomism . . .—

85. For Donne's use of atoms and other scientific imagery in the "Anniversaries," see Harvey and Harrison, "Embodied Resonances." Hirsch points to two additional contemporary definitions of "atomi" as "an anatomical preparation, especially a 'skeleton' or, more loosely, 'an emaciated or withered living body.'" Hirsch, "Donne's Atomies," 74–75.

86. See, for example, Victor Harris's classic study, *All Coherence Gone*, which takes its title from Donne's poem; also Koyré, *From the Closed World to the Infinite Universe*, 29.

87. Guthrie, *History of Greek Philosophy*, 2:471.

each atom may be regarded as an image of every other."[88] But what Conger calls "easy" might be redescribed as the seemingly automatic function of the imagination continuing on its compulsive course with a nearly inconceivable speed. What is *difficult* about the analogy is the way it forces a confrontation of dead matter and organic life. This is not the familiar form of the analogy that insists that man is like the universe and is connected to it through a great chain of being. A stabilizing idea now disturbs. In the first meditation, Donne speaks of his "perplex'd discomposition," which refers to his mental state (troubled with uncertainty) but also evokes the body's decomposition—the very thought that generates it.[89]

Throughout the *Devotions*, Donne repeatedly reminds us that our minds have the power to exalt us—and destroy us. "Our *creatures* are our *thoughts*," he writes in the fourth meditation, "*creatures* that are borne *Gyants*; that reach from *East* to *West*, from *earth* to *Heaven*; that doe not onely bestride all the *Sea*, and *Land*, but span the Sunn and *Firmament* at once."[90] The word "creatures" here aligns the author's art of making with the work of God, but when Donne remembers that such flights are confined to the "prison" of the body, he turns again suddenly to the horror of the involuntary: "And then as the other *world* produces *Serpents*, and *Vipers*, malignant, & venomous creatures, and *Wormes* and *Caterpillars*, that endeavour to devoure that world which produces them, and Monsters compiled and complicated of divers parents, & kinds, so this world, our selves, produces all these in us, in producing *diseases*, & *sicknesses* of all those sorts."[91] By the twisty turns of Donne's analogy, this "sickness" is the illness of the body but also the author's unwanted, monstrous thoughts, which like a disease

88. Conger, *Theories of Macrocosms and Microcosms in the History of Philosophy*, 6.

89. Donne, *Devotions upon Emergent Occasions*, 8.

90. Donne, *Devotions upon Emergent Occasions*, 20.

91. Donne, *Devotions upon Emergent Occasions*, 20.

"insinuat" themselves.[92] "Whats become of mans great extent & proportion," he asks, "when himselfe shrinkes himselfe, and consumes himselfe to a handfull of dust; whats become of his soaring thoughts, his compassing thoughts, when himselfe brings himselfe to the ignorance, to the thoughtlessnesse, of the *Grave*?"[93] Donne vacillates between knowledge of his own agency (he is doing this to "himselfe") and a sense of helpless inevitability. "Thoughtlessnesse" here describes the lack of sense in death, but also the mental stupor with which the author anticipates it.

Donne links his violent experience of thought to his "melancholy"—the "artificiall sicknes" or "unnaturall fever" he says he "joyn[s]" to his natural one.[94] According to Burton, melancholics were particularly vulnerable to the kind of mental distortions that make little things into big ones and symptoms into catastrophes. "As a concave glasse reflects solid bodies," he writes, a mind affected by melancholy "may reflect and shew prodigious shapes, as our vaine fear and crased phantasie shall suggest and faigne."[95] "Many times such terriculaments may proceed from naturall causes," he says, and the devil himself can use the "distemper of humours" to "possesse" us.[96] In a section of the *Anatomy* called "Love of Learning, or overmuch Study. With a Digression of the Misery of Scholars," Burton identifies melancholy as an occupational hazard—"one of those

92. For Donne's use of the word "insinuate," see, for example, Donne, *Devotions upon Emergent Occasions*, 29: "As the ill affections of the *spleene*, complicate, and mingle themselves with every infirmitie of the body, so doth *feare* insinuat it self in every *action*, or *passion* of the *mind*."

93. Donne, *Devotions upon Emergent Occasions*, 21.

94. Donne, *Devotions upon Emergent Occasions*, 8. On Donne's scholarly melancholy, see Trevor, *Poetics of Melancholy in Early Modern England*, 87–115. On the epistemology of melancholy in the period, see Daniel, *Melancholy Assemblage*.

95. Burton, *Anatomy of Melancholy*, 3:442–43; cited in Hankins, "Monstrous Melancholy," 28.

96. Burton, *Anatomy of Melancholy*, 3:443.

five principall plagues of Students . . . almost in some measure an inseparable companion."[97] Burton knew this from personal experience, but in this case he is borrowing the authority of Ficino, who enumerates the physical causes of the scholar's melancholy: lack of sleep, bad diet, and the agitation of the mind, among other (familiar) things.[98]

The mind's agitation is particularly relevant in the present context, for Ficino elsewhere attributes impiety to the "overly curious," "for men who are overly curious in any discipline because of their brain's excessive agitation usually become in a way insane, their brain having dried out. Plato says this in the *Theaetetus* in countering those who used to declare that nothing in nature ever stands still: having been made dizzy by the constant turning around, he says, they thought everything else was turning when they were being turned themselves."[99] Once again, Ficino here is arguing against the "followers of Lucretius," perhaps even implicitly conjuring up the poet's seminal image of restless confusion and agitation: dust in sunlight. An excess of curiosity leads the mind to too much agitation and, in the worst-case scenario, to irreligion or death.[100]

It was perhaps something like an "excessive agitation" that led Donne in the *Devotions* to muse on the mortality of the soul ("Even *Angels*, even our *soules*," he says, would be subject to "*Ruine*" and "*Annihilation*" if not for the constant preservation of God) and also on the plurality of worlds.[101] He laments the extreme solitariness imposed by the illness: "Men

97. Burton, *Anatomy of Melancholy*, 1:302.

98. See Ficino, *Three Books on Life*, 122–29.

99. Ficino, *Platonic Theology*, 4:311; cited and discussed in Hankins, "Monstrous Melancholy," 40.

100. For Augustine, curiosity was a form of lust and pride and a source of distraction. See Augustine, *Confessions* 10.35. See Daston and Park, *Wonders and the Order of Nature*, 122–24. For a wide-ranging account of "the 'trial' of theoretical curiosity," see Blumenberg, *Legitimacy of the Modern Age*, 229–456.

101. Donne, *Devotions upon Emergent Occasions*, 51.

that inhere upon *Nature* only, are so far from thinking, that there is anything *singular* in this world, as that they will scarce thinke, that this world it selfe is *singular*, but that every *Planet*, and every *Starre*, is another *World* like this."[102] Donne here enlists materialist ideas as evidence against solitude, "for *God*, and *Nature*, and *Reason* concurre against it"—attempting to refashion the dizzying thought of infinite space (which Pascal found so empty and terrifying) toward a vision of productive plurality.[103] But it's hard not to feel that Donne's thinking is strained here. The phrase "inhere upon" is an unusual construction in the period—from the Latin *inhaerere*, meaning "to cling or fasten to." While Donne prudently marks his distance, the idea of multiple worlds might be said to have already inhered upon him in the first meditation as an unwanted thought. Unlike in "A Valediction: Of Weeping," where, according to Empson, "we see Donne, as often, first taking this idea [of the microcosm] for granted; then throwing on top of it an idea that the whole earth is only a microcosm too, just as a man is, because it is only one of the globes in the universe," the Donne of the first meditation is not casually "throwing" ideas on top of ideas—not exercising a poetic freedom—but is pulled into his thought like a man struggling to escape from quicksand.[104] The common figure of the body as microcosm yields to other "little worlds," and the idea of the apocalypse is relativized in a sudden and radical shift of scale and perspective.

As David A. Hedrich Hirsch has shown, Donne was both repulsed by the (an)atomizing or cutting up of the body into parts and attracted to the idea of the atom as an indivisible unit that would survive the ravages of time.[105] While he repeatedly imagines the sudden dispersal of the body, he also follows Paul in describing God's "recollecting and reuniting this

---

102. Donne, *Devotions upon Emergent Occasions*, 25–26.
103. Donne, *Devotions upon Emergent Occasions*, 26.
104. Empson, *Essays on Renaissance Literature*, 107.
105. See Hirsch, "Donne's Atomies."

dust againe at the *Resurrection"* as an event that happens with an even greater velocity, "in an atom" (ἐν ἀτόμῳ) of time (1 Cor. 15:52). In interpreting this passage, Saint Jerome attempted to avoid the confusion between temporal and material atoms by translating the phrase as *in momento,* suggesting that Epicurus associated his materialist vision of the universe with the idea of the atom as an indivisible "point in time" (*punctum temporis*).[106] In his treatment of the resurrection, Saint Augustine too had tried to clear up the ambiguity around the phrase: "And to impress upon you the speed of such an atom, after saying *in an atom,* [Paul] straightaway went on to show how much action and movement can occur in an atom of time, by saying *in the twinkling of an eye.* . . . He realized, you see, that saying *in an atom* was rather obscure, and he wanted to say it more plainly so that it could be the more easily understood."[107]

Donne, by contrast, revels in the ambiguity, toggling between a material and a temporal idea of the "atom" "to explain the miraculous speed with which God rejoins these points of matter" at the end of time.[108] As Donne says, "and all shall rise there in a less *Minute,* then any one dies here."[109] "This minute" with which he began the first meditation in a state of terror,

106. Jerome, *Opera omnia,* 22:969. On this point, Jerome is citing the Alexandrian scholar Didymus the Blind. On this passage in Jerome, Don Fowler observes, "The atomist implications are brought out by the discussions in the Fathers of Paul's unusual phrase." Fowler, *Lucretius on Atomic Motion,* 350. Charles Doyle discussed the passage, its relation to atomism, and the fathers' reading of Paul in his 2015 Imbas presentation, "*Sed in Atomo, in Ictu Oculi:* A Proposed Origin for the *Atomus in Tempore.*"

107. Augustine, *Sermons on Various Subjects,* 257.

108. Hirsch, "Donne's Atomies," 83. Hirsch suggests that lines 55–59 from Donne's "Obsequies to the Lord Harrington" ("Yet at the last two perfect bodies rise, / Because God knowes where every Atome lyes; / So, if one knowledge were made of all those, / Who knew his minutes well, hee might dispose / His vertues into names, and ranks") "link the word 'Atome' with the suggestive term 'minutes,' which can be read as both tiny particles of matter and tiny particles of time."

109. Donne, *Devotions upon Emergent Occasions,* 13.

imagining his body instantly dissolved, had already suggested a kind of temporal atomism, a breaking up of time materialized in the choppy lines of the first edition:

> Variable, and
> therefore mi-
> serable con-
> dition of
> Man; this minute I was
> well, and am ill, this
> minute. [110]

In "this minute," at least, the text itself seems to register the earthquake of Donne's thought. But this, we know, is only the beginning of the poet's encounter with his illness. The *Devotions* dramatically refigures the body in crisis to make illness and doubt meaningful, as Achsah Guibbory has shown.[111] As Donne proceeds, the "discomposition" of materialism that opens the text proves instrumental, setting into motion a spiritual process. In this sense, we might read his idea of bodies recomposed in an "atom" of time, like Digges's notion of infinity, as an inversion of and a theological reply to the disturbing experience of materialist catastrophizing that began the text—that is, to the violence of the kind of analogy that simultaneously makes and unmakes the world.

---

110. Donne, *Devotions upon Emergent Occasions* (1624), 1.

111. See Guibbory, *Returning to John Donne*, 7–18. See also Targoff's discussion in *John Donne*, 130–53. For Donne's transformation of the devotional genre, see Goldberg, "Understanding of Sickness in Donne's *Devotions*." On the embodied way that Donne imagines religious identity, see Coles, "Matter of Belief in John Donne's Holy Sonnets."

THREE

Shakespeare's Catastrophic "Anything"

In a passage from Samuel Beckett's novel *Malone Dies* (1951), Malone explains how what seems insignificant can nonetheless produce a sudden feeling of dread or disaster: "I know it is a small thing. But I am easily frightened now. I know those little phrases that seem so innocuous and, once you let them in, pollute the whole of speech. *Nothing is more real than nothing.* They rise up out of the pit and know no rest until they drag you down into its dark. But I am on my guard now."[1] When it comes to such involuntary thoughts, however, it's hard to know if one can successfully guard against them, as Malone says, or if vigilance only makes things worse.

Beckett here reminds us of the all-too-casual way that patterns of thought can circulate. In the phrase "*nothing is more real than nothing,*" for example, we might hear an echo of Shakespeare's King Lear losing control upon hearing the word "nothing" from the mouth of his favorite daughter as if it were an evil charm.[2] "Nothing will come of nothing: speak again," Lear

1. Beckett, *Three Novels*, 192. Malone here is telling the story of Sapo, whose eyes are like "gulls," possibly echoing a line from Proust: "indifferent to everything, sea-like, like a sea-gull" (indifférente à tous, et marine comme un mouette). Cited and translated in Ackerley, *Demented Particulars*, 30. Beckett, who wrote *Malone* first in French, might very well have been thinking of Proust's own "little phrases."

2. According to Dirk Van Hulle and Mark Nixon, *King Lear* was "the play that occupied Beckett most during his life" and that he said was "unstageable." Van Hulle and Nixon, *Samuel Beckett's Library*, 26.

responds, shifting all of a sudden to a philosophical register.[3] Malone too is shifting registers, mixing up at least two sayings from Democritus—his argument that "thing is no more than nothing" (DK 68 B156), which, according to Plutarch, means that the void is as real as atoms—and the expression "In reality we know nothing; for truth is in the depths."[4] As we have already begun to see, such fragments themselves are perfect examples of the seemingly irrational efficacy of certain "little phrases."[5]

We consider now another of these "little phrases that seem so innocuous" but sometimes turn out not to be. I am thinking of a common Renaissance saying, to make *quidlibet ex quolibet*, or "anything of anything." The word *libet* in *quidlibet ex quolibet* signifies whatever "you wish," and it suggests that you are seeing what you *want* to see. To make *quidlibet ex quolibet* is to transpose one thing by interpretive violence into another. It might refer to deliberately dishonest practices of interpretation (i.e., the manipulation of evidence to suit one's needs), but it need not imply a conscious act at all. The catastrophizer, for example, doesn't *think* that she is making "anything of anything"

---

3. Shakespeare, *King Lear*, 1.1.88. Hereafter abbreviated *L* and cited in parentheses. Most editors of *Lear* trace the idea of "nothing will come of nothing" back to the Aristotelian *ex nihilo nihil fit*. L. C. Martin has argued that Lear was channeling not Aristotle but Lucretius, who, "at first or second or tenth hand, may have been among the influences which affected Shakespeare during his mainly tragic period." Martin, "Shakespeare, Lucretius, and the Commonplaces," 178.

4. Taylor, *Atomists*, 142.

5. In *Murphy* (1938), Beckett makes the connection to Democritus explicit, writing of "Nothing, than which in the guffaw of the Abderite naught is more real." Beckett, *Murphy*, 246. Beckett wrote some thirty years after the publication of *Murphy*: "If I were in the unenviable position of having to study my work, my points of departure would be the 'Naught is more real . . .' and the '*Ubi nihil vales . . .*' both already in *Murphy* and neither very rational." Cited and discussed in Durantaye, *Beckett's Art of Mismaking*, 139.

but rather believes she can make out a very specific "something."

For Shakespeare and his contemporaries, I'll argue, "anything of anything" establishes another connection between catastrophizing and the misconstrual of the nature of things— a pattern that stretches from the expression's early history in Scholastic translations and commentaries to descriptions of willful reading in the early modern period. In two subsequent sections, I turn to several pivotal scenes in Shakespeare's plays where "anything of anything" illuminates seemingly inexplicable and disastrous turns to the language of ontology. If anything might be made of anything, the strength of the *attachment* to one's disastrous convictions may be understood as another measure of catastrophic materialism's reach.

QUIDLIBET EX QUOLIBET

A little more than ten years after Thomas Digges viewed the nova in 1572, the astrologer Richard Harvey defended his own use of the stars. His brother Gabriel had pled with him "either not so much to addict to the studie, and contemplation of Judiciall Astrologie, or else by some evident and sensible demonstration, to make certaine and infallible proofe."[6] Not easily swayed by anyone—perhaps especially his older brother— Richard declared that an unthinkable disaster was certainly (or almost certainly) upon them. When Saturn and Jupiter crossed

6. Harvey, *Astrological discourse*, 3. In 1580, Gabriel had published a letter to his friend, Edmund Spenser, on a series of earthquakes that year, taking a rational and witty approach to interpreting the events and concluding with a note of skepticism. It was "almost impossible," he wrote, "for any man, either by Philosophie, or Diuinitie, euermore to determine flatly the very certaintie [of the earthquake's causes] either way." He even enthusiastically endorsed Pico della Mirandola's skeptical argument "against Cogging deceitfull Astrologers, and Southsayers"—the same text his brother was arguing against. Harvey and Spenser, *Three Proper and Wittie Familiar Letters*, 21, 24. On Harvey's letter, see Passannante, "Art of Reading Earthquakes."

paths again in 1588, he predicted, "Greate feare and dreade shal come sodainely upon the people, a great sterilitie and barrenesse of the earth shal ensue, manifold submersions, shipwracks, exustions, burnings, and such other, waterie and fierie calamities wil followe."[7] The only real disaster was his reputation.[8] When the year 1588 came and went not with apocalyptic events but with England's miraculous defeat of the Spanish Armada, Richard would come to regret his disaster-mongering—and not taking his brother's advice.[9]

That same year, the youngest of the three Harvey brothers, John, would condemn those (like Richard) who used the conjunction of 1588 to preach "still more and more dread, suspicion, jealousie, horror, I wot not what: full much adoo, and full little helpe: great stur, to small purpose."[10] John, who had written previously in support of his brother's predictions, was now lamenting an all-too-familiar problem—interpreters who

---

7. Harvey, *Astrological discourse*, 16. For a detailed description of this event and the controversies it inspired, see Aston, "Fiery Trigon Conjunction."

8. In his public feud with Gabriel Harvey, Thomas Nashe would revel in the embarrassment of Richard's failed predictions. He recounts Richard's humiliation: "That the whole Uniuersitie hist at him, Tarlton at the Theater made ieastes of him, and Elderton consumed his ale crammed nose to nothing, in beare-baiting him with whole bundels of Ballads. All this he barely repeates without any disprouement or denudation at all, as if it were so lame in it selfe, that it would adnihilate it selfe with the onelie rehearsall of it." Nashe, *Apologie of Pierce Pennilesse*, sig. 12ʳ.

9. Richard Chambers noted: "Howsoever they might laugh, it was no laughing matter to the Catholike king, and his invincible Navie, who will be famous for that exploit til 88 come againe." See Chambers, *Treatise against Judicial Astrologie*, 43; cited and discussed in Allen, *Star-Crossed Renaissance*, 127–28. According to Howard Dobin, the event of the Armada battle would "vindicate" prophecy in the years following: "A blizzard of new astrological and prophetic publications followed the Armada battle, and—fed by the growing anxiety over the uncertain succession—the storm persisted through the early years of James's reign." Dobin, *Merlin's Disciples*, 109–10.

10. Harvey, *Discoursive probleme*, 2. Aston, "Fiery Trigon Conjunction," 170–71.

make too much of too little: "But what needeth any farther in-
vectiue against so palpable a forgerie? Or what are these cunning Syllogizers, or any like Sophisticall concluders, but even
meere Cabalisticall coiners, and impostural wringers, making
at their own pleasure *Quidlibet ex quolibet*, numbers of cyphers,
bodies of Atomes, or sun motes, something of nothing?"[11] Like
his older brothers, John was well versed in the Renaissance art
of name-calling. In this case, astrological excess attracts a host
of analogies. John, for example, is thinking of the "cunning
Syllogizers" who use arguments that are formally correct but
lead to erroneous conclusions and those "Sophisticall concluders" who employ false reasoning.[12] "Can so heavy Consequents
proceed from so light Antecedents?" he asks with an almost
audible sigh of exasperation.[13] Among the other "bad" interpreters he mentions here are the "Cabalisticall coiners" who
wrest esoteric interpretations from texts, those who produce
numbers out of zero (a "cipher"), the overzealous readers of
Virgil and Homer who find Christianity lurking in every pagan
line, and the philosophers who make "bodies of Atomes, or sun
motes," impiously making "something of nothing"—or almost
nothing.[14]

Though all of the figures Harvey mentions here might be
said to make *quidlibet ex quolibet*, or "anything of anything," in
one way or another, those who make "bodies of Atomes, or sun
motes" stand out from the crowd because they bring us back

11. Harvey, *Discoursive probleme*, 96.

12. Aristotle discusses the various kinds of logical fallacies in *On Sophistical Refutations*. On the medieval background, see Novikoff, *Medieval Culture
of Disputation*.

13. Harvey, *Discoursive probleme*, 2.

14. Cf. Howard, *A defensatiue against the poyson of supposed prophesies*, sig.
Xi^v: "For as it is most free for all men to peruse and reade the word of God,
but not to wrest it to the maintenaunce of Cabalisticall conceyts . . . so we
conjure not to take profite by the meane, without rushing into desperate ex-
tremities; to measure trueth whereas she shines, without regard to shaddowes
where they flicker."

to the phrase's origins, linking it to a question of what bodies (like opinions) are made of.[15] We come upon *quidlibet ex quolibet* first in the earliest Latin translations of a passage from Aristotle's *Physics* that concerns the opinion of Anaxagoras that the matter of all things was contained *in* the matter of all other things (an idea the philosopher founded on that most familiar of premises, "nothing comes from nothing"). As Aristotle explains, "All such things are already there in each other and do not come into existence but are merely sifted out from where they are and take their names from their dominant constituents, and anything can be sifted out of anything (water out of flesh or flesh out of water)."[16] For Anaxagoras, man could call himself a little world or microcosm because his body quite literally contained the matter of everything else—and thus anything could be made of anything, or "ex quolibet quodlibet," as James of Venice rendered the Greek in his twelfth-century Latin translation.[17] For the author of the *Physics*, however, the notion that the bodies of all things were in everything else was absurd—not to mention that Anaxagoras was (for Aristotle at least) something of a closet materialist, positing a notion of mind or intelligence behind the organization of the world and "drag[ging] it in whenever he is at a loss to explain some necessary result; but otherwise [making] anything rather than Mind the cause of what happens."[18] It was easy enough to accuse

15. In the introduction to his 1660 translation of Rabelais's "Pantagruel's prognostication," the author who went by the pseudonym "Democritus Pseudomantis" uses the analogy between atoms and dust in a similar way, condemning the ludicrous astrologer for whom "every Beam of the Sun is a letter, and each Mote in it a Character for thee to uncypher and read over all the dispatches of Fate." Rabelais, *Pantagruel's prognostication*, A4.

16. Aristotle, *Physics* 187b.

17. Aristotle, *Physica: Translatio Vetus* 187b.

18. Aristotle, *Metaphysics* 985a. See also Plato, *Phaedo* 98b–c: "So I thought when [Anaxagoras] assigned the cause of each thing and of all things in common he would go on and explain what is best for each and what is good for all in common. I prized my hopes very highly, and I seized the books very eagerly

Anaxagoras himself of making *quidlibet ex quolibet*—and so the phrase came to refer not only to an argument for the makeup of things but also to the willful derivation of one thing from another. By the time it arrives in the Renaissance, the now-familiar saying suggests all manner of bad or strained interpretation.

This seemingly "innocuous" phrase became especially popular in theological disputes throughout the sixteenth and seventeenth centuries. In this context, it might evoke the Scholastic tradition of "quodlibets," famously subtle and often elaborate disputations on theological and philosophical subjects freely chosen by the speaker or the logical rule *Ex impossibili sequitur quodlibet*, "From the impossible follows anything."[19] As Thomas Bilson once put it, "You remember belike the olde rule, *Ex impossibili sequitur quodlibet, from an impossibilitie supposed any thing will follow*: and seeing your selfe destitute of all proofes for your new Doctrine, you will needs make lotteries of impossibilities, and thence draw what you like best."[20] But one curious feature of the phrase's travels in the early modern period is that it never entirely lost contact with the old philosophical questions about matter and substance to which it had been originally attached. Responding to one of his adversaries, the Anglican divine James Calfhill quipped: "I rather think you to be some scholar of Anaxagoras, which have learned to make *quidlibet ex quolibet*; an apple of an oyster."[21] According to the *American Heritage Dictionary of Idioms*, "an apple of an oyster" is the not-so-distant an-

and read them as fast as I could, that I might know as fast as I could about the best and the worst. My glorious hope, my friend, was quickly snatched away from me. As I went on with my reading I saw that the man made no use of intelligence, and did not assign any real causes for the ordering of things, but mentioned as causes air and ether and water and many other absurdities."

19. For the history and afterlife of the quodlibetical tradition, see, in general, Schabel, *Theological Quodlibeta in the Middle Ages*; and especially Courtenay, "Demise of Quodlibetal Literature."

20. Bilson, *Suruey of Christs sufferings*, 365.

21. Calfhill, *Aunsvvere to the Treatise of the crosse*, 43.

cestor of the still-common expression "comparing apples and oranges."[22] Another clergyman, John Weemes, likewise complained of the excesses of biblical interpreters: "To make divers senses in the Scripture, is to make it like that which *Anaxagoras* dreamed of, making *Quidlibet ex quolibet.*"[23]

Allegorical interpreters and etymologists too were prone to making "anything of anything," as were paranoid or overly scrupulous readers and, as we already know, astrologers. When Harvey uses the phrase *quidlibet ex quolibet* above, he treats it and "something of nothing" as near synonyms.[24] Though he doesn't mention the name Anaxagoras, the philosophical connotations of *quidlibet ex quolibet* bubble to the surface as he arrives at the ancient question of what makes up "bodies." Where making anything of anything was concerned, one "materialist" philosopher speculating about the nature of things was just as good (or bad) as another.[25] As John Harvey would say, if we place our trust in absurd notions like the idea that the world is eternal (Aristotle's) or in the predictions of astrologers, "we may as well conclude with Democritus, Metrodorus, Lucretius, and the ridiculous Epicure that there are innumerable, or infinite worlds, not only one world."[26] Harvey might have added to his list the name Giordano Bruno, who had left England

22. Ammer, *American Heritage Dictionary of Idioms*, 12.

23. Weemes, *Exercitations divine*, 177.

24. Echoing Harvey in the seventeenth century, Henry More would level a similar critique against the astrologers, tracing a line from "anything of anything" to "nothing:" "*Methinks that it ought to be Conviction . . . that the whole business of* Judiciary Astrology *is a mere piece of phantastry, in which they make* quidlibet ex quolibet . . . *and that there is nothing found at the bottom.*" More, *Tetractys anti-astrologica*, 168.

25. Samuel Parker would later associate the phrase not with Anaxagoras but with Epicurus: "And if such a licentious latitude may be allowed in historical guesses, *Quidlibet ex Quolibet* will soon be as warrantable a *maxime* in History, as 'tis in Epicurean Philosophie." Parker, *Free and impartial censure of the Platonick philosophie*, 104.

26. Harvey, *Discoursive probleme*, 30.

only a few years earlier but not before publishing his treatise on infinity.[27] "Infinite worlds" was another example of an interpreter making too much of too little.

The phrase was one way in which early moderns consciously or unconsciously brought the matter of ontology to bear on questions of interpretation (and its limits). Montaigne's accidental habits of mind are once again illuminating here, demonstrating the way the phrase unexpectedly brings different kinds of discourses into contact with one another. In the "Apology for Raymond Seybond," the essayist silently traces the logic of *quidlibet ex quolibet* to its roots, showing how quickly a bad or willful interpretation can devolve into philosophical dogmatism. Unfolding over several pages, the passage begins:

> There is no prognosticator if he has enough authority for people to deign to leaf through him and study carefully all the implications and aspects of his words, who cannot be made to say whatever you want [*à qui on ne face dire tout ce qu'on voudra*], like the Sibyls. For there are so many means of interpretation that, obliquely or directly, an ingenious mind can hardly fail to come across in any subject some sense that will serve his point.[28]

The scene of the unscrupulous (or is it delusional?) interpreter "leaf[ing] through" (*feuilleter*) pages in order to find "whatever [he] wants" recalls Virgil's image of prophetic leaves

---

27. Bruno published his cosmological work, *De l'infinito, universo e mondi*, in London in 1584.

28. Montaigne, *Complete Works*, 442; *Les essais*, 586. Montaigne makes a similar point in the essay "Of Prognostications": "And they have been so strangely fortunate in [making prognostications] in my time as to persuade me that since divination is an amusement of sharp and idle minds, those who are trained in this subtle trick of tying and untying knots would be capable of finding, in any writings, whatever they want." Montaigne, *Complete Works*, 29.

(*folia*) jumbled by the wind.[29] This sense of the phrase *quidlibet ex quolibet* will exfoliate over the next few paragraphs, bringing us from irresponsible readers of prognostications to readers of Homer. Is it possible, Montaigne asks, "that Homer meant to say all they make him say?"[30] Montaigne here is echoing Rabelais: "Now do you really and truly believe that Homer, when composing the *Iliad* and the *Odyssey*, had any thought of the allegories which have been caulked on to him by Plutarch, Heraclides of Pontus, Eustathius or Conutus and which Politian purloined from them?"[31] Bad or dishonest readers of Homer find anything they want in the poet; they make "anything of anything." With his penchant for quoting ancient authors promiscuously, sometimes bending their meaning to its opposite sense, Montaigne knew well of what he spoke.[32]

From a loaded question of literary interpretation, Montaigne moves now, almost imperceptibly, to interpreting the text of the world, demonstrating once again how easily (perhaps unthinkingly) these kinds of substitutions can be made.[33] Here he is drawing a connection between the hermeneutic issue of making anything of anything and the philosophical problem of imagining the makeup of things through the senses. Elaborating on a passage from Sextus Empiricus, he writes: "From

29. See Virgil, *Aeneid* 6.74–75: "Only trust not your verses to leaves, lest they fly in disorder, the sport of rushing winds" (foliis tantum ne carmina manda, / ne turbata volent rapidis ludibria ventis).

30. Montaigne, *Complete Works*, 442.

31. Rabelais, *Gargantua and Pantagruel*, 207–8.

32. As Timothy Hampton explains, "The blade of disfiguration and distortion cuts both ways. To preserve himself and express 'ce qui est mien par nature' [what is naturally my own] Montaigne must run the risk of being disfigured, or at least misunderstood, by his readers. He must open himself to the charge that he has failed to comprehend the 'natural usage' of the passages he borrows." Hampton, *Writing from History*, 178–79.

33. On Homer and ancient philosophy, see Naddaff, "Allegory and the Origins of Philosophy."

the same foundation that Heraclitus had, and that maxim of his that all things had in them the aspects that were found in them, Democritus derived a wholly opposite conclusion, that things had in them nothing at all of what we found in them."[34] Montaigne here identifies one particular species of interpretive waywardness, pointing out that different philosophers draw opposite conclusions from the very same premise, remaking what they perceive according to their own pleasure. Explaining the forking paths of interpretive error, he suggests two meanings of the phrase "nothing at all" (*tout rien*). The first is fairly straightforward: the sensible properties that we perceive in objects don't correspond to the reality of things. As Democritus puts it, "Sweet exists by convention, bitter by convention, colour by convention. Atoms and Void (*alone*) exist in reality" (DK 68 B9).[35] This still leaves open the possibility of knowledge grasped by reason through the senses. A second interpretation of Montaigne's phrase "nothing at all" raises a more disturbing possibility, recalling the most skeptical reading of a fragment I've already discussed, "In reality we know nothing; for truth is in the depths," which casts doubt on our capacity to know anything at all.

We see Montaigne here playing on various meanings of the phrase *quidlibet ex quolibet*, arriving finally at the question of matter and epistemology just beneath the surface. Sextus Empiricus tells us that Democritus approved of the opinion "Appearances are a glimpse of the obscure," which he attributes to Anaxagoras.[36] Like both Anaxagoras and Democritus, Montaigne is also considering the question of what and how much might be made of appearances. At the end of this passage in the "Apology," he will draw our attention to this issue again, this

34. Montaigne, *Complete Works*, 443. Compare to Sextus Empiricus, *Outlines of Pyrrhonism* 2.6.63.

35. Freeman, *Ancilla to the Pre-Socratic Philosophers*, 93.

36. See again Kirk, Raven, and Schofield, *Presocratic Philosophers*, 383; discussed in the introduction.

time citing some lines from *De rerum natura* that begin "Hence what the senses see is always true" (*proinde quod in quoque est his visum tempore, verum est*), and condemning the Epicureans for their delusions with an intensity that feels almost personal: "This desperate and most unphilosophical advice means nothing else than that human knowledge can maintain itself only by unreasonable, mad, and senseless [*forcenée*] reason; but that still it is better for man, in order to assert himself, to use it and any other remedy, however fantastic, than to admit his necessary stupidity."[37] Knowledge from the senses devolves into "unreasonable, mad, and senseless reason," and drawing conclusions from perception becomes a desperate attachment to an untrustworthy image. *This*, he seems to be saying, is how we become enthralled by an idea—how we make anything of anything.

The word *forcenée* suggests a person fanatical, obsessive, without control, frantic. Montaigne here is talking about the fanaticism of philosophers—but what he is saying has urgent implications in sixteenth-century France. "How many quarrels," he writes in another place, "and how important, have been produced in the world by the doubt of the meaning of that syllable *Hoc*!"[38] This is a reference to the theological controversy over the word in "Hoc est corpus meum" (Christ's "This is my body").[39] Like *quidlibet ex quolibet*, this "little phrase" also posed a question of what it was that composed a body (in this case, the Eucharist). In fact, Calvin had made this very point himself when he criticized those who make of "Hoc est corpus meum" what they will:

37. Lucretius, *De rerum natura* 4.509; Montaigne, *Complete Works*, 447; *Les essais*, 592.

38. Montaigne, *Complete Works*, 229.

39. For Montaigne's interest in the controversy surrounding this phrase, see Compagnon, *Nous, Michel de Montaigne*, 32–35. Ulrich Langer finds an echo of the phrase in Montaigne's image of himself in his book. See Langer, *Divine and Poetic Freedom in the Renaissance*, 111–12.

Our faith rests in the saying, "This is my body," so far as to have
no doubt that the communion of Christ is truly offered. In this
way there is no need of subtle arguments as to the quantity of
body. These we are forced to use by the extravagance of those
who, depriving Christ of the reality of his flesh, transform him
into a phantasm. When we say that we are made partakers of
Christ spiritually, we do not mean that his body is held forth to
be eaten only in a figurative, symbolical, and allegorical sense.
This vile falsehood, like the others, sufficiently declares that
those men who thus assume a license of making anything out
of anything [*quidlibet ex quolibet*], have not one particle of in-
genuous shame.[40]

Here Calvin is using the phrase to drive home the point that
some contemporary theologians misunderstand the very nature of the Eucharist, which gives us a sense of the phrase's
reach in the early modern imagination. Writing in the shadow
of the French wars of religion, Montaigne himself was all too
aware of the disastrous consequences of making anything of
anything—the ways a seemingly small issue of interpretation
(in this case, even a single syllable) might lead to catastrophe.

"THE QUALITY OF NOTHING"

Montaigne's sensitivity to the philosophical dimensions of the
phrase takes us now to Shakespeare, in whose plays the potential tragedy of making "anything of anything" can be felt most
acutely. Shakespeare was likewise preoccupied with the problem of bad interpretation and the willful imposition of bad interpretations upon the world. His promiscuous use of words
such as "anything," "something," and "nothing" provide us
with another context for thinking about possible resonances

40. Calvin, *Tracts Relating to the Reformation*, 2:445; *Opera omnia*, 8:711.

of the phrase—and for charting its catastrophic ends. Though he could have come upon *quidlibet ex quolibet* in any number of the sources I mention above, he almost certainly encountered a version of it in Samuel Harsnett's *A declaration of egregious popish impostures*—a source, as scholars have shown, he drew upon in *Lear*.[41] In condemning the ritual of Catholic exorcism, Harsnett writes of priests who "made what they list of any thing" and "would make a faire tale of any thing."[42] Like Montaigne in the passage above, Shakespeare doesn't use the Latin phrase *quidlibet ex quolibet*, but its distinctive set of associations animates critical moments in his plays. While we can hear more gentle echoes of the phrase and its cousins in titles such as *Twelfth Night, or What You Will* (1601–2) and *Much Ado About Nothing* (1598–99), in Shakespeare it is most illuminating in moments of strained or willful interpretation when the language of ontology rises catastrophically to the surface.

We've already seen the example from *Lear* when the word "nothing" sets into motion a precipitous unraveling of the title character's psychic universe. When Othello responds to Iago's deliberately vague insinuations with the phrase "Thou dost mean something," he too is making anything of anything.[43] Even if we place a considerable amount of blame on the villainous Iago for what befalls Othello, we are nonetheless surprised by how *little* it takes for Othello to assume the worst (little more than a subtle echoing of his own words). Iago here is a minimalist, leaving Othello to make "something" of his "exsufflicate and blowed surmises"—a phrase that, once again, recalls the sibyl's scattered leaves and the chaotic wind of hasty

41. See Muir, "Samuel Harsnett and *King Lear*," on the parallels between Harsnett and Shakespeare in the play. See also Greenblatt, *Shakespearean Negotiations*, 94–128.

42. Harsnett, *Declaration of egregious popish impostures*, 188, 282.

43. Shakespeare, *Othello*, 3.3.112. Hereafter abbreviated *O* and cited in parentheses.

interpretation (*O*, 3.3.186).[44] Iago will later use the phrase "what you will" to evoke Othello's worst thoughts about how Desdemona has betrayed him, occasioning an epileptic fit (*O*, 4.1.34). Othello responds: "It is not words that shakes me thus" (*O*, 4.1.39–40). In *Lear*, we find another example in Gloucester reading a forged letter supposedly written by his son Edgar:

> GLOUCESTER: What paper were you reading?
> EDMUND: Nothing, my lord.
> GLOUCESTER: No? What needed then that terrible dispatch of it into your pocket? The quality of nothing hath not such need to hide itself. Let's see. Come, if it be nothing, I shall not need spectacles. (*L*, 1.2.30–35)

While considering this passage, we might recall the title of a volume in Donne's satirical library: *Quidlibet ex quolibet; Or the art of decyphering and finding some treason in any interpreted letter*.[45] But one would hardly require such a book to find treason in the letter in question, which broadcasts Gloucester's worst fear that his only legitimate son would like to see him dead sooner rather than later.

Though the letter itself is hardly ambiguous, the fact that

44. With this image of scattered words like leaves "blown" in the wind, Iago, as Joel Altman has suggested, is a "desacralized Sibyl." Altman, *Improbability of Othello*, 218.

45. Donne, *Courtier's Library*, 32. In *Pseudo-martyr* (1610), Donne defends his practice of citing authors loosely rather than to the letter, calling out "the curious malice of those men, who in this sickly decay, and declining of their cause, can spy out falsifyings in every citation: as in a jealous, and obvious state, a Decipherer can pick out Plots, and Treason, in any familiar letter which is intercepted." Donne, *Pseudo-martyr*, sig. A2ʳ. Acknowledging his own practice of avowedly inexact citation, which we might expect to receive the charge, he instead accuses those who would find him guilty of "falsifyings," of making "anything of anything."

Gloucester is willing to believe its contents so quickly is disturbing. "You know the character to be your brother's?" Gloucester asks (*L*, 1.2.60) — "character" here suggesting "handwriting" but also perhaps something like "the sum of moral and mental qualities" (a meaning, according to the OED, that begins to come into focus in the early seventeenth century).[46] Edmund answers his father, punning on the word "matter," meaning "contents" but also "substance" in a sense that underlies their broader discussion of legitimacy and lineage: "If the matter were good, my lord, I durst swear it were his, but in respect of that, I would fain think it were not. . . . It is his hand, my lord, but I hope his heart is not in the contents" (*L*, 1.2.61–62, 64–65). In the end, Edmund promises the letter will be backed up by "auricular assurance," but that assurance is already unnecessary, for Gloucester's baneful certainty is by now well established (*L*, 1.2.86). The flimsy "matter" of the letter stands in for Edgar and unequivocally declares his guilt.[47]

As in Montaigne's case, we see Shakespeare connecting the dots from a question of interpretation to one of material substance. Though *quidlibet ex quolibet* isn't used in this context, the entire scene is like an elaborate illustration of the phrase. This is particularly the case where one kind of speculative leap is juxtaposed with and analogized to another. Having leapt to conclusions from the forged letter, Gloucester abandons rational explanation for the influence of the stars. In turning to the

46. OED *Online*, s.v. "character, *n.*," 9a.

47. As Richard Meek has argued, "Edmund's forged letter brilliantly generates the illusion of a real, if absent, author." Meek, *Narrating the Visual in Shakespeare*, 121. According to Alan Stewart, letters were "not merely a means to maintain communication across distances, but increasingly taken as documentary evidence of transactions, of responsibility, and ultimately of guilt. . . . Even on those occasions where letters are forged or mistaken . . . the characters still subscribe to their power as evidentiary documents." Stewart, *Shakespeare's Letters*, 299.

stars to moralize, he calls to mind the "impostural wringers" in
Harvey's treatise against prophecies:

> GLOUCESTER: These late eclipses in the sun and moon portend
> no good to us. Though the wisdom of Nature can reason
> it thus and thus, yet Nature finds itself scourged by the
> sequent effects. (*L*, 1.2.95–98)[48]

When he leaves, Edmund notes the absurdity of the practice
of those who "make guilty of our disasters the sun, the moon,
and the stars" (*L*, 1.2.110–11). As Harvey suggested, to make so
much of the stars is to make "something of nothing." The irony
is that the kind of making Edmund describes leads to the denial of human agency:

> EDMUND: As if we were villains on necessity, fools by heav-
> enly compulsion, knaves, thieves, and treachers by spheri-
> cal predominance, drunkards, liars, and adulterers by an
> enforced obedience of planetary influence, and all that we
> are evil in by a divine thrusting on. (*L*, 1.2.111–15)

In other words, we make whatever we like of the stars (or of a
few words or of our own subjective perceptions) and then forget the role we played in our actions. This is one way we dis-
avow our own thoughts and treat them as if they were somehow external to us—like natural disasters.

By making anything of anything, Edmund shows just how
fungible the "matter" of legitimacy really is—and also how in-
tractable it can seem if you don't have the influence or power
to make it stick. His fantasy is that in unmaking his brother's
reputation, he might actually make or remake himself. Nevertheless, Edmund still finds himself constrained by the system
of assurances that is as full of nothing as the letter he forged. In

48. Harvey, *Discoursive probleme*, 96.

the same train of thought he wonders why he is called a bastard by "custom" (*L*, 1.2.3):

> When my dimensions are as well compact,
> My mind as generous, and my shape as true,
> As honest madam's issue? Why brand they us
> With 'base,' with 'baseness, bastardy—base, base'— ...?
> (*L*, 1.2.7–10)

It is as if Edmund were invoking a critique of etymology along with his critique of astrology, laying bare the dubious derivation of "bastardy" from "base."[49] Even if one word doesn't derive from the other, the association still has a palpable force—one he has trouble escaping. A scene about making whatever you like out of whatever you like once again raises a question of ontology. In spite of his best efforts, he remains Edmund the bastard, "base" in that most material sense of the word—literally not made of the same stuff as his brother.

Only slightly later, the poet and satirist Robert Anton would associate those who "boast their *gentry* from a *starre* / Kinde in *coniunction*" with the atomists, linking social status explicitly to matter:

> Laugh, Laugh *Democritus*,
> Heer's a right *Comedie*, though vicious,
> To stretch foorth all thy *powers* to *excesse*,
> And fat thy *heart* with mortall *foolishnesse*:
> These are those *atomes* of *nobilitie*,
> Which in thy *schoole* thou taugh'st erroneously,
> To be the *worlds* beginning.[50]

---

49. On the false connection between "bastardy" and "base," see Palmer, *Folk-etymology*, 23. Edmund is playing on the sound of the word "bastard," evoking the tardiness of the younger in a system of primogeniture. See Gilbert, "'Unaccommodated man.'"

50. Anton, *Philosophers Satyrs*, 25.

We might be reminded of the connection Harvey saw between the absurdity of atomists and astrologers. As Harvey suggested, predicting the end of the world from the configuration of stars was like making "bodies of Atomes, or sun motes." Here, falsely deriving one's nobility from the stars is just as bad as imagining the "*worlds* beginning" from atoms.⁵¹

As we know, Anton is drawing on the idea of Democritus as laughing at the madness of the world—"a right *Comedie*." When his brother Edgar finally arrives on the scene, Edmund also evokes the language of the theater: "Pat, he comes like the catastrophe of the old comedy. My cue is villainous melancholy, with a sigh like Tom o' Bedlam.—O, these eclipses do portend these divisions! Fa, so, la, mi" (*L*, 1.2.122–24). Edmund here uses "catastrophe" explicitly in its theatrical sense, but the word also calls to mind the idea of an "overthrow, ruin, calamitous fate."⁵² In light of Erasmus, Thomas Cooper defined the word in his sixteenth-century dictionary as a "subversion. Also the latter end of a comedie, and, proverbially, the ende of any thing."⁵³ Playing on this "proverbial" sense, Edmund's "catastrophe" echoes his use of "disaster" only slightly earlier ("make guilty of our disasters the sun, the moon, and the stars"), and reminds us both of the dissonant sound of his father's catastrophizing and of Melanchthon's deployment of the word "catastrophe" in an astrological context.

The drama of *quidlibet ex quolibet* that plays out around the interpretation of the letter sets the stage for another scene of disaster. Edmund's raising of "catastrophe" looks forward to the pathetic sight of Lear in the midst of an actual disaster in which he himself is no longer able to make of the world what he will—and his own "*atomes of nobilitie*" are reduced to the

51. William Elton finds another analogue to Edmund's skepticism in a later text by Anton. See Elton, *King Lear and the Gods*, 159.

52. OED *Online*, s.v. "catastrophe, *n.*," 2a.

53. Cooper, *Thesaurus Linguae*, sig. ʀ3ʳ; cited and discussed in Rosen, *Dislocating the End*, 9.

stuff of a quivering body on stage. Here, Lear struggles to make sense of the storm, shifting rapidly between various interpretations—none of which quite hold. He first addresses the storm as follows:

> Blow, winds, and crack your cheeks! Rage, blow,
> You cataracts and hurricanoes, spout
> Till you have drenched our steeples, drowned the cocks!
> You sulph'rous and thought-executing fires,
> Vaunt-couriers of oak-cleaving thunderbolts,
> Singe my white head; And thou, all-shaking thunder,
> Smite flat the thick rotundity o'th' world,
> Crack nature's molds, an germens spill at once
> That makes ingrateful man. (*L*, 3.2.1–9)

As the storm rages on, Lear will try (and fail) to make *quidlibet ex quolibet*. But, after wondering about the storm's motives, imagining the disaster as an instrument of revenge, and regretting that he wasn't more generous to the poor, he addresses the figure of a naked Edgar as follows: "Thou art the thing itself. Unaccommodated man is no more but such a poor, bare, forked animal as thou art" (*L*, 3.4.95–97). In seeing himself in this image, Lear's catastrophic failure to impose his "anything" upon the world resolves into a catastrophe that transforms man into a "nothing" contemplating its very thingness.

"WHY, THEN, THE WORLD AND ALL THAT'S IN'T IS NOTHING"

In Edgar Allan Poe's short story "Ligeia" (1838), a man reflects on the inscrutable mystery of his otherworldly lover:

> What was it—that something more profound than the well of Democritus—which lay far within the pupils of my beloved? What *was* it? I was possessed with a passion to discover. Those

eyes! those large, those shining, those divine orbs! they became to me twin stars of Leda, and I to them devoutest of astrologers.[54]

Poe here brings together again the twin images of the astrologer and the materialist that we've been tracing across these last two chapters—the one reading the future and the other reading the insensible world of matter from visible signs. The figure of the lover here emerges as a ghostly apparition, but Poe's story might suggest the uncanniness of intimacy more generally. The starstruck lover assures us that he is the "devoutest of astrologers." But being "devoutest" might also mean being *too* devout—being "one that loved not wisely but too well," as Othello puts it (*O*, 5.2.353). There are very real dangers to over-reading the stars—or, to recall the etymology of disaster, finding an "ill" star in a lover's eyes.

We may recall that John Harvey himself spoke of those who would produce "still more and more dread, suspicion, jealousie, horror, I wot not what," linking the seemingly automatic fear induced by the doomsday astrologer with the equally violent affections of jealousy and suspicion. To rush to catastrophic conclusions, he said, was to get lost in "the profound deepes of this bottomles pit."[55] Consider now a second example from Shakespeare, which demonstrates how casually a metaphysical dread or horror might be transformed into a matter of "jealousie." The opening of *The Winter's Tale* presents a familiar story: Leontes doubts whether his wife has been faithful. He also doubts whether his son is his own. As in the case of Othello, the doubt comes upon him all at once. As Francis Bacon says, "But in fearful natures [suspicions] gain ground too fast. There

54. Poe, "Ligeia," 65.
55. Harvey, *Discoursive probleme*, 99.

is nothing makes a man suspect much, more than to know a little."[56]

In a moment of wishful thinking, Leontes's wife, Hermione, allows herself to imagine that her husband's jealousy might be explained as an effect of an "ill planet," again evoking the etymology of *disaster*.[57] A little later in the same scene, we see all too clearly that it is Leontes, with the aid of his own passions rather than the stars, who catastrophically converts nothings into somethings, observing his wife's interactions with his best friend and interpreting every little thing they do (every sign, real or imagined) as evidence of infidelity: "Is whispering nothing? / Is leaning cheek to cheek? Is meeting noses?" (*WT*, 1.2.287–88). The list goes on until the sense of his speech breaks down:

> Is this nothing?
> Why, then, the world and all that's in't is nothing,
> The covering sky is nothing, Bohemia nothing,
> My wife is nothing, nor nothing have these nothings
> If this be nothing. (*WT*, 1.2.294–98)[58]

In short, Leontes finds clues everywhere he looks. In Aaron Landau's words, "His methodology is in many respects that of an extremely meticulous, even obsessive, interpreter: he constantly plays around with words, rearranges syntax, recontextualizes statements, reevaluates gestures—everything in the

56. Bacon, *Works*, 12:190.

57. Shakespeare, *The Winter's Tale*, 2.1.107. Hereafter abbreviated *WT* and cited in parentheses.

58. As Paul A. Jorgensen has shown, when Shakespeare evokes "nothing," he is drawing on the "highly potential nature of the word and idea" in contexts such as the *contemptus mundi* tradition as well as the playful literary tradition that produced mock encomia like Edward Dyer's *The Prayse of Nothing* (1585). Jorgensen, *"Much Ado About Nothing,"* 287.

service of his own particular 'reading.'"[59] Translated into the period's terms, Leontes, like the doomsday astrologer or the atomist, is making *quidlibet ex quolibet*, abruptly transforming the language and gestures of courtesy with which the play begins into grist for his jealous mill.[60] He is also catastrophizing in the more familiar sense of the word, leaping from the sensible to the insensible—and from a "small thing" to the worst.

Leontes's habits of mind exhibit a proximity to philosophical argument throughout the play, indicating, as in the case of Montaigne's "atoms," how easily a question of something slight can suddenly assume an outsized significance in a person's mind. We might take, for example, a famously knotty passage from the same scene in which Leontes crudely addresses his young son, Mamillius. His speech begins:

> Thou want'st a rough pash and the shoots that I have,
> To be full like me. Yet they say we are
> Almost as like as eggs. Women say so,
> That will say anything. (*WT*, 1.2.130–33)

Here Leontes is considering the boy's likeness to him in light of his suspicion about his wife's infidelity. The eggs here are proverbial, and Leontes mentions them almost in passing, but the image points us to one of the larger problems of the play: how we know for certain the things we think we know. These eggs, in fact, recall a discussion about the nature of knowledge from Cicero's *Academica* where we find Lucullus, the Stoic representative in the dialogue, debating with the skeptics, who hold that certain knowledge is impossible. The example of the eggs comes up when Lucullus refutes the contention that false

59. Landau, "'No Settled Senses,'" 33.
60. Harold C. Goddard writes of the passage above: "Leontes is exactly right, but not in the sense he intends, for it is precisely out of the vast realm of Nothing—of pure possibility—that he has summoned these nothings." Goddard, *Meaning of Shakespeare*, 2:264.

presentations are not discernible from true ones and responds to the various instances of resemblance that the skeptics used to make their case (twins, eggs, seals in wax). For the Stoics, the experience of examining eggs—which often look alike—shows how close inspection can reveal small differences between seemingly identical objects. Lucullus explains, "These poultry-keepers used to be able to tell which hen had laid an egg merely by looking at it."[61] He is certain, he says, that there is a criterion that would allow him to make meaningful distinctions between eggs—as between true and false claims, "for I possess a standard [*regulam*] enabling me to judge presentations to be true when they have a character of a sort that false ones could not have; from that standard I may not diverge a finger's breadth, as the saying is [*ut aiunt, digitum discedere*], lest I should cause universal confusion [*ne confundam Omnia*]."[62] Moments earlier, Lucullus had referred disapprovingly to the philosophy of Democritus, who, we are told, "says that there are a countless number of worlds, and what is more that some of them to such an extent not merely resemble but completely and absolutely match each other in every detail that there is positively no difference between them, and that the same is true of human beings."[63] The specter of Democritus's philosophical error looms large in the background as Lucullus insists on the importance of making subtle distinctions. His image of

---

61. Cicero, *Academica* 2.18.57; cited and discussed in Eden, *Renaissance Rediscovery*, 120. Erasmus treats this passage under the heading "Non tam ovum ovo simile" (As like as one egg to another); (Chilias 1, Centuria v, Proverbium 10) in *Adages Ii1 to Iv100*, 393. Montaigne recalls the passage at the start of "Of Experience," modifying it slightly as if to drive home the point: "And we ourselves use eggs for the most express example of similarity. However, there have been men, and notably one at Delphi, who recognized marks of difference between eggs, so that he never took one for another; and although there were many hens, he could tell which one the egg came from." Montaigne, *Complete Works*, 815.

62. Cicero, *Academica* 2.18.58.

63. Cicero, *Academica* 2.17.55.

the "finger's breadth" brings home the idea that small things really do matter—that "universal confusion" might actually hinge on the slightest "somethings" or, as it were, "nothings." Leontes too believes that he has a *regulam* for distinguishing truth from falsehood. In the space of a "finger's breadth," Shakespeare shows us how arbitrary (and dangerous) such a standard can be.[64]

The catastrophic pattern of making anything of anything becomes apparent where the mind leaps suddenly (and seemingly without agency) to the end of thought, where it moves with too much confidence from the sensible to the insensible, and where it confuses scale and perspective (shifting, as we've seen, from the thought of a wife's supposed indiscretion to the structure of the world). The pattern also becomes apparent where it leads again to the question of what thoughts and opinions are made of. The implications of *quidlibet ex quolibet* are powerfully felt when characters such as Leontes, Othello, or Lear make too much of too little and the language of "something," "nothing," or "anything" immediately follows—perhaps symptomatically.

In the remainder of the speech that began above, we watch as Leontes passes from the "anything" that women say to "nothing" and then to "something" in the space of thirteen lines, dredging up the old philosophical roots of making anything of anything. Recall that he is still speaking to his son when he falls into this "mysterious, mumbling half-soliloquy" (as Northrop Frye memorably calls it):[65]

---

64. According to the Platonic distinction in the background of Cicero's dialogue, the wise man rejects opinion in favor of true knowledge. In *The Winter's Tale*, Paulina refers pointedly to "the root of [Leontes's] opinion, which is rotten / As ever oak or stone was sound" (*WT*, 2.3.90–91). Leontes believes that he holds a "true opinion," but if we accept the distinction between opinion and knowledge, there is no such thing (*WT*, 2.1.39). See also Cicero, *Academica* 2.21.67–68.

65. Frye, "Recognition in *The Winter's Tale*," 243.

> Can thy dam—may't be?—
> Affection, thy intention stabs the centre:
> Thou dost make possible things not so held,
> Communicat'st with dreams—how can this be?—
> With what's unreal thou coactive art,
> And fellow'st nothing. Then 'tis very credent
> Thou mayst co-join with something, and thou dost—
> And that beyond commission; and I find it—
> And that to the infection of my brains
> And hard'ning of my brows. (*WT*, 1.2.139–48)

Leontes here addresses "Affection," referring to his own jealous passion (*affectio* in the Ciceronian sense of "a disposition or
mutation happening to bodie or minde: trouble of minde"[66]).
Judith Anderson has suggested that the phrase "Thy intention"
"belongs . . . at once to Leontes, whose affection 'thy' references, and to the personified form of an Affection to whose
self-centered power he is surrendering."[67] Apostrophe, it turns
out, is the perfect figure for this kind of making—an act of
making that one accomplishes oneself but that is projected
upon objects or, in this case, abstract beings.[68] Reading Leontes's
speech, Julia Reinhard Lupton has asked: "If the passage indeed
describes adulterous desire, why is the topic pursued in such
contortedly ontological terms ('unreal,' 'something,' 'nothing')
rather than ethical ones?"[69] Lupton finds her answer in the
biblical injunction against idolatry, which is one particularly
fraught way of making anything of anything in the period.[70]

---

66. Cooper, *Thesaurus Linguae*, s.v. "Affectio," sig. E4ᵛ; cited and discussed in
Smith, "Leontes's Affectio," 163.

67. Anderson, "Working Imagination in the Early Modern Period," 204.

68. For a useful discussion of the function of apostrophe in poetry, see
Johnson, *Persons and Things*, 6–10.

69. Lupton, *Afterlives of the Saints*, 187.

70. Lupton, *Afterlives of the Saints*, 189: "Whereas God creates something out

Though Leontes knows that affection is "coactive" with the "unreal" and "fellow'st nothing," he doesn't realize that his own mind is generating "somethings" out of "nothing."[71] Affection's "intention" is a mirror of Leontes's own (disavowed) will.

When Leontes makes "anything" into a test of his knowledge about the world, or indeed when he hangs the world on a "nothing," the object or perception in question tightens its grip on his mind. Experience narrows and catastrophe unfolds with increasing intensity. Leontes here describes (or rather performs) his conviction about his wife's infidelity:

> If I mistake
> In those foundations which I build upon,
> The centre is not big enough to bear
> A schoolboy's top. (*WT*, 2.1.102–5)

The "center" has commonly been taken to mean the earth in the old Ptolemaic system. If Leontes is wrong, he is saying, then the earth is not large enough to support the motion of a toy. With this image of the earth mentally reduced in size and substance, Shakespeare might have had in mind Digges's description of the earth in an infinite (Copernican) universe, which "scarcely retaineth any sensible proportion, so marvelously is that Orb of Annual motion greater than this little dark star wherein we live." Making his own assumptions about the nature of insensible things, Leontes might well have wanted

---

of nothing (the doctrine of creation *ex nihilo*), the false images of the idolater and the false love of the adulterer create nothing out of something by rendering reality itself into a vain fiction."

71. As Philip Lorenz has pointed out, "Generations of scholars have struggled with the passage, trying to clarify how the term 'affection' functions by showing how it must either refer to Hermione's lust or to Leontes's jealousy, but not to both." Lorenz, *Tears of Sovereignty*, 228. As a counterexample, Lorenz cites Christopher Pye, who shows that Leontes is "in the throes of his delirium and [also able] to recognize it as delirium." Pye, "Against Schmitt," 202.

to charge Copernicus or Digges with making anything of anything. This would have been the least of his mistakes.

Though he doesn't know it, the top he mentions can also be understood as an image of the violence of thought working upon (and building upon) itself: Leontes won't let his mind stop spinning. In the midst of perceiving insensible things from sensible signs, his thoughts have seemingly taken on a force of their own. As Montaigne's protégé, Pierre Charron, explains in *De la sagesse*, originally published in 1601 and translated into English in 1608:

> And then euen as a wheele that is alreadie in motion, receiuing another motion by a new force, turnes with farre greater speede; so the *Soule* being already mooued by the first apprehension, ioining a second endeuour to the first, carrieth it selfe with farre more violence than before, and is stirred vp by passions more puisant and difficult to be tamed.[72]

Charron goes on to say that the "tempests of our *Soul*," which "rise" from the "pit," are "nothing else but the opinion (which commonly is false, wandring, vncertaine, contrary to nature, veritie, reason, certaintie) that a man hath, that the things that present themselues vnto vs, are either good or ill."[73] It was, we recall, out of Leontes's uncertain "opinion" regarding his wife's hospitality to his friend that the "tempests" of his soul arose.[74] Charron links the tyranny of such "violent affection[s]" to the figure of prognostication, implicitly invoking *quidlibet ex quolibet*: "[Such men] wax mad if they be contradicted . . . interpret-

---

72. Charron, *Of wisdome*, 74.
73. Charron, *Of wisdome*, 73.
74. Leontes recognizes that "this entertainment / May a free face put on, derive a liberty / From heartiness, from bounty, fertile bosom/ And well become the agent," but he doubles down on his so-called "true opinion" about his wife's infidelity (*WT*, 1.2.113–16, 2.1.39).

ing all prognostications and occurrents *at their owne pleasure*, and making them serue their owne designements."[75]

In pitting his certainty against the structure of a world system, as I suggested earlier, Leontes is implicitly calling to mind the ongoing debates about the Copernican hypothesis. His own logic, for example, loosely recalls Ptolemy arguing against the idea that the earth revolves around the sun. If the earth did, in fact, circulate around the sun, Ptolemy said, "the Earth, being dissolved in pieces, should have been scattered through the heavens, which were a mockery to think of, and much more, beasts and all other weights that are loose could not remain unshaken."[76] His conclusion is that the earth does not (and indeed cannot) move because it remains intact.[77] We find a similar logic in *De rerum natura* where Lucretius argues that the universe is infinite and has no center, though he is using this style of argument to shore up another kind of ground: the atom. Without the notion of the indivisible atom, the poet writes,

> [there is a danger] lest the walls of the world suddenly be dissolved and flee apart after the fashion of flying flames through the void, and the rest follow in like manner, the thundering regions of the sky rush upwards, the earth swiftly slip from under

75. Charron, *Of wisdome*, 250 (emphasis mine).

76. Digges, *Perfit Description*, sig. N4ᵛ. Digges here is translating Copernicus recounting Ptolemy's opinion.

77. As Copernicus (and Digges) answer Ptolemy: "Without cause therefore did Ptolemy fear lest the Earth and all earthly things should be torn in pieces by this revolution of the Earth, caused by the working of nature, whose operations are far different from those of Art or such as human intelligence may reach unto. But why should he not much more think and misdoubt the same of the world, whose motion must of necessity be so much more swift and vehement than this of the Earth, as the Heaven is greater than the Earth. Is therefore the Heaven made so huge in quantity that it might with unspeakable vehemency of motion be severed from the Center, lest happily resting it should fall, as some Philosophers have affirmed?" Digges, *Perfit Description*, sig. O1ʳ.

our feet, and amidst the commingled ruin of sky and all things, letting their elements go free, utterly depart through the empty profound, so that in one moment of time not a wrack be left behind except desert space and invisible elements.[78]

Lucretius is here entertaining a rival theory, but if we accept this other idea (or *any* other, for that matter), he insists, the world will be reduced in a "moment of time" to nothing, "depart[ing] through the empty profound." "For in whatsoever part you shall assume that [atoms] shall first be lacking, that part will be the gate of death for things: by that way the whole mass of matter will disperse abroad."[79]

As the imagery of the passage builds to a climax and Lucretius makes the vision of disaster almost present before our eyes, it begins to sound like a veiled threat: either you be as certain as I am or the world will come to an end in this very instant. This is presumably not what he means—but in the escalation of the imagined disaster, this is what it can *feel* like to read these lines. The materialist is caught between a disaster that he makes and the disaster of uncertainty. If the atom rescues Lucretius by holding the world back from collapsing into emptiness, it is already a figure of the end (a world dispersed into atoms). Leontes parodies this logic, showing just how badly things can go when one holds on to one's convictions about the insensible at the cost of everything else. As Shakespeare's contemporary George Carleton put it, "If a man once give way to unnaturall grounds, his minde can never bee free from superstitious and absurd conceits, which are impediments to faith and good manners, and in the end make shipwracke thereof."[80] Carle-

---

78. Lucretius, *De rerum natura* 1.1102–10.

79. Lucretius, *De rerum natura* 1.1111–13. Porter argues of this passage: "Death here is *of things*, and so too the horror before the void is a fear of death in this one sense—fear of the death of things." Porter, "Lucretius and the Poetics of Void," 224.

80. Carleton, *Astrologomania*, 75–76.

ton was critiquing a 1603 treatise that defended astrology and explaining how one "absurd conceit" can open the door to an army of them.

In *Disowning Knowledge*, Stanley Cavell attributes the precipitous doubt of characters such as Othello and Leontes to what he calls "skepticism," describing it as the misinterpretation of "a metaphysical finitude as an intellectual lack." For Cavell, our external relation to the world is transposed (always inappropriately) to the figure of the other: "the philosopher turns the world into, or puts it in the position of, a speaker, lodging its claims upon us, claims to which, as it turns out, the philosopher cannot listen. Everyone knows that *something* is mad in the skeptic's fantastic quest for certainty."[81] Hearing the language of Othello ("Thou dost mean something") in this last phrase, we might suspect that there is a more-than-ordinary sense conveyed by Cavell's italics. *Quidlibet ex quolibet* emerges here, I would suggest, as a description of the skeptical enterprise and the work of its interpretation. Both are forms of allegoresis: the transformation or conversion of one problem into another and its unveiling as such: "skepticism with respect to other minds as allegorical of skepticism with respect to material objects."[82] Here, the world is transformed into a speaking subject, and the speaking subject (the other) comes to stand in for the world, that is to say, becomes an object.[83] In the course of his readings of Shakespeare, Cavell himself can be said to be making "anything of anything"—not because his self-described "intuitions" are absurd, but because, much like the tragic characters he anatomizes, he substantializes interpretation, transforming questions of hermeneutics into matters of ontology.[84]

Making *quidlibet ex quolibet* can certainly bring upon ruin and, in Shakespeare's tragedies at least, it does more often than

81. Cavell, *Disowning Knowledge*, 7–8.
82. Cavell, *Disowning Knowledge*, 8.
83. Cavell, *Disowning Knowledge*, 19.
84. Cavell, *Disowning Knowledge*, 4.

not. But such making needn't always imply disaster. It might even suggest the creative act of making what we call poetry. In a well-known passage, George Puttenham "reverently" compares the poet to God, "who without any travell to his diuine imagination made all the world of nought."[85] In *A Midsummer Night's Dream*, Shakespeare writes famously, "And as imagination bodies forth / The forms of things unknown, the poet's pen / Turns them to shapes and gives to airy nothing / A local habitation and a name."[86] Shakespeare will again explore the creative potential of making anything of anything in the final scene of *The Winter's Tale* when he transforms the statue of Leontes's long-dead wife, Hermione, into living flesh and brings the play to its miraculous conclusion.

At this point in the play, Leontes has been brought by Paulina, Hermione's lady-in-waiting, to a gallery to find the statue of Hermione, which he hastily attempts to embrace. Paulina stops him, setting the stage for the moment when the statue seemingly comes to life. As Huston Diehl explains, Paulina's theatrical trick echoes the tricks of her biblical namesake, Saint Paul: "Shakespeare appears to claim for the playwright here the power of the [Pauline] preacher to 'do good,' and he locates that power in the impurities of the theatre—its mingling of piercing words and marvelous images, its cunning tricks, illusions and fictions."[87] Writing in 1610, the year or the year before Shakespeare is thought to have composed *The Winter's Tale*, the soon-to-be Dean of Canterbury, John Boys, glosses Paul in 1 Corinthians 13 and gives us a sense of how one might make anything of anything, though this time with love:

85. Puttenham, *Arte of English Poesie*, 3.
86. Shakespeare, *Midsummer Night's Dream*, 5.1.14–17.
87. Diehl, "'Doth Not the Stone Rebuke Me?,'" 82. For the aesthetics of Protestant theater in the play, see Waldron, *Reformations of the Body*, 55–84. For Pauline influence in the period more generally, see Coolidge, *Pauline Renaissance in England*.

If a man could thunder in an Oration, as *Aristophanes* said of
Pericles; or tune his note so sweetly, that hee could moue moun-
taines and stony rockes with *Orpheus*; or fetch soules out of
hell. . . . If a man were so bewitching an Orator . . . so subtill a
disputer, as that he could make *quidlibet ex quolibet*, euery thing
of anything, yet without loue were he nothing.[88]

In the passage to which Boys is referring, Paul celebrates the
virtues of love, arguing that even the so-called gifts of speech
and knowledge (he refers to prophecy) are "nothing" without
it. In the final scene of the play, Paulina translates the powers
that Boys here attributes to the verbal arts of the preacher to
the creative potential of the theater—a power that includes
the Orphic ability to move rocks and bring the dead back to
life.[89] Without love, Hermione's statue is just an empty spectacle—"nothing." With the power of love that Paul describes
and faith awakened through art, another kind of transformation takes place—an internal one. With love, *quidlibet ex quolibet* describes not the idea of a strained interpretation that one
makes for oneself (Leontes's blasphemous *creatio ex nihilo*, as
Frye has it) but rather an act of creative making for the good
of another.[90] The "disasters of speech," as Leonard Barkan has
called the catastrophes with which the play begins, might not
have been entirely banished, though the play leaves us with at
least a hope—if not with any assurance—that we might manage them better in the future.[91]

88. Boys, *Exposition of the dominical epistles*, 272.
89. We might recall that the myth of Pygmalion—another story of a
statue come to life—takes place in the narrative frame of the Orpheus story in
Ovid. Lynn Enterline reads Shakespeare's use of Orpheus and Pygmalion as an
interrogation of the powers of the theater and the "cost to women of Ovid's
foundational tropes for poetic authority." Enterline, "'You Speak a Language
that I Understand Not,'" 44.
90. See Frye, *Fables of Identity*, 115.
91. Barkan, "'Living sculptures,'" 659.

FOUR

The Earthquake and the Microscope

An immigrant to the United States from Armenia in 1960, Hagop Sandaldjian was a concert musician who developed ergonomic techniques for playing the violin. He was also a master of miniature sculpture, which he produced under the lens of a 120-power microscope. A collection of his sculptures is on permanent display in the Museum of Jurassic Technology in Culver City, California.[1] They cover a wide range of subjects—from Snow White and the Seven Dwarfs balanced on the eye of a needle to a figure of Christ suspended on a cross made of a strand of human hair to the twin peaks of Mount Ararat (the snow-capped, volcanic cone in Turkey where Noah's ark is said to have landed) depicted on a grain of rice (fig. 2). In the museum's catalog, Ralph Rugoff describes the practical difficulties of producing such objects:

> Born of obsessive devotion, an individual figure could take as many as fourteen months to finish. Each sculpted micron represented not only endless hours of toil, but exacting travail fraught with peril, as his work could so easily be destroyed or lost. An unexpected sneeze or misdirected breath could blow away a microminiature with hurricane force, while a casual movement could sabotage the work of months. . . . The micro-

1. On the Museum of Jurassic Technology and its uses of fact and fiction, see Weschler, *Mr. Wilson's Cabinet of Wonders*; and Konstantinou, *Cool Characters*, 203–7.

FIGURE 2.   Hagop Sandaldjian, "Eternal Symbol (Mount Ararat)" (ca. 1986). Microminiature sculpture on grain of rice. Text cites the Armenian poet Yeghishe Charents: "On a grain of rice, my beloved mountain. From the times of Noah up to this day, 'you stand supreme and majestic.'" Photograph: © The Museum of Jurassic Technology.

miniaturist must learn to make his decisive movements between breaths, even between heartbeats.[2]

The creation of these sculptures might be understood as a precise response to catastrophizing—even an attempt to master
it. Instead of disasters suddenly befalling the mind, the artist
generates the conditions under which potential catastrophes
might be forestalled by carefully managing the body and the
mind (Rugoff describes the artist's ability "to concentrate his
passionate energy into a laserlike point of calm").[3] Sandaldjian
may occasionally make disasters, but avoiding them is what is
thrilling about his hobby—a pleasure he reproduces with every
stroke.[4]

   The artist's dream of technological mastery leads us back
now to another chapter in the history of catastrophizing—to

2. Rugoff, *Eye of the Needle*, 20, 36.
3. Rugoff, *Eye of the Needle*, 21.
4. Here one might also speak of the desire to destroy the things we make.
See Stewart, *Poet's Freedom*, 1–2.

the birth of the microscope in the seventeenth century and to the intellectual world of the scientific revolution. The echo of Democritus's pit also haunted the minds of early experimenters as they attempted to conceptualize the problem of depth — that is, as they sought to plumb the profundity of matter with their optical machines and to imagine the interior spaces of the earth. Here we will explore how and why the thought of catastrophe was conjured up out of the abyss of technological vision.

The first part of the chapter examines how the metaphor of depth brought together two seemingly separate areas of investigation. Here I will argue that a history of earthquakes began to take shape for the English virtuoso Robert Hooke in dialogue with his more famous microscopic investigations as he confronted the epistemological challenge his instrument dug up. In the second part, I will show how Hooke made much of little, transforming the objects of fossils into instruments of catastrophic vision — lenses through which to view the violent transformations of the earth over time. Much the way the microminiaturist might be said to have contained disastrous thoughts by means of his art, Hooke restaged and disciplined the mind's making of disaster in the service of scientific inquiry. At the intersection of microscopic investigation and geology, catastrophic materialism became the stuff of history.

GOING DEEP

In 1667 Henry Howard presented to the Royal Society a library of books and "neere 100 mss.," including the "Codex Arundel" of Leonardo da Vinci now held at the British Library.[5] Making his way through the pages of the manuscript, a member of the fledgling Society could have stumbled upon any number of Leonardo's catastrophic images, including the description

---

5. Evelyn, *Diary and Correspondence*, 2:122.

of Etna and Stromboli "when their sulphurous flames, having been forcibly confined, rend, and burst open the mountain," and the figure of the cavern that inspired Leonardo's "fear and desire." This latter passage would have been of special interest to John Evelyn, who had convinced Howard to make a gift of the codex.[6] As he reports in a diary entry dated February 7, 1645, Evelyn had himself climbed to the top of Vesuvius to peer "into that most frightfull and terrible vorago, a stupendous pit of neere three miles in circuit."[7] Not two years after Leonardo arrived at the Royal Society, Athanasius Kircher's *Mundus subterraneus* made its debut in English. Kircher's lavishly illustrated book touched on many things—from fossils (which he believed to be *lusus naturae*, or "jokes of nature," rather than the remains of organic bodies) to the flow of subterranean rivers to the network of fires that continually burned like a furnace underground (fig. 3).[8]

Though the English translation of the *Mundus subterraneus* was only partial, focusing especially on volcanoes, it was, like the original, a meditation on what it meant to imagine depth, both literally and figuratively. Though one can only guess at its exact features ("For whoever has seen them?"), the subterranean world, Kircher writes, "is a well fram'd House, with distinct Rooms, Cellars, and Store-houses, by great Art and Wisdom fitted together; and not, as many think, a confused and jumbled heap or Chaos of things."[9] The order beneath the

6. Evelyn makes reference to the drawings and paintings of Leonardo da Vinci several times in his diaries. See, for example, Evelyn, *Diary and Correspondence*, 1:56, 93, 226.

7. Evelyn, *Diary and Correspondence*, 1:153.

8. Around the corner from the microminiatures in the Museum of Jurassic Technology, one comes upon a room of three-dimensional recreations of some of Kircher's illustrations, hinting at the connection between the microscopic view, the image of catastrophe, and the depth of the earth.

9. Kircher, *Vulcano's, or, Burning and fire-vomiting mountains*, sig. A3^r. As William C. Parcell reminds us, "In Kircher's studies, no event is taken in isolation. Behind Kircher's examination of the Earth rests Plato's philosophy that the

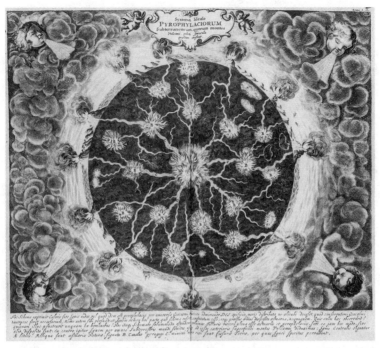

FIGURE 3. Athanasius Kircher, "System of Subterranean Fire," from *Mundus subterraneus* (1620). Bibliothèque nationale de France, Paris. Photograph: Snark / Art Resource, New York.

earth mirrors the divine wisdom that organizes the cosmos, even when the outward appearance of chaos and irregularity (the evidence of erupting volcanoes) might suggest otherwise. The title page of *The vulcano's, or, Burning and fire-vomiting mountains* invites the reader to consider Kircher's "relation of the late wonderful and prodigious eruptions of Aetna" and "thereby to occasion greater admirations of the Wonders of Nature (and of the God of Nature) in the mighty element of fire." It also contains a short poem, which puts another recent catastrophe in perspective:

universe or great world order was fashioned by God the creator as a manifestation and illustration of his own perfection." Parcell, "Signs and Symbols," 68.

> None sadlier knows the unresisted Ire,
> Then Thou, Poor *London*! of th' all-raging Fire.
> But these occasion'd kindlings are but Blazes,
> To th' mighty Burnings, which fierce Nature raises.
> If then a Town, or Hills blaze be so dire;
> What will be th' last, and universal Fire?[10]

The "all-raging Fire" of 1666, which virtually consumed London, was no doubt still fresh in the minds of readers.[11] Many, including Evelyn, viewed the disaster as an act of God, blaming themselves.[12] But in comparing smaller things (the London fire) with bigger ones (the final conflagration), the author of the poem was asking his readers to consider a wider and, as it were, deeper view.[13] If we could take in the whole picture, we'd see that all things serve a purpose in the grand providential scheme. According to Kircher, even events as violent and destructive as volcanoes had their place—for example, diffusing heat for the benefit of all creatures.[14] Natural phenomena that couldn't be explained by their usefulness were beyond our

10. Kircher, *Vulcano's, or, Burning and fire-vomiting mountains*, sig. A1ʳ. Following the example of Seneca in the *Natural Questions*, Kircher wrote the *Mundus subterraneus* in the wake of a real earthquake, in Calabria in 1638. See Fletcher, *Study of the Life and Works of Athanasius Kircher*, 528.

11. The fire started after midnight on Sunday, September 2, and continued through Wednesday, September 5. What most likely began as a small accident in the bakeshop of Thomas Farriner on Pudding Lane left much of the city in ruins. For an account of the fire and its aftermath, see Rideal, *1666*.

12. Evelyn, *Diary and Correspondence*, 2:16: "10th October, 1666. This day was ordered a general Fast through the Nation, to humble us on the late dreadful conflagration, added to the plague and war, the most dismal judgments that could be inflicted; but which indeed we highly deserved for our prodigious ingratitude, burning lusts, dissolute court, profane and abominable lives, under such dispensations of God's continued favor in restoring Church, Prince, and People from our late intestine calamities, of which we were altogether unmindful, even to astonishment."

13. For the Senecan precedent, see again Williams, *Cosmic Viewpoint*.

14. Kircher, *Vulcano's, or, Burning and fire-vomiting mountains*, 3.

immediate apprehension—or what was proper to know.[15] As God had asked Job from the whirlwind, "Hast thou entered into the springs of the sea? Or hast thou walked in the search of the depth?"[16]

In the nascent world of English experimentalism, a vertiginous view of the pit could inspire both faith and despair—or provide a corrective to the presumption of knowing too much. Joseph Glanvill, a clergyman and fellow of the Royal Society, cast his mind into the depths in order to correct the "vain dogmatizing" that he believed had come to obstruct a true "advancement of learning": "We strangely forget our selves when we plead a *necessity* of their being so in Nature, and an *impossibility* of their being otherwise. The *ways* of God in *Nature* (as in *Providence*) are not as *ours* are: Nor are the Models that we frame any way commensurate to the vastness and profundity of his Works; which have a *depth* in them greater than the *Well of Democritus*."[17] Glanvill is using Democritus here to skeptical ends, but in enumerating "the CAVSES of our *Ignorance*, and Mistakes," he isn't advocating a radical skepticism. Instead, he is making a point about our misplaced "confidence in opinions" that pretend to approximate the mysteries of divine order. For

15. Wilkins, *Discourse concerning the beauty of providence*, 68–69: "So is it likewise in the *wayes of Providence*, those designes that in respect of our apprehensions are carried on by a crypticall involved method, are yet in themselves of as excellent contrivance, as any of those, that seem to be of more facile and perspicuous order."

16. Job 38:16 KJV.

17. Glanvill, *Essays on several important subjects*, 15. The passage is an echo of his earlier text, *The vanity of dogmatizing* (1661), but here Glanvill adds a reference to the famed pit of Democritus. Compare to Lactantius, who evokes Democritus's pit only to dismiss the metaphor: "Democritus says that the truth lies sunk in a well so deep that it has no bottom; foolishly, indeed, as he says other things. For the truth is not, as it were, sunk in a well to which it was permitted him to descend, or even to fall, but, as it were, placed on the highest top of a lofty mountain, or in heaven, which is most true." Lactantius, *Works*, 21:205. See Blumenberg, *Paradigms for a Metaphorology*, 34.

all was *not* lost.[18] The "pit" was merely a reminder of man's weakened senses after the Fall, the damage of which the English natural philosopher would help to repair.[19]

When Glanvill turned to Democritus, he most likely had in mind the writings of Bacon, who had said *"that the truth of nature lieth hid in certain deep mines and caves."*[20] The imagery of depth was central to Bacon's philosophy—which sought by induction to penetrate ever more deeply beneath appearances.[21] In *The New Organon* (1620), his aphoristic guide to reforming natural philosophy, the author made a special point of praising the school of Democritus, "which went further [*penetravit*] into nature than the rest."[22] Likewise, in *The wisedome of the ancients* (1619), he suggested an alternative to Scholastic philosophy in the scattered fragments of Empedocles and Democri-

18. Isidore places Democritus in the company of the skeptics for saying that "truth lies hidden, as if in a well so deep that it has no bottom." For Isidore too, however, some things can be recovered: "They [the skeptics] believe that everything is doubtful, but, just as it must be said that many things are doubtful and hidden, which God has wished to be beyond the intelligence of humans, nevertheless there are many things that can be grasped by the senses and understood by reason." Isidore of Seville, *Etymologies*, 179.

19. Glanvill writes: "Adam's natural Opticks shew'd him much of the Coelestial magnificence and bravery without a Galilaeo's tube." Glanvill, *Vanity of dogmatizing*, 5; cited in Harrison, *Fall of Man*, 202. On the tradition of emphasizing the fallenness of man's senses and the possibility of recapturing Adamic knowledge through the labor of natural philosophy, see Harrison, *Fall of Man* and Picciotto, *Labors of Innocence*.

20. Bacon, *Works*, 6:214. Bacon writes in the same place: "It were good to divide natural philosophy into the mine and the furnace, and to make two professions or occupations of natural philosophers, some to be pioneers and some smiths; some to dig, and some to refine and hammer."

21. On the related iconographic tradition of Time rescuing Truth from the pit, see Saxl, "Veritas Filia Temporis"; Panofsky, "Father Time."

22. Bacon, *New Organon*, 45; Bacon, *Works*, 1:258. It was arguably for both practical and metaphorical reasons that Bacon placed laboratories in caves, "some of them, above three miles deep," in his scientific utopia, described in *The New Atlantis* (1626). "The end of our foundation," he wrote, "is the knowledge of causes, and secret motions of things." Bacon, *Works*, 5:398.

tus, "who with great moderation complained that all thinges were inuolued in a mist . . . that wee knew nothing, that wee discerned nothing, that trueth was drowned in the depthes of obscurity, and that false things were wonderfully ioynd and intermixt with true."[23] Adapting a passage from Cicero's *Academica*, Bacon was using the "moderation" of Democritus to encourage natural philosophers to awaken from their complacent stupor.[24]

Bacon's skepticism was hardly radical.[25] Elsewhere he wrote: "Democritus said; *That Truth did lie in profound pits, and when it was got, it needed much refining*."[26] The grandfather of modern science believed that truth could be "got," that is, eventually.[27] Later, in his *History of the Royal-Society* (1667), Thomas Sprat would self-consciously return to this image of the pit, echoing and amplifying Bacon's optimism: "Men commonly think that the pit, in which (according to *Democritus*) Truth lyes hid, is bottomless: and that it will devour, whatever is thrown into it, without being the fuller. This false conception had got so much ground, that as soon as a man began to put his hands to Experiments, he was presently given over, as impoverish't and undone."[28] The

23. Bacon, *Wisedome of the ancients*, 130–31.

24. Cf. Cicero, *Academica* 2.5.14. Bacon is picking up on Cicero's description of the *verecundia* of Democritus, using the same word in the Latin version of *De sapientia veterum*. Bacon, *Works*, 13:47. As Barbour explains, "Poised between the relentness skepticism of the New Academy and the blind confidence of the Peripatetics, the Baconian figure of Democritus is remarkable insofar as his challenge to formal metaphysics and traditional ethics encourages a distrust of received ideas but without impeding the advancement of natural learning." Barbour, *English Epicures and Stoics*, 84.

25. On Bacon's "middle way," and the Royal Society's use and transformation of the idea, see Scodel, *Excess and the Mean*, 48–76.

26. Bacon, *Works*, 13:383.

27. Recall Seneca's praise of the pre-Socratics in the *Natural Questions*: "It took great courage to prize open nature's hiding places, and, not content with her outward appearance, to look inside, and to immerse oneself in the secrets of the gods." Seneca, *Natural Questions* 6.5.2; discussed in chapter 1.

28. Sprat, *History of the Royal-Society of London*, 79.

experiments of the Royal Society would show just how deep one could go.

But how deep was *too* deep? This question would take on a special significance when it came to optical devices that promised new profundities. Elsewhere in *The New Organon*, Bacon exchanged his praise of Democritus for a tone of modern superiority, gently poking fun at the naïveté of the ancient philosopher, who, "if [he] had seen a magnifying glass [*perspicillum*] . . . he would perhaps have jumped for joy, thinking [it] a means of viewing the atom (which he affirmed was quite unseeable)."[29] The word *perspicillum* here can mean either a magnifying glass or a microscope. Bacon was writing in the early days of the microscope and had probably never seen one himself.[30] He said that optical devices were only good for "tiny things" [*minutias*], by which he meant small things such as insects and not the hidden structure of matter.[31] However, the fantasy of seeing the elements of matter up close would quickly come to seem less distant.

When Henry Power published his *Experimental philosophy* in 1663, he reproduced Bacon's line on Democritus jumping for joy on the title page, but with a slight modification: he would gloss the word *perspicillum* with the parenthetical phrase *Microscopicum scilicet* (the microscope, that is).[32] With the in-

29. Bacon, *New Organon*, 171; *Works*, 1:456: "quale perspicillum si vidisset Democritus, exiluisset forte, et modum videndi atomum (quem ille invisibilem omnino affirmavit) inventum fuisse putasset."

30. As G. W. Kitchin explains in a footnote in his edition of the *Novum Organum*, "There is also an account of the 'Perspicillum,' or Magnifying-glass, which Bacon himself (from his language 'Quinetiam aiunt') seems not to have known much about, or to have used himself. It was of course the germ of the Microscope." Bacon, *Novum Organum*, 257n33. Galileo used the word *perspicillum* to refer to his telescope. See Rosen, *Naming of the Telescope*.

31. Bacon, *New Organon*, 171; *Works*, 1:456.

32. Power, *Experimental philosophy*, sig. A1ʳ: "Perspicillum (Microscopicum scilicet) si vidisset *Democritus*, exiluisset forte; & modum videndi Atomum (quam ille invisibilem omnino affirmavit) inventum fuisse putasset."

strument in hand and a new confidence in its powers, he dispensed with Bacon's reservations, prophesying the fulfillment of an ancient dream by "our Modern Engine (the *Microscope*)." In a poem celebrating the microscope, Power boasted of an instrument "by whose augmenting power wee now see more / then all the world Has euer donn Before. / Thy Atomes (Braue Democritus) are now / made to appear in bulk & figure too."[33] The very subtitle of his *Experimental philosophy* advertises experiments and deductions "in avouchment and illustration of the now famous atomical hypothesis." In the text itself, Power goes on to explain:

> Herein we can see what the illustrious wits of the Atomical and Corpuscularian Philosophers durst but imagine, even the very Atoms and their reputed Indivisibles and least realities of Matter, nay the curious Mechanism and organical Contrivance of those Minute Animals, with their distinct parts, colour, figure and motion, whose whole bulk were to them almost invisible.[34]

But even as he dreams of tiny particles (whether atoms or corpuscles) producing effects in the world, he quickly shifts to "Minute Animals" with their subtle bodies, as if dwelling in exquisiteness could somehow make up for the technical limits of the instrument—an instrument that in reality brought the observer only slightly further below the surface of ordinary perception. Detail now stands in for depth.

Power, as we know, is drawing upon not only the empirical observation of insects through the microscope, but also an old Lucretian image that led from the contemplation of tiny creatures to a meditation on atoms.[35] In the end, he will have to admit that this dream of actually seeing atomic reality is "vastly

33. Power, "In Commendation of the Microscope," lines 9–12.
34. Power, *Experimental philosophy*, sig. B2r.
35. See again Lucretius, *De rerum natura* 4.116–22; discussed in the introduction.

hyperbolical." Nevertheless, we are told that if invention keeps progressing at the same rate "we might hope, ere long, to see . . . the constant and tumultuary motion of the Atoms of all fluid Bodies, and those infinite, insensible Corpuscles (which daily produce those prodigious (though common) effects among us)."[36] Power's nesting parentheses mime the sudden move in and out of perspectives, recalling the shift in vision that a microscope or a materialist analogy entails. Both have the capacity to turn "common" effects into "prodigious" ones.

The specter of catastrophizing emerged precisely at the limits of the microscope. As Christoph Meinel has shown, philosophers and scientists reached for the poetry of atoms when the empirical vision of instruments petered out and experiments were inconclusive.[37] At the same time, the microscope stoked the fires of old dreams, even, as Catherine Wilson has explained, "when the Boyle-Descartes version [of materialism] allowed no more practical control over nature and offered no more predictive power than had the original Democritean version or the Lucretian version which had been revived earlier in the Renaissance."[38] Hooke wrote in the *Micrographia* (1665),

36. Power, *Experimental philosophy*, sigs. c2ᵛ–c3ʳ. Even with his own high hopes, Power looks with suspicion on a contemporary who said he could see the effluvia of magnets: "Some with a Magisterial Confidence do rant so high as to tell us, that there are Glasses, which will represent not onely the Aromatical and Electrical Effluxions of Bodies, but even the subtile effluviums of the Load-stone it self, whose Exspirations (saith Doctor Highmore) some by the help of Glasses have seen in the form of a Mist to flow from the Loadstone. This Experiment indeed would be an incomparable Eviction of the Corporeity of Magnetical Effluviums, and sensibly decide the Controversie 'twixt the Peripatetick and Atomical Philosophers. . . . But I am sure he had better Eyes, or else better Glasses, or both, then ever I saw, that performed so subtle an Experiment." Power, *Experimental philosophy*, 57. In one moment, he even casts doubt on whether nature is "stinted at an atom, and must have a *non ultra* of her subdivisions." Power, *Experimental philosophy*, sig. B1ᵛ.
37. Meinel, "Early Seventeenth-Century Atomism."
38. Wilson, "Visual Surface and Visual Symbol," 89.

"By the help of *Microscopes*, there is nothing so *small*, as to escape our inquiry."[39] For Hooke, like Power, the limited reality of the microscope sometimes bled into the dream of a technological future that would allow him "to discover *living Creatures in the Moon, or other Planets, the figures of the compounding Particles of matter, and the particular Schematisms and Textures of Bodies.*"[40]

While Hooke spoke piously of returning to knowledge of the senses and leaving aside speculative fantasies, he didn't hesitate to cast his mind into the hidden world of matter as he gazed through the lens.[41] In one case, for example, he observed a swatch of fabric under the microscope, considering its strength and consistency, which in turn leads him to think of the nature of matter on an even smaller scale: "I am very apt to think, that the *tenacity* of bodies does not proceed from the *hamous*, or *hooked* particles, as the *Epicureans* and some modern *Philosophers* have imagin'd; but from the more exact *congruity* of the constituent parts."[42] Hooke here is revising the atomists on hooks, replacing a theory of atomic shape with a vibration theory of matter: the particles that cohere vibrate in the same

39. Hooke, *Micrographia*, sig. a2^v.

40. Hooke, *Micrographia*, sig. b2^v. In the 1670s, Hooke would follow Anton van Leeuwenhoek's lead to uncover a world of microscopic living creatures or "animacula," though even this didn't quite satisfy his fantasy. Hooke still dreamt of going deeper: "Future improvements of glasses may yet further enlighten our understanding, and ocular inspection may demonstrate that which as yet we may think too extravagant either to feign or suppose." Hooke, *Lectiones Cutlerianae*, 83. Hooke would refer to Leeuwenhoek's discovery again in 1680 in the context of thinking about geometrical "points." See Hooke, *Posthumous Works*, 66.

41. On the return to the senses, see Hooke, *Micrographia*, sig. b1^r: "The truth is, the Science of Nature has been already too long made only a work of the *Brain* and the *Fancy*: It is now high time that it should return to the plainness and soundness of *Observations* on *material* and *obvious* things."

42. Hooke, *Micrographia*, 6.

manner, and the ones that don't are "loosened from each other by every vibrative motion."[43] Body and motion are inextricably bound to one another, if indeed not "one and the same," he explained elsewhere, "for a little body with great motion is equivalent to a great body with little motion as to all its sensible effects in Nature."[44] Hooke made a related point in the *Micrographia*: "Nor can I believe indeed, that there is any such thing in Nature, as a body whose particles are at *rest*, or *lazy* and *unactive* in the great *Theatre* of the *World*, it being quite *contrary* to the grand *Oeconomy* of the Universe."[45]

One key to understanding the connection between a world trembling beneath the surface of perception and "the great *Theatre* of the *World*" was texture. As Wilson reminds us, the observation of the invisible texture of bodies was an essential concept for seventeenth-century thinkers because it gave them an explicit (and tangible) advantage over the Scholastics.[46] In a well-known observation on the point of a needle as seen under the lens, Hooke focuses on the surprisingly variegated surface of the object, drawing a distinction between natural and man-made things—at least provisionally.[47] Through the microscope, natural objects appear to maintain their perfection, but artificial ones (razors, the typographic mark of a period, the point of a needle) reveal a roughness hidden to the naked eye. For John

43. Hooke, *Micrographia*, 16. For a technical description of Hooke's "vibrative" theory of matter, see Gal, *Meanest Foundations and Nobler Superstructures*, 86–88, 127–31.

44. Hooke, *Lectiones Cutlerianae*, 7; cited and discussed in Gal, *Meanest Foundations and Nobler Superstructures*, 86.

45. Hooke, *Micrographia*, 16. Cf. Power, *Experimental philosophy*, sigs. b3ᵛ–b4ʳ.

46. Wilson, *Invisible World*, 57.

47. Hooke, *Micrographia*, 2: "Now though this point be commonly accounted the sharpest (whence when we would express the sharpness of a point the most *superlatively*, we say, As sharp as a Needle) yet the *Microscope* can afford us hundreds of Instances of Points many thousand times sharper: such as those of the *hairs*, and *bristles*, and *claws* of multitudes of *Insects*."

Wilkins, the distinction between the natural and artificial was proof of divine providence:

> I cannot here omit the Observations which have been made in these latter times, since we have had the use and improvement of the *Microscope*, concerning that great difference which by the help of that, doth appear betwixt *natural* and *artificial* things. Whatever is *Natural* doth by that appear, adorned with all imaginable *Elegance* and *Beauty*. There are such inimitable gildings and embroideries in the smallest seeds of Plants, but especially in the parts of Animals, In the head or eye of a small Fly: Such accurate order and symmetry in the frame of the most minute creatures, a *Louse* or a *Mite*, as no man were able to conceive without seeing of them. Whereas the most curious works of Art, the sharpest finest Needle, doth appear as a blunt rough bar of iron, coming from the furnace or the forge. . . . Now I appeal unto any considering man, unto what cause all this exactness and regularity can be reasonably ascribed, Whether to Blind *Chance*, or to Blind *Necessity*, or to the conduct of some Wise Intelligent Being.[48]

The perfection of the book of nature writ small was no small comfort to natural philosophers and historians, for the exquisiteness revealed by the microscope was a telling sign. Defending natural philosophy against the charge of atheism, Hooke's friend Robert Boyle wrote, "A virtuoso, who by manifold and curious experiments, searches deep into the nature of things, has great, and peculiar advantages, to discover, and observe, the excellent fabric of the world."[49] Pointing to the distinction between natural and artificial things, Hooke made similar kinds of arguments about the perfection of God's works, using, for

48. Wilkins, *Of the principles and duties of natural religion*, 80, 83.
49. Boyle, *Christian virtuoso*, 26–27.

example, the magnified head and compound eyes of a drone fly to answer the absurdities of the Epicureans: "So infinitely wise and provident do we find all the Dispensations in Nature, that certainly Epicurus, and his followers, must very little have consider'd them, who ascrib'd those things to the production of chance, that wil, to a more attentive considerer, appear the products of the highest Wisdom and Providence."[50]

Hooke wondered, however, whether this was the bottom of the "pit." If the microscope produced testimony of the exactness of God's handiwork, when the mind traveled still deeper below the threshold of perception, the essential distinction between the natural and artificial began to break down. Discussing the magnification of objects, Bacon observed, "In this matter too men have provided a kind of superstitious commentary (as usual with new and strange matters), viz. that such microscopes illustrate works of nature but discredit works of art."[51] With an *ideal* microscope, Hooke conjectured, even natural objects such as "hairs, and bristles, and claws of multitudes of Insects; the thorns, or crooks, or hairs of leaves, and other small vegetables" would yield to rough surfaces:

> Yet I doubt not, but were we able *practically* to make *Microscopes* according to the *theory* of them, we might find hills, and dales, and pores, and a sufficient bredth, or expansion, to give all those parts elbow-room, even in the blunt top of the very Point of any of these so very sharp bodies. For certainly the *quantity* or extension of any body may be *Divisible in infinitum*, though perhaps not the *matter*.[52]

While Hooke makes his point almost as an aside, it presents a serious challenge to the premise that the perfection of natu-

50. Hooke, *Micrographia*, 177. Power writes similarly of the "stenography of Providence." Power, *Experimental philosophy*, sig. b2ᵛ.

51. Bacon, *New Organon*, 171; *Works*, 1:455–56.

52. Hooke, *Micrographia*, 2.

ral things evinces God's hand. As the surface of even organic matter yields to roughness in his mind, Hooke implicitly raises troubling questions: At what level does organic life become inorganic? What does the earth's variegated surface mean for the origins of the world?[53]

In dreaming of the future of the microscope, Hooke acknowledged the possibility of the atom in the technical sense of a smallest possible ontological unit, suggesting that the "quantity" of a thing is infinitely divisible—but "perhaps not the matter." This question of divisibility also implied a question of texture. As Hooke's contemporary, the physician and natural philosopher Walter Charleton, explained, the "superfice of every thing, seemingly most equal and polite" was interrupted with "asperities, or eminent, and deprest particles."[54] Only infinite divisibility can produce a perfectly smooth surface.[55] "Many small masses of Atoms" generate texture. To drive home the point, Charleton looked through his own microscope, discovering roughness on the surface of a sheet of the smoothest Venetian paper, which he found was "so full of Eminences and Cavities, or small Hills and Valleys, as the most praegnant and praepared Imagination cannot suppose any thing more unequal and impolite."[56] As the telescope had shown the existence of mountains on the moon, the microscope revealed a rough-hewn figure below the threshold of ordinary perception, suggesting an analogy between these two kinds of "landscapes."

In *The Christian virtuoso*, Robert Boyle would argue "that proper Comparisons do the Imagination almost as much Service, as Microscopes do the Eye."[57] Both analogies and micro-

---

53. Marjorie Hope Nicolson points out that for the ancient materialists, imperfect surfaces (i.e., mountains) were "evidence of the fortuitous emergence of [the] earth." Nicolson, *Mountain Gloom and Mountain Glory*, 119.

54. Charleton, *Physiologia Epicuro-Gassendo-Charltoniana*, 267.

55. See Wilson, *Invisible World*, 57–58.

56. Charleton, *Physiologia Epicuro-Gassendo-Charltoniana*, 267–68.

57. Boyle, *Christian virtuoso*, sig. A6ʳ.

scopes make things perceptible—or more perceptible. In Hooke's case, it was also true that analogies tended to prolifer-ate under the lens. A typographic period, for example, looked "like a great splatch of London dirt."[58] "The Eyes of a Fly in one kind of light appeared almost like a Lattice"; in another light they looked like a "Surface cover'd with golden Nails."[59] A louse's legs were "joynted exactly like a Crab's, or Lobster's."[60] In the case of the surfaces of microscopic bodies and the topog-raphy of the earth, however, we discover something more than mere resemblance.[61] Bringing us logically step by step from the smallest particles to a vision of mountains rising up from them, Charleton writes:

> For, since a small stone may be made up of a Coagmentation [mass] of grains of Sand; a multitude of small stones, by co-acervation [accumulation], make up a Rock; many Rocks by aggregation, make a Mountain; many Mountains, by coapta-tion [fitting together], make up the Globe of Earth; since the Sun, the Heavens, nay the World may arise from the conjunc-tion of parts of dimensions equal to the Terrestrial Globe: what impossibility doth he incurr, who conceives the Universe to be amassed out of Atoms?[62]

When Hooke saw the surface of the earth in the texture of in-visible bodies, he was taking for granted the same set of steps that Charleton rehearses here in slow motion. As the analogy between dust and atoms resolves into the realization that even

58. Hooke, *Micrographia*, 3.
59. Hooke, *Micrographia*, sig. f2ᵛ.
60. Hooke, *Micrographia*, 212.
61. Frédérique Aït-Touati has described the relation between the micro-cosm and macrocosm under the lens: "The new symmetry established by opti-cal instruments seeks less for correspondences than for a continuity between the two systems." Aït-Touati, *Fictions of the Cosmos*, 139.
62. Charleton, *Physiologia Epicuro-Gassendo-Charltoniana*, 104–5.

dust is made of atoms, Charleton's comparisons give way to an equivalence at the bottom: everything is made of matter and subject to the same physical principles.

But if Charleton calmly unfolds the logic of this thought experiment, Power, in the pages of his *Experimental philosophy*, describes the full vertigo of the thought, casting his mind over another kind of landscape:

> Who is there that knows not the vast disproportion 'twixt this Speck of Earth, and the immense Heavens, how that it is less than the smallest Mote or Atom, which we see to hover and play in the Sun's beams, in comparison of the Fixed Stars? . . . What are we then but like so many Ants or Pismires, that toyl upon this Mole-hill, and could appear no otherwayes at distance, but as those poor Animals, the Mites, do to us through a good *Microscope*, in a piece of Cheese?[63]

Here, as humans and insects are collapsed into the same conceptual space, the sudden violence and disorientation of Leonardo's prophecies come to mind. By no coincidence, the scalar transformation of Power's instrument evokes the form of the materialist analogy of dust in sunlight. When reduced in scale, the earth itself is made to feel vulnerable to disaster. As Margaret Cavendish wrote a decade earlier of the tiny worlds contained in an earring: "There *Earth-quakes* be, which *Mountains* vast downe sling, / And yet nere stir the *Ladies Eare*, nor *Ring*."[64]

63. Power, *Experimental philosophy*, 164.

64. Cavendish, *Poems, and Fancies*, 45. We might also recall the words of Joseph Hall in his *Occasional Meditations* (1631): "How these little motes move up and down in the sun, and never rest; whereas the great mountains stand ever still, and move not, but with an earthquake!" (269). Hall's point is that it is better to be still and to be moved only by "extreme occasions." Perhaps what stays with you, however, is not the moral, but the implicit analogy between dust in sunlight and the earth trembling.

On the one hand, the microscope might be said to have soothed contemporary anxieties about materialism. The ordinary but exquisite creatures the instrument made visible were clear signs of the hand of God. At the same time, however, one could say that the microscope made the threat of materialism more vivid, creating epistemological uncertainty and conjuring up images of disaster at the threshold of the visible. Whether he liked it or not, the scientist could not yet dispense with the resources of materialist analogy.[65] Nor was he immune to the earthquakes of the mind that sometimes attended dust in sunlight.

Catastrophizing continued to inform the project of looking and thinking deeply—especially as more pressure was put on new technologies of vision to get to the bottom once and for all. In one place in his *Micrographia*, Hooke imagines an ambitious new technology—an "artificial transparent body of an exact Globular Figure"—that would allow him to penetrate ever more deeply "into the center and innermost recesses of the earth, and all earthly bodies," and to open "not onely a cranney, but a large window (as I may so speak) into the Shop of Nature, whereby we might be enabled to see both the tools and operators, and the very manner of the operation it self of Nature."[66] Hooke is talking about seeing into the center of the earth, but the phrase "the very manner of the operation of Nature" also suggests the most fundamental actions of matter—an image of particles working at the micro level, *processes* imagined at every scale. The fantasies of going deeper beneath the surface of perception and deeper beneath the ground begin to blur together.

The minutes of the Royal Society dated May 1663 recall the back-and-forth of a session that included discussions of both microscopic observations and the nature of curious stony

65. See again Meinel, "Early Seventeenth-Century Atomism."
66. Hooke, *Micrographia*, 233–34.

objects.[67] Hooke had grown up near the crumbling, fossil-rich cliffs of the Isle of Wight, building mechanical models and miniature ships and hunting for fossils.[68] He was now examining fossils closely under his microscope in conversation with colleagues who were discussing the question of their origins. His observations would eventually make their way into the *Micrographia*, where Hooke tells us he is able to discern the "pores" in petrified wood, which for him are proof of its organic origin.[69] In the same place, he turns his attention to objects that appear to be shells. He observes their "sutures," marking the connection between chambers on shells, "which I was able to discover plainly enough with my naked eye, but more perfectly and distinctly with my *Microscope*."[70]

But if Hooke didn't need the instrument to identify the sutures of the shells, the microscope was crucial to *thinking* about fossils—objects that directly connected the image of the uneven landscape (the mountains on which they were often mysteriously found) to the idea of what lies beneath. From the discovery of fossilized ammonites on mountains arose a baroque vision of the world in a state of violent motion.[71] A year after the Great Fire, Hooke began delivering his lectures on "earthquakes," which again took up the question of fossils (fig. 4). In one of the earliest lectures from the late 1660s, he spoke of "telescopes and microscopes" that might allow man to "see some hundreds of Years backwards and forward," inquiring "whether by Instruments he may not extend his Power,

---

67. For a discussion of this session and the "collaborative possibilities" in the Royal Society, see Poole, *World Makers*, 118–19.

68. Waller, "Life of Dr. Robert Hooke," iii. On Hooke's childhood on the Isle of Wight and its impact on his thought, see Drake, *Restless Genius*, 60–68.

69. Poole speculates that the roundtable in 1663 may even have "triggered" Hooke's discussion in the *Micrographia*. Poole, *World Makers*, 118.

70. Hooke, *Micrographia*, 110.

71. Hooke, *Micrographia*, 111.

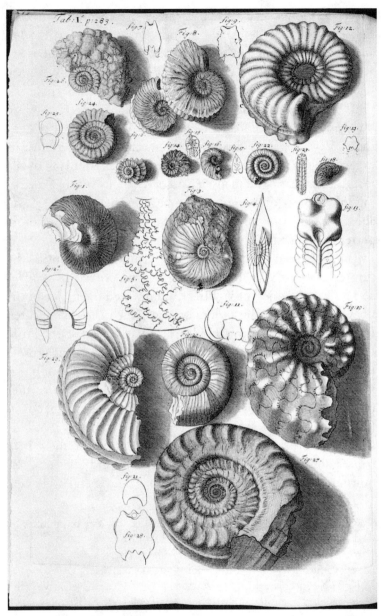

FIGURE 4. Robert Hooke, "Ammonite fossils," from *Lectures and Discourses of Earthquakes, and Subterraneous Eruptions*, in *Posthumous Works* (1705). Photograph: Wellcome Collection.

and reach things far above his Head, and far beneath his Feet, in the highest parts of the Heavens, and the lowest parts of the Earth."[72] Under the lens and under the metaphor of his instrument, petrified objects became high-powered extensions of a form of technological vision that penetrated time in addition to space. When turning his mind to the ambitions of Democritus and the dream of optical technologies, Bacon lamented that "the tumult in the parts of solid bodies . . . is not seen at all."[73] The catastrophic history raised by fossils (from the Latin word *fossilium*, "a thing dug up") lent a visceral expression if not to atoms themselves then to the invisible "tumult" that lay below the surface of perception—a message from Democritus's pit.

"MUCH LIGHTER AND SLIGHTER INDICATIONS"

In the years leading up to the Great Fire of London, the image of earthquakes came to stand for the tumultuous events of the English Civil War, the execution of Charles I, and the aggravated violence of religious schism. The anonymous author of the royalist tract *Eikon e piste* (1649) defended the metaphor as it was used in *Eikon Basilike* (1649), the famous apology for the king allegedly written by Charles I himself and published soon after his beheading:

> The Confuter quarrels at the Book for saying, that these Tulmults *like an Earthquake shook the foundations of all*. If the Church afterwards fell: the Throne brake: the House of Lords came down: if it shook whole families out of their houses: the Major of *London* out of his place: Aldermen into the Tower: the

72. Hooke, *Posthumous Works*, 343. Commenting on this passage, Picciotto has put it nicely: "By displacing his intellectual as well as his visual capabilities onto his instruments, the virtuoso could exult in his superhuman powers without overtly abandoning his humble bearing." Picciotto, *Labors of Innocence*, 220.

73. Bacon, *Works*, 4:221.

Common-councell-men out of their wits: the money out of their purses: and the Chaines off their posts: and if all you were asleep, and did not perceive it: will you not believe when you see all this, that there was an Earthquake that shook all?[74]

In that same momentous year, John Wilkins also called upon an earthquake as a figure of great upheaval, invoking chapter and verse: "*When the mountains are removed, and the pillars of the earth tremble* [Job 9:5, 6]. When Religion and Laws (which are the *foundations* of a people) *are out of course* [Ps. 11:3]. And yet even in all this, there may be a designe of Providence for our good."[75]

Images such as these composed one background for Hooke's lectures on earthquakes, which he began to deliver in the mid-1660s and worked on intermittently for the next thirty years. Another important context was perhaps the apocalyptic enthusiasm that Charles Webster attributed to a series of Puritan reformers who applied their millenarian fervor to the reformation of knowledge. Webster explains, "The great cycles of history would terminate in a spiral of traumatic activity which would destroy the old imperfect order and pave the way for a new age."[76] But if disasters were both useful metaphors for the violent political upheaval of the English Civil War and promising signs of end times, Hooke returned disaster to a literal, geological idiom. In the first series of these lectures, he argued passionately for a vision of earth's continual vicissitude—a history riddled with disasters. As we saw earlier, he derived this history from fossils—phenomena others had long dismissed as the "play of nature" or the effect of celestial influences.[77] Picking up from his description of petrified shells in the *Micrographia*, Hooke described the forms of various fossils in strik-

74. Anon., *Eikon e piste*, 13.

75. Wilkins, *Discourse concerning the beauty of providence*, 70.

76. Webster, *Great Instauration*, 6.

77. On the history of the interpretation of fossils, see Rudwick, *Meaning of Fossils*, 1–100.

ing and often painstaking detail. He then explained the physical processes of petrification. He pointed out that some fossils were broken in parts. It was absurd to think that nature generated simulacra of shells, especially *broken* shells, merely for sport. Looking at another specimen, he conjectured that water had penetrated the surface through cracks, frozen, and then exploded the object from the inside—even more evidence of their organic origin. What drew his attention from the beginning, however, was the discovery of shells on the tops of mountains—objects out of place. The riddle of their location demanded an answer. Like Leonardo, Hooke departed from the old conjecture that Noah's flood was responsible for transporting them so far (the duration of the deluge, he insisted, was not sufficient to explain the stratifications of shells), imagining instead a much longer history of catastrophe following upon the heels of catastrophe. From the study of petrified shells emerged what to some of his contemporaries was an indefinitely long chronicle of disaster—if not "deep time," exactly, then a worrisome gesture in that direction.[78]

The first challenge was to convince fellow members of the Royal Society that the earth had, in fact, changed considerably since the time of Noah's flood.[79] He understood that his conjectures on "first hearing . . . may seem somewhat para-

78. John Wallis, for example, wrote of Hooke's theories in a letter to Edmund Halley in 1687: "So that unless it was before the creation of Adam we cannot find a time wherein the Earth should (so often) have been tossed and turned upside down." The text of this letter is reproduced in Oldroyd, "Geological Controversy in the Seventeenth Century," 210–12.

79. John Woodward was still defending the contrary position in 1695: "There have been some who have made a mighty Outcry about Changes and Alterations in the Terraqueous Globe. The Pretences and Pleas of each I consider in the first Part of this Essay: shewing that they are without any just ground: and that there are no Signs or Footsteps, in all the whole Globe, of any such Alterations." Woodward, *Essay toward a natural history of the earth and terrestrial bodies*, 226. On the invention of an "orthodox" view of the earth's history, see Dal Prete, "'Being the World Eternal,'" 308.

doxical," which was an understatement. Hooke conjured up evidence of earthquakes in spades, exhausting and, I suspect, disturbing some of his audience with a verbal slide show. He reproduced a variety of sources, including accounts from the Jesuit missionary José de Acosta and the English sea captain Sir Francis Drake, all of which provided him with evidence that no place in the world was spared of quakes.[80] Hooke also cited a passage from Samuel Purchas on a catastrophic event in 1591 in which "the earthquake was so strong, that the Ships that lay in the Road, and in the Sea, shaked as if the world would have turn'd round." The report went on: "At the same time they heard such Thunder and Noise under the Earth, as if all the Devils had been assembled together at that Place, where-with many dy'd for fear."[81] Though Hooke disagreed with Kircher's *Mundus subterraneus* on a number of issues, he cited the Jesuit's first-person account of the earthquake in Calabria and its devastating effects: "We prosecuting our Journey . . . found nothing for 200 Miles, but the remaining Carcasses of Cities and Castles, and horrid destructions; the Men lying in the open Fields, and, as it were, dead and withered through Fear and Terror."[82] Hooke followed this passage with a report from a 1665 letter describing a quake in the East Indies that lasted for "32 Days and Nights, without Intermission." The terror concluded with the sinking of "300 Houses, and all the Men": where a town had once stood, now there was a "large Lake some Fathoms deep."[83] In addition to relatively recent events,

80. On this point, Hooke cites the authority of Seneca: "All things are subject to the same chance; tho' they are not yet moved, they are moveable; for we err, if we believe any part of the Earth excused and free from this hazzard; all are subject to the same Law; nothing is made by nature so fixt as to be unmoveable; some sink at one time, some at another." Hooke, *Posthumous Works*, 311; Seneca, *Natural Questions* 6.1.12.

81. Hooke, *Posthumous Works*, 300.

82. Hooke, *Posthumous Works*, 306.

83. Hooke, *Posthumous Works*, 307.

Hooke drew upon historical and literary accounts that bolstered his case against those who wondered why there weren't more written testimonies of the tumultuous earth he was describing. In the same cycle of lectures, for example, he turned to Plato's account of Atlantis, which he took to be more than probable.[84] He even speculated that England and Ireland might have been "rais'd" by the same earthquake that "sunk" the ancient island—bringing the matter home.[85]

In one moment, Hooke draws our attention to the tragic human cost of catastrophe; in another, he puzzles over the means by which inanimate objects traveled to the tops of mountains. This approach to earth science was inherently disorienting. In addition to providing physical accounts of phenomena, the lectures were also experiments in temporal and perspectival relativism. We see the bending of time and space in the rapid movement between ancient and contemporary accounts but also between different kinds of "earthquakes"—some that were all too perceptible to the human senses (the sudden disasters that shook the world), others that were "insensible" (the slow eating away of a cliff or a coastline, the movement of dust).[86] For Hooke, as for Leonardo, the image of sudden catastrophe allowed him to visualize otherwise insensible processes, as if he were imagining them in time lapse.[87] Out of this tumult arose even more bracing thoughts like the birth and extinction of species: "There have been many other Species of Creatures in former Ages,

84. Hooke, *Posthumous Works*, 319–20.

85. Hooke, *Posthumous Works*, 320.

86. As Drake explains, "By earthquakes, [Hooke] meant every manner of movement of the terrestrial crust, whether violently by slipping, sliding, or subsiding (faulting) or by volcanic eruptions; or slowly and imperceptibly by degrees, such as those changes effected by wind, water, waves or ice." Drake, *Restless Genius*, 84.

87. For an insightful discussion of the challenge of picturing nature's slow processes in the seventeenth century, see Nicholson, *Mountain Gloom and Glory*, 155.

of which we can find none at present; and that 'tis not un-
likely also but that there may be divers new kinds now, which
have not been from the beginning."[88] Hooke also flirted with
potentially heretical conjectures about the age of the earth,
wondering how much of this lost world of catastrophes had
escaped human memory.

Hooke's thinking on this issue recalls a passage from Montaigne. Invoking the catastrophe of Atlantis and inviting us to
imagine the time before Homer, Montaigne calls up a vision
of atoms colliding in the void. Adapting a quotation from
Cicero, he writes: "If we could view that expanse of countries and ages [*et temporum*], boundless in every direction, into
which the mind, plunging and spreading itself, travels so far
and wide that it can find no limit where it can stop, there
would appear in that immensity an infinite capacity to produce innumerable forms."[89] Montaigne adds the words *et temporum*, making Cicero's description of Epicurean matter in infinite space into a vision of indefinite time. Montaigne then asks
us to envision a history of inventions lost and discovered anew
through potentially endless cycles: "We exclaim at the miracle
of the invention of our artillery, of our printing; other men in
another corner of the world, in China, enjoyed these a thousand years earlier. If we saw as much of the world as we do not
see, we would perceive, it is likely, a perpetual multiplication
and vicissitude of forms."[90] In a similar vein, Hooke writes:

88. Hooke, *Posthumous Works*, 291. As Poole rightly points out, "Hooke's
originality lies not in voicing variation . . . but in combining it with his rarer
views on extinctions and new creations." Poole, *World Makers*, 127.

89. Montaigne, *Complete Works*, 692; *Les essais*, 907: "*Si interminatam in omnes
partes magnitudinem regionum videremus, et temporum, in quam se injiciens animus et
intendens, ita late longeque peregrinatur, ut nullam oram ultimi videat, in qua possit insis-
tere: in hac immensitate infinita, vis innumerabilium appareret formarum.*" Cf. Cicero,
De natura deorum 1.20. On what I take to be Bacon's response to this passage in
Montaigne, see Passannante, *Lucretian Renaissance*, 123–38.

90. Montaigne, *Complete Works*, 692; cf. Bacon, *New Organon*, 94.

'Tis not impossible that there may have been a preceding learned Age wherein possibly as many things may have been known as are now, and perhaps many more, all the Arts cultivated and brought to the greatest Perfection, Mathematicks, Mechanicks, Literature, Musick, Opticks, &c. reduced to their highest pitch, and all those annihilated, destroyed and lost by succeeding Devastations. Atomical Philosophy seems to have been better understood in some preceding time, as also the Astronomy evinc'd by *Copernicus*, the *Aegyptian*, and *Chinese* Histories tell us of many thousand Years more than ever we in Europe heard of by our Writings.[91]

Hooke ends this reflection by suggesting there is "great reason to question" the chronology of the Chinese, but he has already raised more than a little doubt about our own.[92] He mentions a number of "Arts cultivated" here, but the choice of atomism and Copernican astronomy are particularly significant in this context. Both, as we know, involve appeals to the insensible that contradict the ordinary experience of the world—much like the story Hooke is telling about the earth.

But if disaster had cast some ancient knowledge of materialist philosophy back into the pit, it was also the key to its recovery.[93] In fossils, Hooke unearthed a moving picture of earthquakes, which is to say, an image of materialist philosophy. Though it may seem odd to think of the history of earthquakes as a mode of catastrophizing, that is precisely what

91. Hooke, *Posthumous Works*, 328.

92. See Drake, *Restless Genius*, 217.

93. In one of the later lectures, Hooke quotes the following passage from Lucretius, "Nam Res accendunt lumina Rebus" (So clearly will truths kindle light for truths), to which he adds, "And the understanding of History of the Course and Progress of Nature preceding will afford sufficient information of the Method of proceeding." Hooke, *Posthumous Works*, 341; Lucretius, *De rerum natura* 5.1117.

it was: a way of conjuring up disasters in order to make sensible the insensible. By relegating the disaster to history, Hooke transformed the seemingly automatic violence of a catastrophic analogy into an object of scientific inquiry.

As David Oldroyd reminds us, Hooke's plan for his "Philosophical Algebra" promised to describe both a method of collection and the formation of hypotheses from the store of observations.[94] He seems to have written only the first part.[95] His lectures on earthquakes, however, put the second part into practice. In the scope of his research, these lectures were specifically an occasion to answer the questions of what method was and what place there was for conjecture within an empirical approach. From the very beginning, he defended the importance of hypothesis in experimental science:

> And though this Honourable Society have hitherto seem'd to avoid and prohibit pre-conceived Theories and Deductions from particular, and seemingly accidental Experiments; yet I humbly conceive, that such, if knowingly and judiciously made, are Matters of the greatest Importance, as giving a Characteristick of the Aim, Use, and Significancy thereof.[96]

Fossils helped frame hypotheses, but they also provided ample opportunity for empirical investigation (they could be found all around the world). Gradually, by the comparison of specimens and the systematic elimination of false hypotheses, Hooke imagined, a picture of a lost world would arise ever more clearly from the abyss. He was in many ways echoing the sentiment of Digges, who, as we recall, had sought to prove the Copernican hypothesis by gathering observations of the supernova of 1572, encouraging fellow astronomers across Europe to

94. Hooke, *Posthumous Works*, 6–7; Oldroyd, "Robert Hooke's Methodology of Science," 119.

95. Hooke, *Posthumous Works*, 65.

96. Hooke, *Posthumous Works*, 280.

do the same. Like fossils discovered on the tops of mountains, a new star suddenly appearing in what were once thought to be immutable heavens was also a thing out of place. Unlike a fading nova, however, fossils didn't disappear. While Hooke in the *Micrographia* had used his instruments to give material weight to his speculations, the fossil would serve as a kind of imaginary instrument with which he might steer a course between speculative and empirical knowledge.

Yet an anxious question remained for Hooke and his contemporaries: Could so much really be built on so little? Hooke's colleague at the Royal Society, Samuel Parker, was among those who had doubts about the grounds of conjecture. Parker advocated the mechanical philosophy over the Scholastic alternative, but he worried about the limits of experiment and observation. In his critique of Platonic philosophy, we watch him shift from the vain speculations of metaphysics to the more solid matter of experiment but then doubt whether even these more reliable procedures could ever successfully shore up the premises of their practitioners:

> For though I preferre the Mechanicall Hypotheses before any other, yet methinks their contexture is too slight and brittle to have any stress laid upon them; and I can resemble them to nothing better than your *Glasse drops*, from which, if the least part be broken, the whole *Compages* [structure] immediately dissolves and shatters into Dust and Atoms; for their parts, which rather lie than hang together, being supported only by a thin film of brittle Conjecture (not anneal'd by experience and observation) if that fail anywhere, the whole Systeme of Hypothesis unavoidably shatters.[97]

97. Parker, *Free and impartial censure of the Platonick philosophie*, 44–45. A year later, Richard Baxter would cite this passage from Parker in his defense of the immortality of the soul against the Epicureans. Baxter, *Reasons of the Christian religion*, 497. Parker's misgivings about speculative philosophy are discussed in Gaukroger, *Emergence of a Scientific Culture*, 354–55.

Under the slightest pressure, the mechanical philosophy crumbles into the very particles it imagines — "if the least part be broken," the whole thing shatters. Though, Parker says, "we may rationally expect a greater Improvement of Natural Philosophie from the *Royal Society*, (if they pursue their design) then it has had in all former ages," he remains skeptical about the possibility of joining experimental findings to theory, "so that though the *Hypothesis* may have a firm *Basis* to bottome upon, yet it can be fastned and cemented to it no other way, but by conjecture and uncertaine (though probable) applications."[98]

Though hardly naïve, Hooke was more optimistic — he believed that a combination of scientific instruments and method might add some heft to the mechanical philosophy and lead to a "true and certain knowledge of the Works of Nature."[99] For him, the petrified stuff of fossils gave a decidedly more "solid," experimental dimension to picturing what lay beneath perception. But even as Hooke hoped one day to assemble an actual "chronology" of the earth's history out of shells, the fossil sometimes appeared less like an object of scientific inquiry than like an old materialist thought dressed up in stone. On the credit of future instances (a dream collection), Hooke allowed his imagination to take a huge leap. In his *Experimental philosophy*, Power writes of the "Springy Intellect," which "flye[s] out into its desired Expansion," the "vigorous and active Reason" that seeks to "unriddle All Nature," the "Elastical Souls of the world" who unveil reality.[100] Power knows that "elastical" and "springy" are terms his contemporaries use to picture the behavior of air.[101] Reason here assumes the properties of matter as

98. Parker, *Free and impartial censure of the Platonick philosophie*, 45–46.

99. Hooke, *Posthumous Works*, 330. Cf. Power, *Experimental philosophy*, sigs. c4^{r-v}: "Though [the philosopher] superstructed upon his Experiments, yet the Foundation being solid, a more wary Builder may be very much further'd by it, in the erection of a more judicious and consistent Fabrick."

100. Power, *Experimental philosophy*, 191–92.

101. Boyle published his *New Experiments Physico-Mechanicall, Touching the*

it contemplates it. Similarly, in the *Micrographia*, Hooke writes of the tincture, which from a single drop can "disperse and expand it self into a vast space, if it have room enough, and infect, as it were, every part of that space."[102] The action of the tincture provides Hooke with an analogy to understand the movement of the air or ether, but he might as well be describing the nature of his own mind reaching and spreading outward.[103] This capacity of the imagination to expand instantly, combined with arduous observation, would allow men like Hooke to go deeper. Power says encouragingly: "And, certainly, there is no Truth so abstruse, nor so far elevated out of our reach, but man's wit may raise Engines to Scale and Conquer it: Though *Democritus* his pit be never so deep, yet by a long *Sorites* [heap] of Observations, and chain of Deductions, we may at last fathom it, and catch hold of Truth that hath so long sitt forlorn at bottom thereof."[104]

For Hooke, the fossil was the perfect springboard, but the conjectures that took flight from fossils again raised concerns

---

Spring of the Air, and its Effects in 1660. See Power, *Experimental philosophy*, 101–2: "So that all the particles of this *Atmosphaere* (especially the inferiour sort) strive at all times to expand and dilate themselves: and when the circumresistency of other contiguous Bodies to them is removed, then they flye out into their desired expansion (or at least will dilate so far as neighbouring Obstacles will permit:) Just like the Spring of a Watch (which if the String be broke, presently flyes out into its fullest expansion:) which Elastick motion in the Ayr then ceases, when it comes to an aequilibration with those circumjacent Bodies that resisted it."

102. Hooke, *Micrographia*, 13–14.

103. The tincture is a classic example of perceiving invisible things in *De rerum natura*. See, for example, Lucretius, *De rerum natura* 4.223–24. In discussing Democritus in *Thoughts on the Nature of Things*, Bacon uses the example of tinctures to illustrate the invisible dissemination of subtle bodies in the air (*Works*, 9:431), though elsewhere he writes critically of the "tincture" (*infusio*) of the affections that distorts the understanding. Bacon, *Works*, 1:169. Hooke's own subtle mind vacillates between the senses and the kind of untamed speculation that Bacon thought was dangerous. See Wilson, *Invisible World*, 47.

104. Power, *Experimental philosophy*, 191.

about how much the mind could legitimately lay claim to—
and by what means. Hooke's contemporary Nicolas Steno
(whom Hooke sharply accused of plagiarizing his lectures) was
especially sensitive to the dangers of overreaching.[105] Steno had
himself speculated about the nature of fossils, which he found
buried in Tuscany—but he did so somewhat more modestly
than Hooke (not to mention that Steno was keen to keep his
speculations within the biblical chronology).[106] Chastising pre-
mature speculators, he writes:

> It often befalls Travellers in unknown Countries, that hasten-
> ing thorow a Mountanous Tract unto a Town standing on the
> top of an Hill, they think it hard by, as soon as they come in
> sight of it; although the manifold windings and turnings of
> the ways leading thereto, retard their hopes even to a trouble.
> For they have only a view of the nearest tops, but they cannot
> guess what is hidden by the interposition of these high places;
> whether they be lower Hills, or deep Vallies, or plain Fields,

105. Oldenburg had Hooke's early lectures on earthquakes specifically in
mind when he presented Steno's text in its English translation, reminding the
reader in his preface of the fact that "Mr. Robert Hook had at that time ready
some Discourses upon this very Argument, which by reason of the many avo-
cations he hath met with in the rebuilding of the City of London, and his
attendance on the R. Society, he hath not yet been able quite to finish for
the Press." Steno, *Prodromus*, sig. A4ʳ. In a manuscript sent to John Ray, John
Aubrey implicitly suggests that Hooke's ideas had been plagiarized. Drake
observes, "There is some suspicion, at least on the part of Hooke and Aubrey,
that Oldenburg might have deliberately sent Steno Hooke's ideas and cham-
pioned Steno's book." Drake, *Restless Genius*, 108. On the relationship between
Hooke and Steno, see Eyles, "Influence of Nicolaus Steno"; Oldroyd, "Geological Controversy in the Seventeenth Century," 217. Poole finds Hooke's
accusation of Steno's plagiarism to be unfounded. Poole, *World Makers*, 120.

106. Steno was careful to position his thinking within an orthodox frame:
"But least there should be apprehended any danger in the novelty, I shall in
short lay down the agreement of *Nature* with *Scripture*, reciting withall the
chief difficulties, that may be raised about each Face of the Earth." Steno, *Prodromus*, 99.

because with their flattering hopes they measure the distances of places by the eagerness of their desires. 'Tis no otherwise with those, that travel to the true knowledge of things by *Experiments*: For no sooner have they the least stricture of a truth unknown, but they imagine, the whole shall immediately open it self to them; nor can they make a true estimate of the time requisite to solve that continued *series* of difficulties, which by little and little, rising out of hidden depths, and stil casting new impediments in the way, slacken the pace of those that made so much haste to attain the end of their course.[107]

The passage begins with the idea of seeing something from a distance and the impulse to grasp it. Steno is describing how easily (and often wrongly) men jump to conclusions from the "the least stricture of a truth unknown." He stresses the difficulty that becomes clear when one considers the task at hand: "I found my self wandering in a Labyrinth, where, the nearer you are to the out-let, the more windings you finde your self engaged in."[108]

Steno's thinking here resonates with that of Descartes. In *Rules for the Direction of the Mind*, an unfinished treatise written before 1628, Descartes instructs "anyone who sets out in quest of knowledge of things" to proceed step by step "as he would [with] the thread of Theseus if he were to enter the Labyrinth."[109] He condemns those men who behave "as if they

107. Steno, *Prodromus*, 1–2.
108. Steno, *Prodromus*, 4.
109. Descartes, *Philosophical Writings*, 1:20. For Descartes's image of the labyrinth and its bearing on his ideas about knowledge, see Harries, "Descartes and the Labyrinth of the World." While he was in many ways the object of this kind of criticism, Hooke had much in common with Steno. In his "Lectures of Light," which, like the lectures on earthquakes, were also published posthumously, Hooke too describes the "Works of Nature" as a labyrinth. He even chides the person who would "think immediately to fly and transport himself over these Walls, and set himself in the very middle and inmost Recess of it, and thence think himself able to know all the Meanders and Turnings, and

were trying to get from the bottom to the top of a building at one bound, spurning or failing to notice the stairs designed for that purpose."[110] Among them he singles out astrologers who "do not know the nature of the heavens and do not even make any accurate observations of celestial motions, yet they expect to be able to delineate the effects of these motions."[111] The astrologers lead him to a critique of the philosophers who "think that truth will spring from their brains like Minerva from the head of Jupiter."[112] Steno is also drawing attention to the seemingly automatic springing of the mind—and to those who, with a few scattered clues (or a handful of fossilized shells), leap to conclusions. In the same text, he brings us back not surprisingly to the grandfather of atomism: "Nor was it amiss that Democritus made use of the similitude of a Pit, where a Man can hardly make a right estimate of the labour & time of drawing thence, but by having actually drawn up the things in it; for as much as the number and plenty of the latent Veins leave it very uncertain, what store there is of the subterraneous matter."[113]

Steno converted to Catholicism in 1667, largely abandoning his scientific studies (he would eventually become a bishop). Meanwhile, Hooke kept harping on earthquakes—much to the dismay of some of his contemporaries.[114] In a lecture deliv-

---

Passages back again to get out." For these men, the "labyrinth was in their own Mind, and not of Nature's making. . . . Thus the Pythagoreans were puzzled with their Numbers; the Peripateticks with their Four Elements; the Epicureans with their Atoms." Hooke, *Posthumous Works*, 84. The passing reference to the Epicureans, like the mention of Democritus in Steno, seems designed to preempt the accusation of materialism or atheism—an accusation that Hooke might well have anticipated in his lectures on earthquakes.

110. Descartes, *Philosophical Writings*, 1:20.
111. Descartes, *Philosophical Writings*, 1:20.
112. Descartes, *Philosophical Writings*, 1:21.
113. Steno, *Prodromus*, 2–3.
114. I have focused so far on the first series of lectures from the late 1660s. As I mentioned above, Hooke continued to pursue his interest in fossils and

ered at Oxford in 1686, the mathematician John Wallis accused
Hooke of seeing whatever he wanted wherever he happened to
look. Wallis himself was not willing "to turn ye world upside
down . . . to serve an hypothesis."[115] The remark clearly both-
ered Hooke, who would echo it the following year in a lecture
before the Royal Society:

> And tho' possibly some may say, I have turned the World upside
> down for the sake of a shell, yet, as I think, there is no one has
> reason for any such assertion from any action I have hitherto
> done; yet if by means of so slight and trivial Signs and Tokens
> as these are, there can be Discoveries made and certain Con-
> clusions drawn of infinitely more important Subjects; I hope
> the attempts of that kind do no ways deserve reproach, since

---

earthquakes over a period of thirty years. Some features of his argument
evolved. As scholars have emphasized, in the 1680s Hooke became increasingly defensive, attempting to make his ideas look more orthodox in response
to his critics. He also gave more subtle accounts of what caused the earthquakes that moved the shells (he pursues, for example, a theory of "polar wandering," the gradual shifting of the earth's magnetic poles, which he said affected both the interior and the exterior of the earth, generating earthquakes).
One thing, however, remained the same: his fixation on petrified stones as
the solution to the world's history. On the evolution of Hooke's thinking, see
Rappaport, "Hooke on Earthquakes."

115. Wallis to Halley, Oxford, March 4, 1686/87. This letter may be found
in Turner, "Hooke's Theory of the Earth's Axial Displacement," 167–69. With
a heavy dose of sarcasm, Wallis recounts a story of what appeared to be a shell
that had been removed from a woman's kidney, "which yet me thought more
likely to have been formed there, than that this kidney had once been Sea"
(Turner, 169). As Hooke himself points out, there was a good deal of personal
animus motivating Wallis. Hooke wrote in 1687: "And upon the whole I must
needs say that I find [Wallis's letter] to be made up partly of misrepresentation,
partly of designed Satyr[, a]rising as I conceive partly from a misunderstand-
ing of what I have here deliverd but chiefly from some prejudice conceived
against me and my performances, which has formerly Discovered it self in
print and has not it seems as yet all spent its self." Hooke, "Ansr to Dr Wallis
& Ways to find ye Meridian. Read to ye RS Apr. 27. 1687"; cited in Oldroyd,
"Geological Controversy," 213.

possibly 'tis not every one that takes notice of them, nor one of a hundred that does, that will think of a reason; besides, much greater conclusions have been deduced from less evident and more inconsiderable Marks . . . and much more weighty Consequences may, and will in time, be drawn from seemingly more trivial, and much lighter and slighter Indications, yet where the Testimonies are clear, certain and self-evident, they are not to be rejected for their bulk, tho' it be so small as no Eye or Sense can reach it unless assisted by Engines, as the Sight by a Microscope, Telescope, and the like.[116]

As we know, Hooke's *ideal* version of his method depended on a collection that would allow him to "peruse, and turn over, and spell, and read the Book of Nature, and observe the Orthography, Etymologia, Syntaxis, and Prosodia of Natures Grammar."[117] He imagined men all around the world industriously collecting fossils and making observations with their instruments, reading the lost history of the earth together (a vision of scientific collaboration). In his official answer to Wallis, Hooke stressed the importance of the empirical confirmation of his hypotheses about the axial rotation of the earth, hoping that, in the progress of time, measurements might be taken, experiments done.[118] But when he returned to the controversy the following year, the emphasis changed. In the passage above, he shifts from a question of quantity to one of size, stressing the heightened attention and perspicacity of the lynx-eyed interpreter and reminding us again how much can be made of small things. Much more, he predicts, will one day hang on much less.

As Hooke reaches for the microscope while defending his use of fossils, something of his distinctive epistemological fan-

116. Hooke, *Posthumous Works*, 411–12.
117. Hooke, *Posthumous Works*, 338.
118. See Oldroyd, "Geological Controversy," 216.

tasy about the instrument comes again into view. In the next breath, he expounds on the virtues of small things, looking to another kind of shell to make clear exactly how much can be contained in little:

> In how few Letters, Words, or Characters is the History of the World before *Noah's* Flood? Is it therefore not to be believed because we have not as many Volumes of its History as there are now to be found words? In how little room will the History of the Flood be contained if *Homer's* Iliads could be boxed in a Nutshell?[119]

Hooke is here making reference to an ancient story in Pliny's *Natural History*, which tells of a copy of the *Iliad* written in letters so small that the entire poem fit in a nutshell.[120] If Homer could be compacted to so small a size, how small would the very few testimonies of the history of the earth before the flood (and the history of the flood itself) be if they were similarly miniaturized? The answer is very small indeed. Hooke's point is that size is not proportional to significance. The mere mention of Homer also unlocks a question of depth and perspective. Hooke, we recall, has just moments before men-

---

119. Hooke, *Posthumous Works*, 412.

120. Pliny, *Natural History* 7.21. Cf. Hooke, *Micrographia*, 153: "Should a Lemmon or Nut be proportionally magnify'd to what this seed of Tyme is, it would make it appear as bigg as a large Hay-reek, and it would be no great wonder to see *Homers Iliads*, and *Homer* and all, cramm'd into such a Nut-shell." The story was a familiar one in the Renaissance, when the printing press made the production of miniature books more common. Like Power, Hooke mentions several examples of such books in the *Micrographia*, the title of which means both "writing about the small" and "small writing." Hooke, who once used microscopic evidence to argue that the human brain could potentially hold hundreds of millions of ideas, understood well the old saying *multum in parvo*. See Yeo, *Notebooks, English Virtuosi, and Early Modern Science*, 241. On the image of Homer in a nutshell in the Renaissance, see Wolfe, *Humanism, Machinery, and Renaissance Literature*, 161–202.

tioned the opportunities afforded by his optical devices. That he pairs them now with Homer—that most encyclopedic of poets—is significant. Homer himself was a master of shifting perspectives—dramatic similes that moved from the very smallest detail to the image of the world. The bard was long thought to be a kind of *vates* for his ability to capture a God-like viewpoint, ranging over time and space with a seemingly otherworldly gaze. Robert D. Lamberton has described in Homer "the raising of the narrator to a level of perception for which the most obvious analogy is that of the gods. Thus the narrative voice does in some sense assimilate 'divine' wisdom and adopt a privilege that implies such wisdom."[121] I suspect it was something like this mode of "assimilation" that Democritus was trying to express when he called Homer's poetry a *kosmos*, as if reading Homer could lead one to the contemplation of invisible things, and perhaps even to an understanding of the material formation of the universe (DK B21).[122] By invoking the name of Homer alongside the microscope and telescope, Hooke points to a perspective that he himself hopes to inhabit—one that would allow him to "see some hundreds of Years backwards and forward" (to see the world unfolding). In this context, "Homer" might even be understood as the name for an obsolete form of technology. If the expansive vision of Homer can be housed in a nutshell, Hooke argues that fossils contained a much longer epic.

In conjuring up catastrophe, Hooke brought an empirical emphasis to the speculative history of the earth. At the same time, as I've been suggesting, he was answering the deep call of the microscope, which, by failing to get to the bottom of things, made the groundlessness of knowledge more vivid. To recall the words of Pascal, "We burn with desire to find a firm foundation, an unchanging solid base on which to build a

121. Lamberton, *Homer the Theologian*, 6.
122. Dio Chrysostom, *On Homer* 53.1.

tower rising to infinity, but the foundation splits, and the earth opens up to its depths." As philosophers such as Hooke went progressively deeper with their instruments, the earth did open up—or at least a history of earthquakes did. From one perspective, Hooke's was a strictly scientific endeavor with explicit empirical ambitions: an attempt to test the validity of speculations against the weight of material evidence. From a different point of view, his earthquakes can be read as expressions of the metaphysical disaster threatening the foundations of experimental science, the absence of a "firm basis to bottome upon." These possibilities, of course, are not mutually exclusive. For Hooke, digging up earthquakes from the evidence of fossils was, among other things, a way of grasping the groundless as a sensuous image—of holding it in his hands.

CODA

In the century after Hooke delivered his lectures on earthquakes, while working to build the highways that cut across the countryside of France, the architect and engineer Nicolas Boulanger came across fossilized seashells on mountaintops.[123] Prompted to understand the meaning of these objects, Boulanger took it upon himself to absorb a dizzying range of ancient languages and traditions, expounded his own geological system to explain the transformations that had befallen the earth, and developed a theory of language, religion, and psychology that connected the events of disasters and terrestrial upheavals across a comparative history of human culture.[124] Eventually, he would attempt to show how the origins of all

123. On Boulanger's life and work see Hampton, *Nicolas-Antoine Boulanger et la science de son temps*; Manuel, *Eighteenth Century Confronts the Gods*, 210–27; Rossi, *Dark Abyss of Time*, 101–7.

124. In 1761, two years after Boulanger's death, Baron d'Holbach would publish his controversial (and atheistic) work *Christianisme dévoilé* falsely under Boulanger's name.

religions (including Christianity) could be traced back to an encounter with the flood—a disaster that haunted human memory and kept man in a state of perpetual fear and vulnerable to manipulation.[125] According to Boulanger, in the face of catastrophe men gave up their natural freedom and turned to the gods for shelter, which in turn led to the horrors of political despotism. The world, he insisted, was still living in the pall of ancient disaster, having been "penetrated profoundly."[126]

Boulanger was echoing (and amplifying) Hooke's own late thinking on the anthropology of catastrophe, which Hooke had used to fill out the historical record and explain to his contemporaries the absence of more explicit witnesses. In the same lecture in which Hooke wrote of microscopes and telescopes extending our gaze backward and forward in time, for example, he also recounted the story of one particular shell, which he found mentioned in Pliny—a kind of nautilus (now extinct) called *Cornua Ammonis*, also known as "snake-stones" for their large, winding coils, which can sometimes exceed a foot in diameter.[127] Whenever these stones were found, he tells us, they were buried in the temple of Jupiter Ammon (whence they derived their name), having been carried in a procession that involved a miniature ceremonial ship:

> This was carried in Procession by the Priests in a guilded Ship hung with Bells on both sides, &c. by which it should seem that the very Idol itself was nothing but such a *Nautilus* Petrify'd, as I have produced, beset round with Jewels for ornament, and carry'd in a Ship possibly as a Hieroglyphick, to signifie the manner of some eminent Deliverance of that Country from a

125. Boulanger explained: "We compare traditions with traditions and fables with fables, and by their mutual testimonies we wrest them of their secret in spite of themselves." Boulanger, *Oeuvres*, 1:26 (my translation).
126. Boulanger, *Oeuvres*, 1:11 (my translation).
127. Hooke, *Posthumous Works*, 299.

former Flood, or the use of Ships in that place, whilst an island and that Desert was cover'd with Water.[128]

Hooke's first biographer reports that, as a child on the Isle of Wight, he had made a miniature toy ship, which he sailed in the water among the crumbling cliffs.[129] One wonders if even back then Hooke didn't imagine a tiny vessel moving through time like the one on the title page of Bacon's *Instauratio Magna*.

Obsessively reconstructing a psychological history of the flood from ancient accounts, Boulanger had taken Hooke's hermeneutic procedures to their outer limits—and perhaps their breaking point. Once again, the question was, could so much really be made of so little? The answer, of course, depended on whom you asked. According to one acquaintance, namely Jean-Jacques Rousseau, Boulanger was a man who "no longer saw anything in nature but shells, and he ended up really believing that the universe was nothing but shells."[130] In other words, Boulanger was making anything of anything. For Denis Diderot, however, the story was more complicated. In his preface to Boulanger's posthumously published *Antiquité dévoilée* (1766), Diderot describes the elusive author to whom he says he was "intimately tied:"[131]

I have hardly ever seen a man who withdrew so suddenly into himself when he was struck by some new idea, whether it occurred to him, or someone else offered it to him: the change

128. Hooke, *Posthumous Works*, 244.

129. Waller, "Life of Dr. Robert Hooke," iii.

130. Rousseau, *Oeuvres complètes*, 1:373; cited and translated in Rossi, *Dark Abyss of Time*, 102.

131. Boulanger, *Oeuvres*, 1:xi (my translation). Boulanger wrote several entries for Diderot's encyclopedia, including the entry on the flood. As Paul Sadrin has suggested, Boulanger appears to have gotten more interesting to Diderot after he died. Sadrin, "Diderot et Nicolas-Antoine Boulanger," 44.

that came across his eyes was so marked that it seemed like his soul had quit him to hide in a fold of his brain. With a strong imagination that was attached to various extensive pieces of knowledge and an unusual subtlety, he elaborated the fine links and points of analogy between the distant objects. . . . Sometimes I liked to compare him to that solitary insect covered with eyes who drew from its intestine a silk, which it is able to attach from one point in the vastest space to another distant point, and using that first thread to base its beautiful and subtle work, throws right and left countless other threads and eventually occupies the entire space with its web; and this comparison did not offend him a bit. It is in the interval between the ancient and the modern world that our philosopher built his web, seeking to travel back from the current state of things to how they had been in the most ancient times.[132]

Here Boulanger is portrayed as a kind of shaman whose physical demeanor transforms when he is possessed by an idea—a man in a state of pleasure or ecstasy, standing outside of himself and the world of people and things. Diderot perhaps betrays a hint of skepticism when he compares Boulanger to a spider, but the association here is overwhelmingly positive.[133] Diderot is dazzled by the art of his friend's subtle web—that is, by Boulanger's rare ability to command a world of discourse with the speed that Homer attributed to the horses of the gods: "As far as the eye discovers far off space in the skies, these heavenly messengers cross with a single bound."[134] In weaving together a story of the interconnectivity of human culture, Boulanger is both applying a materialist perspective to the history of religion and writing a history of the philosophical imagination of

132. Boulanger, *Oeuvres*, 1:xii–xiii (my translation). Cited and discussed in Vila, *Suffering Scholars*, 121.

133. Bacon, *Works*, 3:286. On Diderot's use of the spider analogy, see Vila, *Suffering Scholars*, 8, 108, 115, 121–22.

134. Boulanger, *Oeuvres*, 1:viii (my translation).

which he is himself a part. If his philological gymnastics often strain the limits of decorum and credulity, even hermeneutic excess can sometimes have its uses, as Diderot seems to recognize. In the end, Boulanger's catastrophizing discloses a certain truth about the nature of historical memory and forgetting—if not in the stuff of the web itself, then in the act of spinning it. Spiders' webs naturally cannot catch everything, but they catch some things; and they make both light and space perceptible in a different way.

FIVE

Disaster before the Sublime;
or, Kant's Catastrophes

In a footnote added to the second edition of the *Critique of the Power of Judgment* (1793), Kant takes up the question of our control over the faculty of desire—the way "man" vainly tries to bring his desires into existence through the representations of his imagination:

> Now, conscious as we are in such fantastic desires of the ineffi-
> ciency of our representations, (or even of their futility,) as *causes*
> of their objects, there is still involved in every *wish* a reference
> of the same as cause, and therefore the representation of its *cau-
> sality*, and this is especially discernible where the wish, as *long-
> ing*, is an affect. For such affects, since they dilate the heart and
> render it inert and thus exhaust its powers, show that a strain is
> kept on being exerted and re-exerted on these powers by the
> representations, but that the mind is allowed continually to
> relapse and become languid upon recognition of the impossi-
> bility before it.[1]

We cannot grab ahold of the objects of our desire by representation alone. The mind's pursuit of its images is a matter
of involuntarily doing (and unconsciously repeating) what we
already know can't help us.

Writing on the Kantian sublime, Jean-François Lyotard
picks up on the theme of the mind's compulsive behavior, sug-

---

1. Kant, *Critique of Judgment*, trans. Meredith, 13n1.

gesting that "we have to conclude that it is essential for thought to feel reflexively its heterogeneity when it brings itself to its own limits (something it cannot avoid doing)."[2] Lyotard is referring to the double experiences of dissonance and synthesis that the sublime generates in the mind. My interest is in how and why this reflexivity emerges in Kant's thought long before he theorizes his famous notion of the sublime in the third *Critique*. In what follows, I will explore one origin of Kant's catastrophic reflex in his early encounters with materialism and place the figure of the sublime within the history we've been tracing in this book.

I've divided this chapter into two parts that correspond to the "before and after" of the Lisbon earthquake of 1755, which Kant observed from a distance in Königsberg. The first part looks at Kant's staging of disaster as a response to—and repetition of—the reflex of the materialist analogy in his *Universal Natural History* (1755), a text that was published less than nine months before the earthquake. Here we'll explore how he developed a taste for the affective structure of catastrophizing— one he would find hard to give up. The second part shows how catastrophic materialism continued to exert its force on Kant's mature philosophy, helping us understand what Lyotard meant when he suggested that the sublime might be construed as a "philosophical neurosis."[3]

BEFORE

In the *Universal Natural History*, the thirty-year-old philosopher was attempting a reconciliation. Newton and Leibniz would

2. Lyotard, *Lessons on the Analytic of the Sublime*, 149–50.

3. While Lyotard ultimately lands on another formulation, I am interested in exploring the implications of his initial suggestion: "One might consider this a philosophical neurosis. Rather, it is a faithfulness par excellence to the philosophical feeling, 'brooding melancholy.'" Lyotard, *Lessons on the Analytic of the Sublime*, 150.

finally settle their feud, and, with their help, Kant could dispel once and for all the idea that "accidental chance . . . made the atoms come together so fortuitously that they constituted a well-ordered whole."[4] The book was supposed to launch his career. It might very well have done so if his publisher hadn't suddenly gone bankrupt.[5]

The idea for Kant's system appears to have emerged from a few hints he had come upon in the Hamburg account of Thomas Wright's *An Original Theory or New Hypothesis of the Universe* (1750).[6] In the context of this German précis, Kant absorbed Wright's discussion of the infinity of worlds, "crowded full of beings" and "tending to their various states of a final perfection," and it was here that he read of the proper affective response to such a vision.[7] Of those who would contemplate this "stupendious sphere of primary bodies . . . [and] the general laws and principles of nature," Wright asks, "Who can avoid being filled with a kind of enthusiastic ambition, to be acknowledged one of the number, who, as it were, by thus adding his atom to the whole, humbly endeavors to contribute towards the due adoration of its great and Divine Author?"[8] "Who can avoid being filled"—the phrase suggests an affective overriding of objections or doubts (to be "filled" is also to be evacuated of one's thoughts). It was a rhetorical question, but

4. Kant, *Universal Natural History*, 198. See Schönfeld, *The Philosophy of the Young Kant*, 107.

5. For the circumstances surrounding the publication of the text and its later reception, see Watkins's introduction in Kant, *Universal Natural History*, 186–87.

6. Kant says, "Herr *Wright of Durham*, with whose treatise I became acquainted through the *Hamburg Freie Urteile* of the year 1751, first gave me cause to regard the fixed stars not as a scattered milling mass without any visible order, but rather as a system with the greatest similarity to a planetary one." Kant, *Natural Science*, 201. A translation of the Hamburg account to which Kant refers here may be found as an appendix to *Kant's Cosmogony*, 180–91.

7. *Kant's Cosmogony*, 180–81.

8. *Kant's Cosmogony*, 181.

both the "atom" and the view of infinity that Wright evokes here point to materialists as the answer. *They* could "avoid" reaching for the idea of God. The question recalls Melanchthon's anxiety about Epicureans who divest the stars of providence and "defend wildly [the notion] . . . that all things are brought together fortuitously from atoms, that all things are moved and joined without order and without a guiding mind, and that continually other worlds and other species come into being."⁹ If the materialists had a way of gripping the mind with thoughts of atoms and catastrophes, Wright too would offer an alternative feeling of (pious) rapture—one derived from the light of Newtonian principles. He acknowledged that many of Newton's discoveries, "such as relate particularly to the Planetary System, are but as so many confirmations of the conjectures and imaginations" of the ancients.¹⁰ As the Hamburg account is quick to note, however, unlike Newton, the ancients had "employed merely an analogical way of judging."¹¹

That Kant responded with such eagerness to the clues he found in this description of Wright's system suggests that he was reacting to something he already deeply felt. We are told that Lucretius was his favorite poet as a youth—and that he could recite his favorite authors by memory into adulthood.¹² The poem stayed with him. Kant meets the question of Lucretian influence head-on in the *Universal Natural History*. There

9. Melanchthon, *Orations on Philosophy and Education*, 94; discussed in chapter 2.

10. Newton traces his idea of universal gravitational force back to the Epicureans in notes prepared for the second edition of the *Principia*. See my discussion in Passannante, *Lucretian Renaissance*, 198–215.

11. *Kant's Cosmogony*, 182.

12. Hettner, *Geschichte der deutschen Literatur im Achtzehnten Jahrhundert*, 2:160: "Auf der Schule war Lucrez, auf der Universität Newton sein [i.e. Kant's] Lieblingsstudium." Cited in Nisbet, "Lucretius in Eighteenth-Century Germany," 100n20. On Kant's engagement with Lucretius and Epicureanism, see Aubenque, "Kant et l'épicurisme"; Porter, "Lucretius and the Sublime," 176–84; Wilson, "Presence of Lucretius," 81–84.

was no denying, he says early, as if to ward off imagined objections, "that Lucretius' theory or that of his predecessors, Epicure, Leucippus, and Democritus, has much in common with mine." Kant knows he sounds like an Epicurean when he describes the "dispersion of original material of all world-bodies, or atoms as they call them."[13] In light of Newtonian mechanics, he understands the heaviness Epicurus attributed to bodies as being "not very different" from Newtonian attraction and even finds a way to make some sense of the infamous Epicurean swerve, which, he suggests, "to some extent corresponds to the change in the straight fall that we attribute to the repulsive force of the particles."[14] Though Kant again admits that his own arguments have "the greatest similarity" with those of the materialists, he assures us that he has the matter under control: "The close relationship with a doctrine that was the proper theory of the denial of the divine in antiquity, will not, however, drag mine into association with their errors."[15]

In the context of this discussion of ancient influence, the *clinamen* or swerve suggests at least two things at once: a physical principle that might be explained (and explained away) by Newtonian laws and the involuntary force of an unwanted thought that might "drag" the mind into error. In the first case, as we'll see, the swerve mirrors the characteristic form of the philosopher's thought throughout the *Universal Natural History*, leaping from one small thing (or law) to the beginning of the world and its end. Kant says he won't be dragged off course, but he is attracted precisely to what is most coercive about Epicurean thought—the catastrophic feeling of an idea's inevitability. It is arguably to this feeling (rather than to any philo-

13. Kant, *Universal Natural History*, 198.
14. Kant, *Universal Natural History*, 198.
15. Kant, *Universal Natural History*, 198. Wilson has described Kant's "virtual obsession with the moral problematic posed by Epicurean materialism and the pessimistic view of history as undirected by Providence." Wilson, "Presence of Lucretius," 81.

sophical principle) that he is "compulsively drawn," to borrow Peter Fenves's description of Kant's attraction to the swerve.[16] But even as the philosopher partially reinscribes the swerve within a Newtonian universe, saving the Epicureans from themselves, he reaches for its catastrophic structure to explain the insinuating nature of philosophical error: "One false principle or a few ill-considered connecting principles will lead men from the path of truth via imperceptible errors into the abyss."[17] Just as the poet of *De rerum natura* had defined the *clinamen* as the smallest possible digression from the course of an atom's fall—"just so much as you might call a change in motion"—Kant reflects on how even one slight error can lead the mind "imperceptib[ly]" to certain disaster. As Melanchthon had said, "Men often carelessly attract to themselves deadly danger by a slight mistake."[18] Like Melanchthon, Kant is talking about the materialists, but he is also anticipating the worst for himself. In raising catastrophes out of the stuff of Newtonian laws, he too would come to know the mixed inheritance of Democritus—the dream of the pit from which truth might be recovered and the abyss of skepticism that threatens to pull you down into the dark.

Several aspects of Kant's materialist inheritance become visible in the way he treats his own philosophical predecessor. As Lucretius had sought to explicate Epicurus in verse and Newton later translated Epicureanism into mathematics, Kant translated Newton from mathematics into another philosophical idiom.[19] Like both the swerve and the atom, the idea of which Kant contemplates in the sense of a minimum component, Newtonian mechanics demands the end in the beginning. Kant explains: "If a systematic constitution . . . brings

16. Fenves, *Peculiar Fate*, 28.

17. Kant, *Universal Natural History*, 198.

18. Melanchthon, *Orations on Philosophy and Education*, 94; discussed in chapter 2.

19. See Passannante, *Lucretian Renaissance*, 211.

even the tiniest part one can imagine closer to the state of its confusion, then in the infinite passage of eternity there must surely be a point in time [*Zeitpunkt*] when the gradual diminution has exhausted all motion."[20] To know a physical law is also to know its end. For, indeed, "*Newton*, that great admirer of God's qualities from the perfection of his works, who combined the most profound insight into the excellence of nature with the greatest reverence towards the revelation of divine omnipotence, saw himself obliged to proclaim to nature its decay through the natural tendency that the mechanics of motion has."[21] If the word *Zeitpunkt* suggests a future point in time, it also evokes the pointedness of the *punkt*, that is, the swiftness with which the mind is asked (or compelled) to imagine the imminent catastrophe in a "moment" or "atom" of time. Kant's sense of the slowness of the world's demise ("perhaps a thousand, perhaps a million centuries will not destroy it") only amplifies by contrast the speed of the thought.[22]

In this example and throughout the *Universal Natural History*, Kant was performing an upgrade, taking an Epicurean style of analogy and supercharging it with Newtonian laws. If the ancient materialists had relied upon images such as "specks of dust in sunlight" to conjure up a hidden world of matter, Kant would derive his image of "world systems" coming together and apart from what had already been blessed by the light of mathematics, supplying the same basic structures of thought with sturdier material.[23] Physical principles now replaced the shaky ground of the atom. Thus Kant could repeat the style of Epicurean analogy without the uncertainty—and without the guilt. We've already seen this pattern at work in Digges,

20. Kant, *Universal Natural History*, 269; *Immanuel Kants Schriften*, 1:318 (the Akademie-Ausgabe edition is hereafter cited as AK followed by volume and page numbers).
21. Kant, *Universal Natural History*, 269.
22. Kant, *Universal Natural History*, 269.
23. Kant, *Universal Natural History*, 295.

whose leap to infinity was, among other things, a reaction to the spring-loaded violence of materialist thought. Kant's leap was another attempt to answer the sudden grip of catastrophic materialism by repurposing and retrofitting its intellectual machinery. Though he makes a show of quoting the pious lines of Alexander Pope and other poets to convey reverence for the great "chain, which from God its beginning takes," beneath the hood Kant was relying on the catastrophic engine of Lucretius to transform an abstract set of ideas into an embodied experience of thought.[24]

The idea of catastrophe organizes Kant's cosmogony at its most basic level. Where the image of disaster isn't on the surface of the text, we can sense it in Kant's impulse to confirm Newtonianism. The disasters of catastrophic materialism allow Kant to experience Newtonian mechanics as an affective proposition. In the *Universal Natural History*, Kant repeatedly induces the involuntary thought of catastrophe. At one point, he even anticipates the reader's response to the horror of catastrophizing, perhaps recalling something of his own initial feeling. "We must not lament the end of a world structure as a true loss of nature," he says, rushing to console with another kind of analogy:

> What a countless mass of flowers and insects does not a single cold day destroy; but how little do we miss them even though they are splendid artworks of nature and proofs of divine omnipotence! In another place this loss is replaced again with abundance. Human beings, who appear to be the masterpiece of creation, are themselves not excluded from this law. Nature shows that it is just as bountiful, just as inexhaustible in the production of the most excellent of creatures as it is in that of those of low regard, and that even their end is a necessary gradation in the diversity of its suns, because their creation costs

24. Kant, *Universal Natural History*, 306.

it nothing. The deleterious effects of infected air, earthquakes, floods eradicate whole peoples from the face of the earth, but it does not appear that nature has any disadvantage through this.[25]

The analogy between men and insects might remind us again of Leonardo's prophecies, though Kant says explicitly what Leonardo only implies. As "whole peoples" are destroyed by earthquakes and other catastrophes, he says with the wry matter-of-factness of a sixth-grade science teacher, "in a similar way, whole worlds and systems leave the scene after they have finished playing their roles."[26]

Here too the philosopher is following an old script, replaying the ancient dialectical drama of horror and consolation. As Kant conjures up disasters like an Epicurean, like an Epicurean he will attempt to put them in their cosmic place. But if this seems like cold comfort—as chilly as that "single cold day" or the embrace of an Epicurean atom—we might consider the possibility that catastrophizing was for Kant less about arriving at a state of tranquility than it was about the affective dynamics of thinking—what certainty feels like.[27] In this regard, we might view his cosmogony not only as a set of discrete ideas (a philosophical "treatise") but as an essay in catastrophic knowing—a *testing* of Newton's laws through the experience of their apprehension. If William Shea is right that there is "no doubt that [Kant] did not acquaint himself with Newtonian natural

25. Kant, *Universal Natural History*, 270.

26. Kant, *Universal Natural History*, 270. See Lucretius, *De rerum natura* 5.243–46: "When I see the grand parts and members of the world being consumed and born again, I may be sure that heaven and earth also once had their time of beginning and will have their destruction."

27. Fenves sees Kant's fascination with catastrophe as an expression of his ambivalence about "grounding": "Ambiguity therefore belongs so essentially to the catastrophe that Kant's fascination with catastrophes should be understood not as a lurid impulse but as a demand on interpretation itself, namely, that the interpreter be without a secure location." Fenves, *Peculiar Fate*, 64.

philosophy in the mathematically forbidding pages of the *Principia Mathematica*," the reflexive immediacy of catastrophizing would supply the requisite feeling.[28]

This experience of passivity would become central to Kant's thinking. He would elaborate on it later, for example, in the pages of the third *Critique* where he argues against the common view that Newton was a genius, writing, "Everything that Newton expounded in his immortal work on the principles of natural philosophy, no matter how great a mind it took to discover it, can still be learned."[29] Kant here contrasts the workmanlike greatness of Newton to a poet such as "Homer or Wieland," whose genius eludes instruction, "because he himself does not know it and thus cannot teach it to anyone else either."[30] Genius befalls the poet, enabling increased powers of perception, a kind of supercognition, or as Kant describes it, "a faculty for apprehending the rapidly passing play of the imagination and unifying it into a concept."[31] Kant elaborates on this idea in his *Anthropology from a Pragmatic Point of View* (1785):

28. Shea, "Filled with Wonder," 115.

29. Kant, *Critique of the Power of Judgment*, 187. Compare this to David Hume, who described Newton as the "greatest and rarest genius that ever rose for the ornament and instruction of the species." Hume, *History of England*, 8:326. On Kant's idea of genius and its relation to Newton, see Hall, "Kant on Newton, Genius, and Scientific Discovery."

30. Kant, *Critique of the Power of Judgment*, 187–88. As Cassirer says, "This insight as to the 'unconscious' creativity of artistic genius becomes yet more meaningful where it comprises less the opposite to theoretical grounding than the opposite to the intent of desire and action." Cassirer, *Kant's Life and Thought*, 325.

31. Kant, *Critique of the Power of Judgment*, 195. The genius produces "beautiful art," which is not mutually exclusive from the sublime. Kant writes, "The presentation of the sublime, so far as it belongs to beautiful art, can be united with beauty in a *verse tragedy*, a *didactic poem*, an *oratorio*." Kant, *Critique of the Power of Judgment*, 203. For the concept of genius in Kant as a response to the crisis of grounding the feeling of the sublime, see Wang, *Romantic Sobriety*, 36–60.

But how the poets also came to consider themselves as inspired (or possessed), and as fortune-tellers (*vates*), and how they could boast of having inspirations in their poetical impulses (*furor poeticus*), can only be explained by the fact that the poet, unlike the prose-orator who composes his commissioned work with leisure, must rather snatch the propitious moment of the mood of his inner sense as it comes over him, in which lively and powerful images and feelings pour into him, while he behaves merely passively, so to speak. For as an old observation goes, genius is mixed with a certain dose of madness.[32]

Kant associates genius with an experience of involuntariness—a feeling of being "poured" into, overwhelmed by "powerful images." He imagines the way in which the inner sense works unconsciously in the *vates* or poet—"snatch[ing] the propitious moment" with what would appear to be a mind of its own. To imitate it would be to lose its essence, but to "emulate" the involuntary is another story. Through the act of emulation, Kant says, "another genius . . . is awakened to the feeling of his own originality."[33] When Kant mentions that "genius is mixed with a certain dose of madness," he is referencing an "old observation" that was attributed not only to the divine Plato but also to Democritus. Cicero writes: "For I have often heard that—as they say Democritus and Plato have left on record—no man can be a good poet who is not on fire with passion, and inspired by something very like frenzy [*furoris*]" (DK 68 B17).[34]

The name Democritus and the idea of poetic "frenzy" bring us back to the world of the *Universal Natural History*—and to the question of Lucretian influence. As we know, Kant could have easily found a working model for "awakening" in Lucretius, who lent poetic expression to the ecstatic apprehension of Epi-

32. Kant, *Anthropology from a Pragmatic Point of View*, 81.
33. Kant, *Critique of the Power of Judgment*, 195.
34. Cicero, *De oratore* 2.46.194.

curean thought—what Statius described as the poet's "tower-ing frenzy [*furor*]."[35] We recall that Lucretius had imagined the mind's experience of nature "uncovered in every part" both as a "divine delight" (*divina voluptas*) and as a "shuddering" (*horror*). Drawing upon the language of Empedocles, he too had fash-ioned himself as a kind of poetic *vates*—a prophet who could read the past and future of matter. Once again, Kant was closely following his lead. As the "sublime Lucretius" (as Ovid called him) had transformed the bitter philosophy of Epicurus into the sweet stuff of poetry, Kant would capture the feeling of Newton, becoming in turn a kind of rational oracle in what Coleridge would later describe as his "astonishing *prophetic work*."[36] It was the shock of the "prophetic" that Kant sought to reproduce in the pages of his cosmogony—an involuntari-ness to which he submitted, as if by willing the involuntary he might master it. If this sense of shock or "horror" is at the root of Kant's desire in the *Universal Natural History*, it suggests that the text is as much about translating Newtonian laws into the key of infinity as it is about submitting those same laws to a ritual of knowing in which the mind feels its certainty as a "rapidly passing play of the imagination."

Catastrophic materialism emerges again when Kant at-tempts to confirm the universality of Newton's laws—indeed, much as Lucretius had sought to confirm the ground of the atom. In the following passage, for example, Kant is consider-ing the possibility of multiple systems, as opposed to one con-

35. Statius, *Silvae* 2.7.73.

36. Ovid, *Amores* 1.15.23–25: "Carmina sublimis tunc sunt peritura Lu-creti, / exitio terras cum dabit una dies" (The verses of sublime Lucretius will perish only then when a single day shall give the earth to doom). Cole-ridge to C. A. Tuck, January 12, 1818 (*Collected Letters*, 4:808). Coleridge plays on the idea of "prophetic" in at least two senses here. First, Kant has written a book that tells of the history and future of matter; second, he has written a book that anticipated the *Traité de mécanique céleste* (1798–1825) of Pierre-Simon Laplace, which Coleridge calls "an unprincipled plagiarism." Cited in Shea, "Filled with Wonder," 96.

stant system across the universe, which leads him to another disastrous thought:

> If there were only separate galaxies that, between them, have no unified connection to a whole, then, if one were to assume this chain of links to be actually infinite, one could well think that an exactly equal attraction of parts from all sides could keep these systems safe from the destruction with which the inner reciprocal attraction threatens them. This, however, would require such a precisely measured determination of the distances balanced according to the attraction, that even the slightest disarrangement would bring about the destruction of the *universe* and deliver it into collapse in long periods that would ultimately still have to come to an end.[37]

"Even the slightest disarrangement" would bring the world to ruin. But the world stands before us, the universe has not collapsed — at least not yet. If he is wrong about the uniformity of laws across space and time, the universe is nothing. We might remember just how desperate this logic felt in Lucretius in spite of the poet's Epicurean sangfroid. In repeating this line of thought, however, it would have been difficult for Kant to avoid a certain irony — namely, that Lucretius himself had *felt* the same threat of disaster guiding (and constraining) his thought, had manufactured the feeling of certainty on lesser principles. Along with Wright, Kant might very well have believed that Newton had simply "proven" what the Epicureans knew only by analogy. Then again, there was always the disturbing possibility that his certainty was never anything more than a feeling he produced for himself — as Kant would put it in a different context, "what in reality he has forced on himself."[38]

The philosopher's romance with the materialist style might

37. Kant, *Universal Natural History*, 264.
38. Kant, *Anthropology from a Pragmatic Point of View*, 54.

help explain what Susan Meld Shell has called his "rhetorical unevenness" in the *Universal Natural History*: "a tendency to insist on the certainty of his position, even as he admits, almost in the same breath, to its excessive boldness."[39] "I will not," Kant says in one place, "be deprived of the right that Descartes always enjoyed from fair judges when he dared to explain the formation of the heavenly bodies from purely mechanical laws."[40] In other parts of the treatise a more modest posture prevails—for example, when he encourages future philosophers and scientists to take up what can be known only through conjecture and analogy, fostering a "well-founded hope."[41] Still in other places, the philosopher allows himself the space to indulge in a more speculative mood. In chapter 5, for example, where he attempts to explain the mechanical origins of the rings of Saturn, he offers a disclaimer: "Let us, with the approval of our obliging readers, carry it further to the point of excess as much as we like so that, after we have abandoned ourselves in a pleasant way to arbitrary opinions with a kind of lack of restraint, we can return again to the truth with all the greater care and caution."[42] In what follows, he imagines that the earth itself once had rings that held moisture, which was released at the proper moment, a natural philosophical explanation for Noah's flood: "The water of the firmament mentioned in Moses' description has already caused the interpreters some effort. Could one not use this ring to help to get oneself out of this difficulty?"[43] Kant wonders whether it might have been a passing comet that had released the waters, gesturing to the theories of the Newtonian acolyte William Whiston, who held that Noah's flood was the result of a comet (Whiston

39. Shell, *Embodiment of Reason*, 33.

40. Kant, *Universal Natural History*, 199. See Shea, "Filled with Wonder," 105–6.

41. Kant, *Universal Natural History*, 219.

42. Kant, *Universal Natural History*, 257–58.

43. Kant, *Universal Natural History*, 258–59.

himself had caused a panic in London when he suggested that another comet in October 1736 might bring about the end of the world).[44] Kant suggests that the rainbow that followed the flood might have been a memorial to the rings that had once encircled the earth and brought disaster, though he quickly adds that he will "forgo the fleeting applause such correspondences might arouse for the true pleasure that arises from the perception of regular connections when physical analogies support each other to designate physical truths."[45] In the end, Whiston's speculations were only a pale shadow of the certainty of physical truths arrived at by ironclad analogies. Thus even this speculative excursion into science fiction had a purpose: to reinforce the feeling of catastrophic intuition.

What kind of pleasure does catastrophe afford Kant? The question takes on special significance in light of a style of thinking that seems to demand repetition. Kant reflects on disaster's iterability in both the physical terms of his system (the infinity of the universe) and his own mental economy, asking us to picture another catastrophe—the instant when "the final exhaustion of the orbital motions in the solar system has hurled the planets and the comets altogether down onto the sun," the fire of which will "dissolve everything into the smallest elements again" and "renew the original combination."[46] Satisfaction in the spectacle of nature's violence, he says, transforms into heightened pleasure when we picture the end of the world (or worlds) as another beginning.[47] He calls this cyclical image

44. Whiston's *A New Theory of the Earth* (1696) was praised by both Newton and Locke. In no small part due to the success of this work, Whiston would take over the Lucasian Chair of Mathematics from Newton in 1702. For Whiston's ideas about the end of the world, see Whiston, *Astronomical Year*.

45. Kant, *Universal Natural History*, 258–59.

46. Kant, *Universal Natural History*, 271.

47. Schönfeld has described it nicely: "This pulse of outward evolutionary rises and inward entropic falls, of big bangs and big crunches, is to Kant the eternal dialectic chain of self-perfecting cosmoi." Schönfeld, "Kant's Early Cosmology," 58.

of destruction and renewal the "phoenix of nature" that "burns itself only to rise rejuvenated from its ashes to new life through all infinity of time and space."[48] But here, again, the philosopher is describing not only the cycles of nature across the universe but also the repetitive structure of thought through which the mind makes a world and destroys it in a moment.

In an ideal world, the knowledge of firm Newtonian laws would be enough for the mind to rest secure and give up its compulsive conjuration of disaster. But for some (and one suspects Kant is already among them), the mind is never really allowed to rest in its knowledge—a knowledge that it must repeatedly *test*—and the feeling of satisfaction is momentary at best. Thus just as soon as Kant imagines satisfaction in the inevitability and repetition of Newtonian laws, he turns to look for another ground (as if the one he's described is already not enough): "Then the mind that contemplates all this sinks into a profound astonishment; and yet still unsatisfied with this so great object, whose transience cannot satisfy the soul sufficiently, he wishes to get to know at close quarters that being whose understanding, whose greatness is the source of that light which spreads over all of nature as though from one centre point."[49] This "profound astonishment" echoes Wright's affective response in the German précis. But "astonishment" here also suggests an exhaustion of the faculties—what Kant will later describe as a cognitive "sacrifice" or "deprivation."[50] In the desire to know God, Kant is narrating the end of the process of the mind's encounter with Newtonian physics. The rapid movement between astonishment and disappointment points not just to a singular event but to the cumulative effect on the mind of an endless cycle of repetition demanded by the appli-

48. On Kant's notion of the "phoenix of nature" and its relation to other contemporary theories, particularly Wright's, see Schaffer, "Phoenix of Nature."

49. Kant, *Universal Natural History*, 272; AK 1:321.

50. Kant, *Critique of the Power of Judgment*, 152.

cation of Newtonian physics across an infinite universe. Recall Kant's description of what it is like to long for something even if we know our representations cannot answer our longing: "For such affects, since they dilate the heart and render it inert and thus exhaust its powers, show that a strain is kept on being exerted and re-exerted on these powers by the representations, but that the mind is allowed continually to relapse and become languid upon recognition of the impossibility before it." This pattern appears to be woven into the very texture of his cosmogony and its economy of catastrophe and "relapse."

Looking back now to the *Universal Natural History*, the thought of catastrophizing ad infinitum begins to look like something else: a repetition ad nauseam. Kant says that contemplating nature's vicissitudes inspires in him a wish to be closer to God. But it is notably not God to whom he shifts his attention but again to the scene of disaster—and the materialist baggage he can't quite leave behind even as the soul ascends to celestial heights: "O happy if, among the tumult of the elements and the ruins of nature, [the soul] is always positioned at a height from which it can see the devastations that frailty causes the things of the world to rush past under its feet, so to speak! A happiness such as reason may not even have the temerity to wish for, revelation teaches us to hope for with conviction."[51] The reference is unmistakable. As we know, in the original passage in *De rerum natura* that Kant is recalling here, Lucretius imagines the view from a distance as the view of suffering men who have not yet achieved tranquility— a metaphor for philosophical truth: "Pleasant it is, when over a great sea the winds trouble the waters, to gaze from shore upon another's great tribulation."[52] In Kant's hands, the figure becomes literal. The wind troubling the waters is now the fluid

51. Kant, *Universal Natural History*, 273.
52. Kant gestures again to the proem to book 2 of *De rerum natura* in his *Anthropology from a Pragmatic Point of View*, 135, noting, "So it is not luck but only wisdom that can secure the value of life for the human being; and its

turbulence of worlds: the soul *witnesses* what the mind can only imagine.

We might be tempted to read the image as simply another rebuke to Epicurean impiety: Kant is putting an immortal soul where Lucretius had insisted there was none.[53] But the soul towering over disaster is also another figure for the observation of the self—one that appears to arise out of the compulsion of a catastrophic style of knowing. In the first *Critique*, Kant will return pointedly to the image of the turbulent sea as seen from a distance, but now it is explicitly the "great tribulation" of the metaphysician that is at stake. The "land of pure understanding . . . is an island"—a "land of truth (a charming name), surrounded by a broad and stormy ocean, the true seat of illusion, where many a fog bank and rapidly melting iceberg pretend to be new lands and, ceaselessly deceiving with empty hopes the voyager looking for new discoveries, entwine him in adventures *from which he can never escape yet also never bring to an end*."[54]

The ancient materialists insisted on a hard-won tranquility in the here and now of earthly existence (the end of a rigorous therapy). Kant gestures at a similar state of *ataraxia* when he invites us to "accustom our eye" to the great upheavals of nature, yet he still reaches for the promise of an afterlife.[55] "The changeable scenes of nature," he says, "are not capable of disturbing the peace of happiness of a spirit that has been raised to such heights," which suggests perhaps that he was still disturbed in spite of himself.[56] Kant refers to this as the time "when the

---

value is therefore in his power. He who is anxiously worried about losing his life will never enjoy life."

53. The image of the soul observing the rush of worlds "under its feet, so to speak" is perhaps Kant's answer to Lucretius trampling *religio* underfoot (*pedibus subiecta*). See Lucretius, *De rerum natura* 1.78–79.

54. Kant, *Critique of Pure Reason*, 338–39 (emphasis mine). For Kant's repeated use of the trope and its development in his thought, see Poggi, "Standing in Front of the Ocean."

55. Kant, *Universal Natural History*, 270.

56. Kant, *Universal Natural History*, 273. As Fenves has suggested, where

shackles that hold us to the vanity of creatures have fallen off at the moment that has been determined for the transfiguration of our being."[57] The question is, why would the soul, in the state of its eternal rest, need these catastrophic spectacles (the soul "is always positioned at a height from which it can see the devastations")? Why would the philosopher?

Kant provides us with the beginnings of an answer in a late satirical essay called "The End of All Things" (1794). When it comes to contemplating the end of the world, Kant says, "reason does not understand either itself or what it wants, but prefers to indulge in enthusiasm rather than—as seems fitting for an intellectual inhabitant of a sensible world—to limit itself within the bounds of the latter."[58] Kant dismissively cites the example of Eastern philosophers who "contemplate nothingness"—and manages to get in a dig at Spinoza's philosophical system, though he might as well be describing his earlier self in the *Universal Natural History* when he writes: "People would like at last to have an eternal tranquility in which to rejoice, constituting for them a supposedly blessed end of all things; but really this is a concept in which the understanding is simultaneously exhausted and all thinking itself has an end."[59] What else is the dream of pure vicissitude perpetually flowing beneath the soul's feet if not an imagined *relief* from the violent rise and fall of catastrophizing—from the *turba* of compulsive thinking that has no end in sight?

In an essay on the idea of pleasure in De Quincey and late Kant, David L. Clark has narrated the intimate dance between the sage and the opium eater, showing how De Quincey's am-

---

the soul represents both the necessity and the impossibility of self-grounding, "the *Universal Natural History* radicalizes and exceeds the problematic of classical metaphysics, even as it grants the foundation on which a renewed elucidation of its principles can be carried." Fenves, *Peculiar Fate*, 69.

57. Kant, *Universal Natural History*, 273.
58. Kant, *End of All Things*, 228.
59. Kant, *End of All Things*, 228.

bivalence about Kant betrays a startling identification with the philosopher's pathologies.[60] As Clark has shown, Kant was no stranger to the dialectic of will and compulsion that the experience of addiction entails. At one point in his *Anthropology from a Pragmatic Point of View*, Kant tellingly remarks on "the attempt to observe oneself by physical means, in a condition approaching derangement into which one has voluntarily placed oneself in order to observe better even what is involuntary."[61] Here he is imagining philosophers taking drugs so they might better understand what it means to will involuntariness.

In light of this remark, we might return to Kant's addictive use of catastrophic materialism and recall the old story that the author of *De rerum natura* had himself gone mad from drinking a love potion administered by his wife, writing his verses between the bouts of madness ("per intervalla insaniae").[62] As we know, Ficino had suggested this experience as the very *cause* of the poem and treated the poem itself as a kind of dangerous narcotic (an object of lethal "curiosity" that one would do well to avoid). But did Kant imbibe the "genius" of Lucretius uncovering the secrets of nature, or did he partake in the poet's derangement? As Kant will warn later on, as if speaking from personal experience, "An artificially induced dementia could easily become a genuine one."[63]

Following the dream of the soul's ascension, Kant appends

60. Clark, "We 'Other Prussians.'"

61. Kant, *Anthropology from a Pragmatic Point of View*, 111.

62. See, again, Eusebius, *Eusebii Pamphili Chronici canones*, 231; discussed in chapter 2. In the *Anthropology*, he classifies "Dementia" among the kinds of melancholy, which, he says, "accompanied by affect is madness, whose fits, though involuntary, can often be original and which then, like poetic rapture (*furor poeticus*), border on genius." Kant, *Anthropology from a Pragmatic Point of View*, 97.

63. Kant, *Anthropology from a Pragmatic Point of View*, 111. Though Kant is talking about physical substances here (narcotics), Clark has shown how closely connected the discourse of substance abuse is for Kant to "reason's prescription." Clark, "We 'Other Prussians,'" 279.

a "supplement" to the chapter, which brings us to the image of the sun and to the question of orientation that will become central as the philosopher stages a "Copernican revolution" of his own.[64] The topic is now "Why is the centre point of every system occupied by a flaming body?"[65] Coming down from the soul's dizzy flight, he reminds us how matter is dispersed into space and how it organizes itself. He speculates on the nature of the sun's atmosphere, describing its surface to be like the surface of the earth in at least one regard: "Precisely this atmosphere is not free from the motions of the winds for the same reasons as on our earth, but which from all appearances must greatly exceed in vehemence everything the imagination can picture for itself."[66] Then he attempts to picture exactly this unimaginable scene:

> Finally, let us have our imagination represent a wonderfully strange object such as a burning sun as it were from close up. In one glance, we see broad lakes of fire lifting their flames up to the sky, raging storms whose fury redoubles the violence of the former, which, by making them swell up over their banks, now cover the raised areas of this celestial body, now make them sink back to within their borders; burnt-out rocks that stretch their terrible peaks out of the flaming maws, and whose flooding or uncovering by the fiery element is the cause of the alter-

64. Kant, *Critique of Pure Reason*, 110: "Hence let us once try whether we do not get farther with the problems of metaphysics by assuming that the objects must conform to our cognition, which would agree better with the requested possibility of an *a priori* cognition of them, which is to establish something about objects before they are given to us. This would be just like the first thoughts of Copernicus, who, when he did not make good progress in the explanation of the celestial motions if he assumed that the entire celestial host revolves around the observer, tried to see if he might not have greater success if he made the observer revolve and left the stars at rest. Now in metaphysics we can try in a similar way regarding the intuition of objects."
65. Kant, *Universal Natural History*, 273.
66. Kant, *Universal Natural History*, 275–76.

nating appearance and disappearance of sunspots; dense vapors that choke the fire and, raised by the force of the winds, constitute dark clouds which in turn crash down in fiery showers of rain and, in the form of burning rivers, pour into the flaming valleys from the heights of the firm land of the Sun, the crashing of the elements, the detritus of burnt-out matters, and nature wrestling with destruction, which even in the most loathsome state of its disorder brings about the beauty of the world and the benefit of the creatures.[67]

Like Milton's Satan, Kant lands on the surface of the sun. His description of fiery storms would seem to be prophetic, looking forward to the image of the city of Lisbon on fire that would capture the imagination of Europe following the quake that same year. But there is no suffering in this solar landscape, no bodies suspended in the grip of nature's fury. This is an image of pure destruction and creation, removed from the earth and all earthly things. Yet the image begins with (and inescapably relies on) a terrestrial analogy, flickering between an ordinary disaster, an impossible view, and an image of the future. If catastrophe emerges earlier in the text as a reflex following from the contemplation of necessary laws, Kant now inverts that logic, conjuring up disaster as if it were itself a marker of necessity—*an internal compulsion rather than a Newtonian one*. His reverie responds to the mind's "longing" to validate the image of the world's destruction and cyclical renewal with a physical description—to ground it in the force of a purifying image. The intensity of his imaginative labor is one index of that longing.[68]

But, no more than the fantasy of the soul's panoptic perspective, this image of the sun's surface cannot meet the de-

67. Kant, *Universal Natural History*, 277–78.

68. On Kant's imaginary voyage to the surface of the sun, Willi Goetschel writes, "Poetic fantasy is literally in danger here of getting too hot to handle." Goetschel, *Constituting Critique*, 33.

mands of either mathematical certainty or theological proof. Turning again to Wright's flawed example, Kant concedes, as if coming out of a trance: "We do not wish to allow free rein to the boldness of our conjectures, which we perhaps have permitted only too much, to the point of arbitrary inventions."[69] As he would later say to the overzealous Platonists, "To look *into* the sun (the super-sensible) without being blinded is not possible."[70]

AFTER

Though one could trace any number of genealogies for the visual convention of "before and after"—beginning, perhaps, with depictions of Adam and Eve's fall or the London fire of 1666—no event quite captured the form like the Lisbon earthquake of 1755, a disaster that lasted about five minutes and killed an estimated sixty thousand people. Many of the "before and after" images of Lisbon come down to us as simple juxtapositions. Some feature legends or "keys" marking specific buildings (such as the churches where many died attending Mass). One image (fig. 5) borrows a bird's-eye view from the sixteenth-century atlas of Georg Braun but superimposes a picture of a tumultuous sea over the bottom half of the cityscape.[71]

While most likely born of necessity or convenience (i.e., the paucity of up-to-date maps), the image asks us to reconsider the ways we think about time and history. In "before" images, we normally understand what we see as *just* before. Yet this composite "before and after" is only one of several early modern representations that offer an alternative experience of

69. Kant, *Universal Natural History*, 279.

70. Kant, "On a Recently Prominent Tone of Superiority in Philosophy," 439. See Fenves, *Peculiar Fate*, 208.

71. Braun's map of Lisbon was one of over five hundred images of cities in his *Civitates Orbis Terrarum*.

Tab. III

Vorstellung des Erdbebens zu Lißabon

FIGURE 5. Anon., "Fürstellung des Erdbebens zu Lissabon" (1756). Copper engraving, from Anon., *Physikalische Betrachtungen von den Erdbeben und den daraus erfolgten außerordentlichen Bewegungen der Gewässer wie auch von den anderen Naturbegebenheiten, welche am 1ten Nov. 1755 den größten Theil von Europa und andere Welt-Theile betroffen.* Frankfurt/Leipzig (1756). Plate III. Courtesy Lisbon City Council. Photograph: Museu de Lisboa.

FIGURE 6.   After Jacques Philippe Le Bas, "Basilica de Santa Maria. Ruins of Lisbon as appeared immediately after the Earthquake and Fire of the 1st November 1755." Copper engraving, England. Photograph: © The Trustees of the British Museum.

the time of disaster. In England and France, for instance, one popular genre of contemporary images represented the ruins of Lisbon inhabited by well-dressed tourists, as if the city had already become an ancient site (fig. 6).

As David Hume said a few years before the Lisbon quake, our knowledge of cause and effect is really just a matter of "CUSTOM OR HABIT."[72] It is only when out-of-the-ordinary events such as earthquakes occur that we give this problem any mind.[73] Hume himself makes much of such interruptions,

72. Hume, *Enquiry Concerning Human Understanding* 5.5.

73. Hume, *Enquiry Concerning Human Understanding* 7.21: "[Men] acquire, by long habit, such a turn of mind, that upon the appearance of the cause, they immediately expect with assurance its usual attendant, and hardly conceive it possible that any other event could result from it. It is only on the discovery of extraordinary phenomena, such as earthquakes, pestilence, and prodigies of any kind, that they find themselves at a loss to assign a proper cause, and to

discovering an abyss opening out in the space between cause and effect. He reminds us, echoing Democritus: "If truth be at all within the reach of human capacity, 'tis certain it must lie very deep and abstruse."[74] The classic structure of disaster's "before and after," one might say, draws its energy from the pit. As the eye takes in both images in figure 7 in quick succession (or nearly simultaneously), the mind is compelled to reproduce the disaster as an event of thought. Together the images dare us *not* to conjure up the disaster in our heads. On an eighteenth-century tobacco box we come upon another Lisbon "before and after" (fig. 8). The accompanying inscription suggests a *memento mori*, but one wonders if, by some hidden logic, the addictive pleasure of nicotine might not be connected to the compulsive experience of the images themselves.

In mechanically inducing the thought of catastrophe, the before and after might even be said to resemble the addictive structure of materialist catastrophizing that we've been exploring in this book. Both the before and after and the materialist analogy make *conventional* the experience of thought's involuntary force. As the analogy of dust in sunlight reflexively fills the imagination, the sharp movement between the before and

---

explain the manner in which the effect is produced by it. It is usual for men in such difficulties to have recourse to some invisible intelligent principle as the immediate cause of that event which surprises them, and which they think cannot be accounted for from the common powers of nature." On the immediacy of this expectation, P. J. E. Kail explains, "The immediacy of the inference mimics the 'reading off' of an effect from cause, and the psychological difficulty of thinking of the effect without its cause mimics the genuine inconceivability or inseparability, mimic what a true grasp of necessity would entail." Kail, "Efficient Causation in Hume," 244.

74. In 1750, a real earthquake would halt the publication of the second edition of *An Enquiry Concerning Human Understanding*, bringing the metaphor home. Hume writes of his publisher, Andrew Millar, that he "had printed off some Months ago, a new Edition of certain philosophical Essays; but he tells me very gravely, that he has delay'd publishing because of the Earthquakes." Hume to John Clephane, April 18, 1750, *Letters of David Hume*, 1:141; cited in Hume, *Enquiry Concerning Human Understanding*, xxxvi–xxxvii.

1. Die Vorstadt, 2. Der Königliche Pallast, 3. Franciskaner, 4. Carmeliter, 5. Das Hospital, 6. Der Dom, 7. Das Castell, 8. S! Thomas 9. S! Vincent, 10. Die Mauth, 11. Der Tago Fluß, 12. Der Kriegshafen.

Joh. Andreas Stesslinger, excudit. Aug. Vind.

Joh. Andr. Stesslinger, excud. A. V.

FIGURE 7. Johann Michael Roth, "Lisbon before and after." From *Augsburgische Sammlung derer, wegen des höchstbetrübten Untergangs der Stadt Lissabon, vornemlich aber des in denen Königreichen Portugall und Spanien, ja bey nahe in allen Welt-Theilen die Winter-Monathe des 1755ten and 1756ten Jahres hindurch sich geäuserten gewaltigen Erdbebens*. Augsburg (1756). Photograph: Basel University Library.

FIGURE 8. Johan Henricus Giese, Tobacco box (late eighteenth century), Germany. Brass lid and base with copper sides; lid embossed with scene showing Lisbon before and after earthquake of 1755; figure of Neptune; inscription interior with original woodblock printed paper lining; (signed) Iserlohn, Germany. Dutch inscription reads: "Having risen in honor and esteem, I possessed more than kingdoms. But, alas, in what short time I was reduced to ashes and rubble." Photograph: © The Trustees of the British Museum.

after suggests another seemingly inevitable thing. Both generate catastrophic fantasies of knowing what lies beyond experience and perception. In the case of materialism, it is the insensible world of matter. The before and after also generates an image of unwitnessed (and for most people, unwitnessable) events. It might even dramatize the rush of receiving news from afar—another kind of horror. But there are also differences between these two experiences—and at least one that will illuminate our subject. The rapid succession of before and after rehearses the compulsiveness of the catastrophic thought without making any metaphysical claims upon the world. The before and after can suggest only a formal resemblance to the catastrophes of materialism, and it is in this sense that we might understand it as a different model. In what follows, I want to trace Kant's thought after the collapse of his precritical project, exploring how the Kantian sublime reproduces the style of catastrophic materialism, but without the content. While Kant publishes three short essays for popular consumption on the Lisbon disaster and the physical causes of earthquakes in 1756, it is in his later philosophy that we see him return to the problems posed by catastrophic materialism.[75]

The *Universal Natural History* was not very far from Kant's mind in 1790. In the following year, he would allow J. F. Genischen to publish an excerpt from the text as an appendix to a

75. Kant's three essays, *On the causes of earthquakes on the occasion of the calamity that befell the western countries of Europe towards the end of last year* (1756), *History and natural description of the most noteworthy occurrences of the earthquake that struck a large part of the Earth at the end of the year 1755* (1756), and *Continued observations on the earthquakes that have been experienced for some time* (1756), can be found in *Natural Science*, 327–36, 337–64, 365–73, respectively. Martin Schönfeld writes of these essays, "A superior methodological approach distinguished Kant's assertions from the guesses of his contemporaries. Instead of appealing to theological fantasies, or indulging in astrological superstitions, Kant searched for the facts and advanced empirically testable claims." Schönfeld, *Philosophy of the Young Kant*, 76

German translation of three essays by William Herschel.[76] The excerpt, however, only went as far as chapter 5 with an added footnote by Kant. Genischen reports that Kant would not let the remainder be reproduced, "for it contained too much that was mere hypothesis for him to be able to wholly approve of it still."[77] This certainly makes sense regarding what Kant had already called "arbitrary opinions" (the rings of Saturn reverie, the surface of the sun, his speculations about extraterrestrials, etc.), but also missing were Kant's reflections on the affective experience of catastrophizing. As we'll see, he would take up this problem in a different way in his account of the sublime.

Kant divides his conception of the sublime into the mathematical (which deals with quantity and extension—the idea of absolute greatness) and the dynamic (which concerns nature considered "in aesthetic judgment as a power that has no dominion over us").[78] In the latter, he explains, the mind seeks the images of nature's magnitude and violence outside of itself—images as found instruments of thought. Stripped of all their metaphysical and teleological ends, disasters and the grand spectacles of nature do not lead to any knowledge of the world beyond perception. They serve only to activate a kind of reflex. Kant explains:

> The *astonishment* bordering on terror, the horror and the awesome shudder, which grip the spectator in viewing mountain ranges towering to the heavens, deep ravines and the raging torrents in them, deeply shadowed wastelands inducing melancholy reflection, etc., is in view of the safety in which he knows himself to be, not actual fear, but only an attempt to involve ourselves in it by means of the imagination, in order to feel the

76. Herschel, *Über den Bau des Himmels*.
77. Herschel, *Über den Bau des Himmels*, 201. Genischen is cited and translated by Hastie in the introduction to Kant, *Kant's Cosmogony*, lviii.
78. Kant, *Critique of the Power of Judgment*, 153.

power of that very faculty, to combine the movement of the
mind thereby aroused with its calmness, and so to be superior
to nature within us, and thus also that outside us, insofar as it
can have an influence on our feeling of well-being.[79]

As the philosopher describes it, the mind sinks in relation to
the spectacle of natural violence such as a raging torrent, but
the phoenix (to recycle his earlier metaphor) rises again with
new powers. But this time the equivalent of the phoenix is
discovered *within* our minds rather than in the idea of nature
or in the soul. In the face of our failure to resist the violence
of nature's forces, we "discover within ourselves a capacity for
resistance of quite another kind, which gives us the courage
to measure ourselves against the apparent all-powerfulness of
nature."[80] Though the common usage of the word might suggest otherwise, the object of nature itself cannot be called sublime.[81] What is properly sublime in Kant's sense of the word is,
rather, the rational disposition revealed in the one who judges.

We might begin to compare the maker of Newtonian disasters in the pages of the *Universal Natural History* with this
seeker of aesthetic experience. In the first case, the image of disaster follows from the mind's contemplation of physical laws.
Disaster is the experience of the gravity of thought—an event
that appears to befall the mind. In the second case, the image
is already given: a gift from the world. We need only seek out
the violent and majestic spectacles of nature. The characteristic feeling of immensity that emerges from an encounter with

79. Kant, *Critique of the Power of Judgment*, 152.
80. Kant, *Critique of the Power of Judgment*, 144–45.
81. Kant explains: "Thus the feeling of the sublime in nature is respect for
our own vocation, which we show to an object in nature through a certain
subreption (substitution of a respect for the object instead of for the idea of
humanity in our subject), which as it were makes intuitable the superiority of
the rational vocation of our cognitive faculty over the greatest faculty of sensibility." Kant, *Critique of the Power of Judgment*, 141.

nature's violence is still of our own creation (the imagination rushing from an empirical view to what lies beyond the senses). But since writing his cosmogony, Kant seems to have discovered that one can achieve the highs and lows of catastrophizing without the commitment. The affective structure remains intact, and this is what counts. Like the formal juxtaposition of before and after, the sublime isolates and distills the structure of catastrophizing into a kind of pantomime—an empty parody of materialist catastrophizing raised to the level of pure form.

To understand the images of nature's magnitude or their affective experience as anything other than vehicles of reason, Kant says, would be to indulge a "delusion of the mind," which has the capacity to "destroy" it.[82] He might very well be thinking of Spinoza, a "great artist in delusions," whose "syncretistic talk" he describes in a letter to Friedrich Heinrich Jacobi as "magic lanterns, [which] make marvelous images appear for a moment but which soon vanish forever, though they leave behind in the minds of the uninformed a conviction that something unusual must be behind it all—something, however, that they cannot catch hold of."[83] By contrast, the sublime, he says, "carries with it no risk of *visionary rapture* [*Schwärmerei*], which is *a delusion of being able to see something beyond all bounds of sensibility*, i.e., to dream in accordance with principles (to rave with reason)."[84]

For Kant, *Schwärmerei*—a word that evokes the swarming of bees—connotes a religious or spiritual fanaticism.[85] Kant

82. Kant, *Critique of the Power of Judgment*, 157.
83. "Letter to F. H. Jacobi, August 30, 1789," in Kant, *Philosophical Correspondence*, 158; AK 11:76; discussed in Mensch, "Intuition and Nature in Kant and Goethe," 440.
84. Kant, *Critique of the Power of Judgment*, 156.
85. See the entry on "Madness/Insanity" in Cassin, Apter, Lezra, and Wood, eds., *Dictionary of Untranslatables*, 615: "Originally, the German noun *Schwärmerei* meant the agitation of bees, which move about without stop-

famously treats the question of *Schwärmerei* in a text that concerns the Swedish doctor and mystic Immanuel Swedenborg.
In addition to having partially anticipated Kant's own nebular
hypothesis (about the dispersion of primordial matter) in the
Universal Natural History, Swedenborg claimed he could com-
municate with the spirits of the dead. Kant, in a letter to Charlotte von Knobloch in 1763, recounts Swedenborg's vision of
a fire in Gothenburg in 1756 at fifty miles' distance, which was
later confirmed.[86] A more skeptical (and ironic) mood pervades
the *Dreams of a Spirit Seer* (1766), in which Kant links Swedenborg's fanaticism to the delusions of metaphysics and holds
the mirror up to himself.[87] There he writes: "So far we have
been wandering, like Democritus, in empty space, whither the
butterfly-wings of metaphysics have raised us, conversing there
with spirit-forms."[88] The irony of Kant comparing himself to
an atomist while speaking of "spirit-forms" demonstrates the

ping; more precisely, on the one hand, it means the disorderly movements of
each of the bees considered independently, and on the other hand, it means
the compact flight of the swarm forming a group, equally uncontrollable."

86. "Letter to Charlotte von Knobloch, August 10 1763," in Kant, *Correspondence*, 70–76.

87. Kant, *Dreams of a Spirit-Seer*, 343: "However, since the philosophy, with
which we have prefaced the work, was no less a fairy-story from the *cloud-
cuckoo-land* of metaphysics, I can see nothing improper about having them
make their appearance on the stage together. And, anyway, why should it be
more respectable to allow oneself to be misled by credulous trust in the soph-
istries of reason than to allow oneself to be deceived by an incautious belief
in delusory stories?"

88. Kant, *Dreams of a Spirit-Seer*, 354–55. Abbé Barruel would later argue
that Swedenborg's so-called spiritualist universe was just materialism by another name: "Swedenborg, anterior to the derangement of his mind, had
formed a system leading to Materialism; and this continued deeply rooted in
his mind after his illness. He then added his male and female spirits, and some
extravagances of the same nature. With respect to the remainder of his system, he follows up his principles in a consequent manner, and unfortunately
the whole tends to Materialism." Barruel, *Memoirs*, 3:90.

extent to which *all* metaphysics—including the metaphysics of materialism—was beginning to feel like a dream.[89] In another context, Kant's contemporary Moses Mendelssohn cites Democritus as an authority on the difference between dreaming and sleeping: "When one dreams, each of us possesses his own world, and when we awaken, we all cross over to a common world."[90] But to rove through empty space "like Democritus" was already to dream while awake—to "rave with reason." As Kant explains elsewhere, "The play of fantasy with the human being in sleep is called dreaming . . . ; on the other hand if it happens while the human being is awake, it reveals a diseased condition."[91]

Kant knew very well how easily one might find oneself in such a condition. In "On the Power of the Mind to Master Its Morbid Feelings by Sheer Resolution," the philosopher gives us an anatomy of his own melancholy, particularly the experience of "hypochondria," which he describes as "the exact opposite of the mind's power to master its pathological feelings . . . , the weakness of abandoning oneself despondently to general morbid feelings that have no definite object (and so making no

89. In *Metaphysical Foundations of Natural Science*, Kant argues against the tradition of atomism "from Democritus of old, up to Descartes" and the need for "fabrications" such as empty space: "Everything that relieves us of the need to resort to empty spaces is a real gain for natural science, for they give the imagination far too much freedom to make up by fabrication for the lack of any inner knowledge of nature. In the doctrine of nature, the absolutely empty and the absolutely dense are approximately what blind accident and blind fate are in metaphysical science, namely, an obstacle to the governance of reason, whereby it is either supplanted by fabrication or lulled to rest on the pillow of occult qualities." Kant, *Metaphysical Foundations of Natural Science*, 71.

90. Mendelssohn, *Last Works*, 47. As the editor points out in the notes, Mendelssohn has his pre-Socratics mixed up; these words are attributed to Heraclitus, not Democritus (*Last Works*, 188n2).

91. Kant, *Anthropology from a Pragmatic Point of View*, 68.

attempt to master them by reason)."[92] Kant attributes his own hypochondria to purely mechanical (physical) causes that allow him to ignore it by "diverting my attention from this feeling, as if it had nothing to do with me."[93] This may have been easier said than done. As his eighteenth- and nineteenth-century biographers report, Kant continued to suffer from hypochondria in various ways later in life—for example, believing that the "electric condition of the atmosphere" was making him sick after a learned paper he had read on the topic suggested the possibility to him.[94] "Now he ascribed nearly everything to the electricity of the atmosphere," one early biographer reports, "and though the sky might be perfectly clear or in any measure cloudy, it was equally regarded by him as an indication of that state of the air which was dangerous to life."[95] It was apparently an idea that he clung to with such great "tenacity that no amount of argument could change his opinion."[96]

In his *Anthropology from a Pragmatic Point of View*, written around the same time he was apparently worrying about electricity in the air, Kant returns to the subject of melancholy and the disorders that follow from it. Among those he lists here are "*insania*," "a deranged *power of judgment* in which the mind is held in suspense by means of analogies that are confused with concepts of similar things."[97] The "power of the imagi-

92. Kant, "On the Power of the Mind to Master Its Morbid Feelings," 318. See also Kant's discussion in "Essay on the Maladies of the Head," in *Observations on the Feeling of the Beautiful and the Sublime*, 211–12. On Kant's experience of hypochondria, see Shell, *Embodiment of Reason*, 264–305.

93. Kant, "On the Power of the Mind to Master Its Morbid Feelings," 319. Clark links Kant's phrase "as if it had nothing to do with me" to the idea of "negative attentiveness"—"the ability to attend to something by holding it away." Clark, "We 'Other Prussians,'" 272.

94. Stuckenberg, *Life of Immanuel Kant*, 439.

95. Stuckenberg, *Life of Immanuel Kant*, 439; cited and discussed in Johnson, "Tree of Melancholy," 53–54.

96. Stuckenberg, *Life of Immanuel Kant*, 439.

97. Kant, *Anthropology from a Pragmatic Point of View*, 109.

nation," he explains, "in a play resembling understanding, conjures up a connection of disparate things as universal."[98] Another is *"vesania,"* a "sickness of a deranged *reason,"* which is when the patient "imagin[es] that he conceives the inconceivable," including "the unveiling of the supersensible forces of nature."[99] This latter kind he classifies as *"systematic,"* hinting at the ways in which mental illness coincides with philosophical system making—and with his own practice of it in the *Universal Natural History*.[100] As we have seen, Kant revisits the matter of pathological thoughts in the first footnote to the third *Critique*, describing a "causality which not even the consciousness of inefficiency for producing the effect can deter from straining towards it."

Catastrophizing is one such "causality," which suggests another way of understanding what Kant means by *"a delusion of being able to see something beyond all bounds of sensibility."* While he links the notion of *Schwärmerei* to the Platonists and to spiritualists like Swedenborg, there is also the kind of rational "seeing" by analogy he himself had been exploring in the *Universal Natural History*—a "seeing" that closely aligns him again with the "sublime" or deranged poet of atoms and the void. According to Lucretius himself, the task of the poet was to seek "by what words and what poetry at last I may be able to display clear lights before your mind, whereby you may see into the heart of things hidden."[101] Kant begins the second part of the

98. Kant, *Anthropology from a Pragmatic Point of View*, 109–10.

99. Kant, *Anthropology from a Pragmatic Point of View*, 110.

100. Kant, *Anthropology from a Pragmatic Point of View*, 110. Alexander M. Schultz has put it nicely: "The inmate of the mental hospital, who suffers from *vesania*, 'the sickness of a deranged *reason*'—'die Krankheit einer gestörten Vernunft'—is the twin brother of the systematic philosopher." Schlutz, *Mind's World*, 117.

101. Lucretius, *De rerum natura* 1.143–45. Schrijvers has noted, "Lucretian expressions such as *mente (animo) videre* ('to see with the mind,' cf. 1.143–5; 5.149); and the phrases *oculi animi (mentis)*, *acies mentis (animi)* ('the eyes/sight

Universal Natural History with lines from Pope's *Essay on Man* instructing the reader repeatedly to "see" with the mind's eye.[102]

In the *Universal Natural History*, as in *De rerum natura*, we recall, this kind of seeing with the mind is made possible by the instrument of analogy.[103] That Kant may still have had this kind of analogy on his mind in the third *Critique* is suggested by the conspicuous return to the problems raised in the *Universal Natural History*, which we are invited to look at again with fresh eyes. With respect to the sublime, he insists, we must judge the heavens not as we did earlier, as "worlds inhabited by rational beings, taking the bright points with which we see the space above us to be filled as their suns, about which they move in their purposively appointed orbits," but only as a "broad, all-embracing vault," that is, as raw sensory data.[104] If he has once again taken the mental structure of catastrophizing from the Epicureans (the seemingly automatic shudder), this time he has made sure to empty it of its metaphysical content. The idea of

---

of the mind'), used frequently by Cicero, seem to a great extent to have been introduced into Latin by these authors." Schrijvers, "Seeing the Invisible," 280.

102. Kant quotes the following lines: "See plastic Nature working to this end, / The single atoms each to other tend / Attract, attracted to, the next in place, / Formed and impelled its neighbour to embrace, / See Matter next, with various life endu'd, / Press to one centre still." Kant, *Universal Natural History*, 225. Kant is using Brockes's German translation of Pope. Pope, *Aus dem Englischen übersetzter Versuch vom Menschen des Herrn Alexander Pope*, 59. It is as if Kant is once again using Pope to supply a Newtonian riposte to the vatic poetry of Lucretius.

103. In the first *Critique*, Kant would severely limit his claims for the use of such analogies: "The rungs of such a ladder, such as experience can give them to us, stand too far apart from one another, and what we presume to be small differences are commonly such wide gaps in nature itself that on the basis of such observations . . . nothing can be figured out about the intentions of nature." Kant goes on to say that such methods provide "a legitimate and excellent regulative principle of reason," but "[go] much too far for experience or observation ever to catch up with it." Kant, *Critique of Pure Reason*, 604. See Shea, "Filled with Wonder," 114–15.

104. Kant, *Critique of the Power of Judgment*, 152.

freedom that proceeds from the sublime, he insists, "entirely precludes any positive presentation. . . . The moral law is sufficient in itself in us and originally determining, so that it does not even allow us to look around for a determining ground outside of it."[105]

But to keep things empty (that is, free of concepts) and to keep us from "looking around," Kant must carefully manage the narrative of this reflex. To better understand why and what he means by the "risk of *visionary rapture*," we might turn briefly to another early text, *The Only Possible Argument for the Existence of God* (1763), in which we find him rehashing many of the arguments of his still little-known *Universal Natural History*. I am thinking now of his reflection in a note on what is good about traditional physicotheology. The short answer is not much. But one thing that Kant points to is the sudden stroke of imagination that overtakes the mind with an "intuitive concept." He explains:

> When, among other things, I consider the microscopic observations of Dr Hill, which are to be found in the *Hamburger Magazin*, when I see numerous animal species in a single drop of water, predatory kinds equipped with instruments of destruction, intent upon the pursuit of their prey, but in their turn annihilated by the still more powerful tyrants of this aquatic world; when I contemplate the intrigues, the violence, the scenes of commotion in a single particle of matter, and when from thence I direct my gaze upwards to the immeasurable spaces of the heavens teeming with worlds as with specks of dust—when I contemplate all this, no human language can express the feelings aroused by such a thought; and all subtle metaphysical analysis falls far short of the sublimity and dignity of such an intuition.[106]

105. Kant, *Critique of the Power of Judgment*, 156–57.
106. Kant, *Only Possible Argument*, 159.

If this is an example of the "intuitive concept" of physicotheology, it is a curious one. While Kant concludes with a turn to the notions of "sublimity" and "dignity," the passage feels as chaotic as the roving dust it unsettles. We know from experience, for example, that the dust Kant evokes here might suddenly send our imaginations rushing from the idea of motes in the sun to an unseen world of matter. What's to keep a materialist thought from co-opting this "intuitive concept," or a philosopher like Pascal from falling suddenly into despair from a similar kind of encounter? In his *Anthropology from a Pragmatic Point of View*, Kant will explicitly distance himself from Pascal's "terrifying and fearful" ideas when he warns against "concern-[ing] oneself in the least with spying" into oneself, and producing, "as it were, the affected composition of an inner history of the *involuntary* course of one's thoughts and feelings."[107] What's to keep a philosopher from turning to a hylozoist model of the universe?[108] These kinds of sensible presentations threaten to devolve into any number of "arbitrary opinions." The discoveries of Newton were meant to provide a more solid support to intuition (i.e., transforming the image of the night sky as vast

107. Kant, *Anthropology from a Pragmatic Point of View*, 22; discussed in the introduction. Kant would appear to return to the dreadful vision of Pascal's eternal silence in infinite space in his recounting of "Carazan's dream": "As I approached the most extreme limit of nature, I noticed that the shadows of the boundless void sank into the abyss before me. A fearful realm of eternal silence, solitude and darkness! Unspeakable dread overcame me at this sight." Kant, *Observations on the Feeling of the Beautiful and the Sublime*, 17. This is fitting, for Kant uses Pascal to warn against the dangers of too much introspection, and "Carazan's dream" is an allegory about the value of other people. On Carazan's dream, see Arendt, *Lectures on Kant's Political Philosophy*, 11–12; Fenves, *Peculiar Fate*, 73.

108. As Kant wrote, with Leibniz possibly as his target, in *Metaphysical Foundations of Natural Science*, "The possibility of a proper natural science rests entirely and completely on the law of inertia (along with that of the persistence of substance). The opposite of this, and thus also the death of all natural philosophy, would be hylozoism." Kant, *Metaphysical Foundations of Natural Science*, 84. See Mensch, "Intuition and Nature in Kant and Goethe," 442.

expanse into a system ordered by principles), but metaphysics, as Kant had discovered, was a wide and dangerous sea—and he was already feeling seasick. Even defining the basic objects of inquiry was a difficult (if not impossible) task. As he says elsewhere in *The Only Possible Argument*, reaching again for the microscope, "The so very abstract nature of the object itself obstructs every effort at greater clarification, just as the employment of microscopic devices for seeing both enlarges the image of the object so that its minute parts can be discerned but it also proportionally diminishes the brightness and vivacity of the impression."[109]

The sublime focuses the affective structure of catastrophizing by eliminating the possibility of the mind leaping abruptly to metaphysical conclusions or falling into doubt. Divested of all rational principles and teleology, the sky is now simply a wide expanse, a "mirror," and the sea is the sea as the "poets describe it"—a suggestion that led Paul de Man to reflect on the nature of what he called Kant's "materialism." De Man explains: "The sea is called a mirror, not because it is supposed to reflect anything, but to stress a flatness devoid of any suggestion of depth."[110] Attending to the same passage in the third *Critique*, Porter has argued for a more specific debt, drawing an analogy between Kant's transcendental conditions and the insensible world of matter: "The parallels with Lucretius, echoes indeed, ought to be plain—so plain, in fact, that one has to suspect a certain awareness on Kant's part that he is working in a Lucretian, or at the very least atomistic, tradition."[111] Kant had already said as much himself in the *Universal Natural History*. But, as we know, to be "aware" of one's influences is not the same thing as to be in control of them.

Notably, according to Porter, Kant had already stumbled

109. Kant, *Only Possible Argument*, 125.
110. De Man, *Aesthetic Ideology*, 83.
111. Porter, "Lucretius and the Sublime," 180.

upon an aspect of the sublime in the problem of temporal succession, reaching for the Epicurean idea of "prolepsis," or "anticipation," in the first *Critique*. Porter observes: "Every moment of sensation is inhabited or inhibited, from the perspective of critical philosophy, by the sublime, in the form of its anticipation."[112] To put it another way, the most ordinary experience of perception was full of earthquakes to come. The sublime that emerges out of "anticipation" and the gaps in experience raises an important question about the temporality of the sublime itself—and the ways that Kant attempts to narrate it. As he says in one place, "That is sublime which pleases immediately [*unmittelbar*] through its resistance to the interest of the senses."[113] The sense of "immediately" here is simply "unmediated," and need not imply a temporal dimension.[114] But time creeps into the story—as time so often does. Elsewhere in the third *Critique*, Kant tells us that the feeling of the sublime "is a pleasure that arises only indirectly, being generated, namely, by the feeling of a momentary [*augenblicklichen*] inhibition of the vital powers and the immediately [*sogleich*] following and all the more powerful outpouring of them."[115] As Paul Guyer has noted, Kant describes the sublime as both a "single yet complex feeling" and a "sequence of feelings."[116] Kant wants it both ways.

We see this ambivalence most vividly in his discussion of the mathematical sublime where Kant compares the movement of the sublime to an *Erschütterung*, "a vibration, i.e., to a rapidly

112. Porter, "Lucretius and the Sublime," 183.
113. Kant, *Critique of the Power of Judgment*, 150; AK 5:267.
114. In the *Critique of Pure Reason*, Kant defines intuition with regard to space and time as a form of "immediate" and singular perception: "In whatever way and through whatever means a cognition may relate to objects, that through which it relates immediately to them, and at which all thought as a means is directed as an end, is intuition." Kant, *Critique of Pure Reason*, 155.
115. Kant, *Critique of the Power of Judgment*, 128–29; AK 5:245.
116. Guyer, *Kant and the Experience of Freedom*, 204.

alternating repulsion from and attraction to one and the same object," consciously or unconsciously evoking the image and language of earthquakes.[117] The "thing" from which the mind is repulsed, he says, is "as it were an abyss, in which it fears to lose itself."[118] The idea of a vibration also suggests a temporal succession, though, Kant explains, what begins as a "vibration" resolves into a cancellation—an annihilation of time: "The comprehension in one moment [*Augenblick*] of that which is successively apprehended, is a regression, which in turn cancels the time-condition in the progression of the imagination and makes *simultaneity* intuitable."[119] The idea of this "regression" will ultimately allow him to argue that the "exposition of the judgments on the sublime in nature was at the same time [*zugleich*] their deduction. . . . [It] immediately [*sofort*] contains the deduction, i.e., the justification of the claim of such a judgment to universally necessary validity."[120] Here, too, Kant finds the beginning in the end.

It is thus with precise irony that the Kantian sublime—with

---

117. Kant, *Critique of the Power of Judgment*, 141; AK 5:258. For the natural philosophic use of the word *Erschütterung*, see, for example, the title of one of Kant's three treatises on the Lisbon disaster: *Geschichte und Naturbeschreibung der merkwürdigsten Vorfäelle des Erdbebens, welches an dem Ende des 1755sten Jahres einen größen Teil der Erde erschüttert hat* (1756). Gene Ray has argued, "Unmistakably, we can feel the memory of Lisbon in Kant's metaphor and word choice: the sublime moves the mind like the tremors or deep shudders of an earthquake. Amidst all the vibrating, gushing and shaking, this natural object that defeats the imagination opens up like an abyss." Ray, "Reading the Lisbon Earthquake," 10. However, Ray goes on to note, nowhere does Kant explicitly mention the disaster at Lisbon in the third *Critique*—an absence that is "surely symptomatic of an 'interest,' if not remembered anxiety" (10).

118. Kant, *Critique of the Power of Judgment*, 141; AK 5:258.

119. Kant, *Critique of the Power of Judgment*, 141; 5:258–59. As Rudolf Makkreel has argued, "The comparison with a convulsion is used only as an image for the movement. . . . Kant's full analysis indicates that he maintains the simultaneity of the displeasure and pleasure in the feeling of the sublime." Makkreel, *Imagination and Interpretation in Kant*, 78–79.

120. Kant, *Critique of the Power of Judgment*, 161; AK 5:280.

its conspicuous debts to catastrophic materialism—effects a kind of philosophical amnesia: a forgetting of the history of disaster's making and a burying of Kant's own disasters. What Ernst Cassirer once wrote of the difference between aesthetic consciousness and practical consciousness applies here: "The aesthetic consciousness possesses in itself that form of concrete realization through which, wholly abandoned to its temporary passivity, it grasps in this fleeting passivity a factor of purely timeless meaning. The 'before' and 'after' that we objectify conceptually in the idea of causal relation and shape into the empirical time sequence and time order, are here blotted out and brought to a standstill equally with that foresight and aiming at a goal which characterizes our desire and willing."[121] In this sense, aesthetic consciousness is also a relation to history—a forgetting that translates the before and after into the timeless. But the afterimage of "vibration" persists—a memory of desire and willing, a memory of earthquakes. Alfredo Ferrarin has written of the first *Critique*, "Kant's project of a critique of pure reason takes on so many forms and changes aspect so many times that its land should be studied the way the earth is studied by seismologists."[122] The same might be said of the third. When the philosopher's "vibration" admits of time, the sublime suggests the continued importance of the materialist's catastrophic style—a style he restages in his mind (albeit under more carefully controlled conditions). If the idea of the sublime emerges at least in part as a reaction to the compulsive structure of catastrophizing, it also preserves its addiction.[123] In this sense, to remember the making of disaster *before* the sublime is to dig up the problematic at its heart. As

121. Cassirer, *Kant's Life and Thought*, 310.

122. Ferrarin, *Powers of Pure Reason*, 4.

123. Clark brilliantly describes the relation between "the 'aesthetically consuming subject' that is modelled in the *Critique of Judgment*, and the subject metabolizing drugs as it is described in the *Anthropology*." Clark, "We 'Other Prussians,'" 273.

Kant says in his *Anthropology from a Pragmatic Point of View,* "We play with the imagination frequently and gladly, but imagination (as fantasy) plays just as frequently with us, and sometimes very inconveniently."[124] Needless to say, we are still catastrophizing—both in sympathy with and in spite of Kant.

124. Kant, *Anthropology from a Pragmatic Point of View,* 68. We find a similar thought articulated in one of Kant's notebook reflections from the 1670s: "We play with images, or images play with us." Cited and discussed in Shell, *Embodiment of Reason,* 271–72.

Catastrophizing in the Age of Climate Change

The word "catastrophizer" has recently become an accusation on the part of climate deniers and others who would say that there's no reason to believe the worst (i.e., either that climate change doesn't exist or that its costs may be real but not unmanageable).[1] The implication is that the prophets of ecocatastrophe are making too much of too little—or even something out of nothing. On the other end of the spectrum, some ecocritics have suggested that a preoccupation with the end or the catastrophic worst is bad for environmental thinking and therefore bad for us: an addictive plot that makes us both despairing and indisposed to action.[2] In these final pages, I want to make a different proposal: that we may not be able to avoid catastrophizing in spite of our best efforts, and that, as we face the frightening effects of climate change, catastrophizing may be something we can't do without.

1. See, for example, Cass, "Problem with Climate Catastrophizing."
2. Catherine Keller has written, for example, "As to scary weather, those in the state of unacknowledged apocalypticism will simply not perceive any possible connection between an old text and the current reality, but they may be inclined to *expect* the burning of the rainforests, for instance. And they may feel some mix of foreboding and inevitability about the 'the environment,' enabling their own numbed complicity in the economic system that is causing the end of the world for so many Amazonian species, and threatening it for innumerable ethnic minorities." Keller calls for a rhetoric of "counterapocalypse," which "recognizes itself as a kind of apocalypse; but then it will try to interrupt the habit." Keller, *Apocalypse Now and Then*, 8, 19.

In this book, I have tried to recover a history of catastrophizing in the early modern period as a way of seeing and feeling beyond the sensible that returns us to fundamental questions about the nature of the world and the mind's desire and capacity to grasp it. I've argued that the idea of catastrophizing helps us to rethink what we mean when we talk about materialism—to understand materialism less as an intellectual or philosophical commitment (a thing we might consciously affirm or deny) than as an epistemological style, a mental reflex with purchase well beyond its native discourses of philosophy and science. The question now is, what can this history say to our current moment of unprecedented "environmental crisis"—a phrase perhaps already "inflected" by the catastrophic imagination?[3]

As I was writing this book, I watched Hurricane Irma barreling toward Tampa, where much of my family now lives—before it swerved slightly east and lost some of its momentum. Hurricanes such as Irma are becoming increasingly more frequent—and global warming has had a decisive hand in their making. However, if anticipating the potential havoc of such a storm is not catastrophizing in the sense of making too much of too little, it might be catastrophizing in the other sense to which this book has called attention: an experience of the imperceptible mediated by the image of disaster. A hurricane exists in the mind both as a real event (an imminent threat to oneself or one's family) and as an image—a vehicle for imagining and feeling what we can't see with our eyes or touch with our hands. With the slightest coaxing, the mind leaps from the event to the idea of a system of invisible causes.

But catastrophizing, as we know, does not require actual disasters. A catastrophic image might spring to mind even from the most ordinary of perceptions. Timothy Morton has recently

3. Garrard, *Ecocriticism*, 93.

pointed out that global warming has made it increasingly difficult to talk about even "everyday" weather innocently.[4] The
perception of an unusually hot (or cold) day can suddenly set
into motion unbidden thoughts of the hidden world beyond
us—the catastrophe that is global warming and the disasters for
which it is and will be responsible. The most common of social
pleasantries has become a lesson in catastrophizing.

For environmental critics such as Bill McKibben, the figure
of extreme nature vacillates between the realm of physical
event and sign or metaphor, materializing the imperceptible
even as it short-circuits the possibility of assurance. Reflecting
on living in the Adirondack Mountains, for example, he writes:
"In the past decade, a great windstorm and an epic ice storm
have passed through here, leveling thousands of square miles
of forest. By the old way of reckoning, these were not disasters,
just extreme incidences of the powerful forces that made this
place. But now who knows what mixture of 'nature' and of 'us'
they embody? Who knows what they mean?"[5] Disaster ma-
terializes scientific data into feeling; in this case, it also prompts
epistemological modesty.

Still, for some critics, McKibben is a "catastrophizer" in the
more negative sense of that word. Greg Garrard observes: "*The
End of Nature* . . . is haunted by both the ubiquity and unreli-
ability of the 'signs' of climatic change. . . . McKibben's apocalyptic rhetoric effectively produces the irreparable crisis it
claims only to identify."[6] Garrard is right to point us to the
potential dangers of such rhetoric, but here he misses the
critical (and perceptual) function of "produc[ing]" disaster in
McKibben's account. Catastrophizing opens up the spatial and

4. Morton, *Hyperobjects*, 99: "A hyperobject has ruined the weather conversation, which functions as part of a neutral screen that enables us to have a
human drama in the foreground."

5. McKibben, *End of Nature*, xix.

6. Garrard, *Ecocriticsm*, 106.

temporal frame of the picture; at the same time, reflection on the uncertainty born of the mind's catastrophes keeps the window open for investigation.

The truth of the matter—the truth of *matter*—is that we have never really stopped catastrophizing—that is, generating the image of disaster in order to see and feel beyond the sensible. Catastrophizing is a kind of laboratory for feeling that helps us mentally grasp the nature of things—a reflexive reminder that induction often requires an affective process. Thus, even as Morton himself casts the idea of disaster aside for what he calls "hyperobjects"—entities such as global warming that are "massively distributed in time and space relative to humans"—he can't help but reach for the metaphor of disaster to describe the *experience* of coming into contact with such outsized "objects."[7] The first chapter of *Hyperobjects* is called "A Quake in Being." If it is true that new concepts such as climate change "put unbearable strains on our normal ways of reasoning," as Morton suggests, it is perhaps more important than ever to recapture the history of the mind's making of disaster, lest our catastrophizing be of the less reflective—or even world-negating—kind.[8]

7. Morton, *Hyperobjects*, 1. Morton writes: "There's no doubt that cosmic phenomena such as meteors and blood-red Moons, tsunamis, tornadoes, and earthquakes have terrified humans in the past. Meteors and comets were known as disasters. Literally, a disaster is a fallen, dysfunctional, or dangerous, or evil star (*dis-astron*). But such disasters take place against a stable background in at least two senses. There is the Ptolemaic-Aristotelian machinery of the spheres, which hold the fixed stars in place. . . . Meanwhile, back on Earth, the shooting star is a portent that makes sense as a trace on the relatively stable horizon of earth and sky. . . . It seems as if there is something about hyperobjects that is more deeply challenging than these 'disasters'" (*Hyperobjects*, 15–16).

8. Morton, *Hyperobjects*, book copy. Porter usefully connects the notion of the "hyperobject" to the work of the Aetna poet in Porter, *Sublime in Antiquity*, 511n388.

This history presents us with several useful ideas. The first is that we are not always in control of when or how we catastrophize. In his 1964 essay, "The Ecology of the Mind," Harry Berger describes the mind's desire to verify the real through confrontation: "The real as such is indeterminate until the mind confronts it, or feels that it is itself confronted, and the content is determined by what the mind is looking for in a particular case—it may be an atom, the prime mover, gravitation, a person, God, etc."[9] One might easily add climate change to this list. The mind *feels*—and confirms—events it can't grasp with the senses. This is not in the least to suggest that climate change is a fiction. It is simply to pay attention to the action of the mind when we contemplate the insensible. Our affective encounter with the otherness of what lies beyond our senses cannot *prove* the existence of either atoms or global warming. In other words, it cannot replace scientific data. When we are self-conscious about its involuntariness, however, catastrophizing can put us in the right frame of mind for apprehending the reality of such outsized "things"—with or against our visceral feeling about what is real. In this way, it can make them thinkable.

In the face of so much resistance to the very idea of climate change, this capacity for imaginative thought can hardly be underestimated. To counteract what is unthinkable about global warming, as the contemporary novelist Amitav Ghosh has suggested, may mean taking off the blinders of gradualism. It may mean becoming catastrophists, or rather paying attention to the imaginative disasters we already make. Ghosh remarks, "I suspect that human beings were generally catastrophists at heart until their instinctive awareness of the earth's unpredictability was gradually supplanted by a belief in uniformitarianism—a regime of ideas that was supported by scientific theories . . . and also by a range of governmental practices

9. Berger, "Ecology of the Mind," 413.

that were informed by statistics and probability."[10] According to Ghosh, our own narrative habits are at least part of what has made the idea of global warming difficult to imagine. As we've seen, conjuring up catastrophe (whether in the deep past or imminent future) has a way of relativizing time and space, of reminding us that what we perceive before us is only a fraction of the whole, and of putting us in our place. If the sensational immediacy of events of natural catastrophe has occluded the "slow violence" of environmental disasters, the effects of which have been unevenly distributed across populations, catastrophizing might make such effects visible and felt by reconfiguring "environmental time."[11] Thus even the mental catastrophes that in moments seem to befall us can be instruments of ecological thought, transforming the imperceptible into an affective experience.

Yet catastrophizing also reminds us of the dangers of becoming too attached to our disastrous fantasies—of mistaking such compelling images for the end of thought or the impossibility of action. In this sense, catastrophizing embodies both the possibility and the risks of an environmental discourse yoked to the idea of crisis—demonstrating the troubling intimacy between perceiving what lies beyond our senses and the sense of paralysis (or, even worse, appetite for denial) that experience can induce. We are reminded again of the double lure of Democritus's pit—the fantasy that we might perceive the insensible world with something like certainty and the equally stupefying thought that we can know nothing at all. The history of catastrophizing we've traced in this book shows how easily (and indeed unexpectedly) catastrophizing can shift from a mode of confronting the insensible to a bad habit or compulsion—and how looking at something can blur into a reaction against having to look straight at it. In the case of cli-

10. Ghosh, *Great Derangement*, 25.
11. Nixon, *Slow Violence*, 64.

mate change, the vehemence of one's willful blindness in the face of so much scientific evidence might be one index of the strength of the mind's initial confrontation. To be touched by the feeling of the ungraspable is not necessarily to be enlightened by it.

The history of catastrophizing teaches us, however, that there are opportunities for agency in the moment of response—if not in the initial experience. Perhaps more than anyone in this story (one possible exception is Montaigne), Leonardo models a form of detachment that allows us to perceive our relation to the insensible as an object of thought—and to take advantage of the perceptual and critical powers of catastrophizing without losing ourselves to fictions of mastery. The artist's notebooks capture the contingency of thought responding to the world and reflexively to itself, showing how one might be possessed by the idea of disaster in one moment only to discover an opening for reflection in the next. Perhaps the thing I admire most about Leonardo is the way he makes a home between perspectives. If we are to understand a phenomenon such as climate change and our "particles of implication" in what is happening all around us, we too must find a way to be at home between shifting frames—to be both the catastrophizer and the calm observer of mental catastrophe at once.[12] Learning to make disaster in this sense might very well be a matter of survival.[13]

12. I'm borrowing the phrase "particles of implication" from the poet Brenda Hillman, who writes: "We find ourselves amidst conditions on earth that involve not only the ignorant choices we have made as humans but a kind of dispersal of those activities, in tiny particles of implication, throughout the planet." Hume, "Imagining Ecopoetics," 754. I am grateful to Anna Goodson for pointing me to this source.

13. My argument here is not that catastrophic thinking fuels the environmental movement, but only that catastrophizing opens up a possibility for self-reflection. Cf. Veldman, "Narrating the Environmental Apocalypse," 17: "With both the weight of tradition and the power to bind people together,

In closing, I will suggest that one way to cultivate our habits of catastrophizing—to make them work for us—is to look back to the history of the mind's disasters. I don't mean history here as a definitive tale of origins—a genealogy of how we got to where we are. As I said at the start, my interest has been less in the familiar narratives of progress that bring us from superstition to the triumph of reason than in ordinary habits of mind and patterns of thought that represent different solutions to the enduring problem of perceiving what lies beyond our grasp. The "old" materialism teaches us that catastrophizing is a sign of the mind attempting to come into contact with the insensible by means of its own devices. We are right to be "haunted" by it, for we can neither dismiss such a sign nor mistake it for a certain prediction. We can, however, learn to make good use of it.

In our present moment, catastrophizing reminds us of something that should seem obvious but rarely is: that we've had a hand in making the disaster we feel befalling us—a lesson that translates from the realm of imagination to the physical world in which our destructive impact is all too real. In these pages, I've attempted to show how excavating the history of catastrophizing in materialist thought is one way of harnessing its critical potential. In this regard, this book has sought to participate in the shift of attention that it describes. By following a principle of resonance in lieu of causal connection, by emphasizing a practice of juxtaposition and analogy in place of genealogy, and by encouraging the cultivation of imaginative projection into experiences mediated to us by art, I have tried to suggest that looking back may itself be one act of ecocritical awareness. For in inhabiting the catastrophes of other minds we put our modern habits of creating disasters into relief, at once making

---

the narrative of environmental apocalypse is thus a potent source for motivating environmentally ethical behavior."

the critical potential of catastrophizing more readily available and allowing us to see its dangers with clearer eyes. In the war on sensibility—and the war on reality—that is currently being waged, the imaginative thought of the past remains one of our most vital resources. It is also a portent of the intellectual pitfalls we face as we come to terms with our disastrous present and future.

ACKNOWLEDGMENTS

I am thankful for the extraordinary community of scholars and friends near and far who have played a role in the making of this book. For their generosity in engaging with my work in progress, for the example of their scholarship, and for their insights, I want to thank Lydia Barnett, Brooke Belisle, Raz Chen-Morris, David Clark, Martin Clayton, Deborah Coen, Jeffrey Jerome Cohen, Sam Cohn, Jeff Dolven, Kathy Eden, Claire Farago, Hal Foster, Andrea Frisch, Meredith Gill, Robert Goulding, Miguel A. Granada, Kenneth Gross, Achsah Guibbory, Tim Harrison, Christopher Johnson, Jacques Lezra, Megan Marshall, Alessandra Natale, Anahid Nersessian, Joanna Picciotto, Steven Pincus, Jay Reed, Josh Scodel, Anita Sherman, Bill Sherman, Dan Shore, Susan Stewart, Richard Strier, Jean Strouse, Gordon Teskey, Henry Turner, Jennifer Waldron, Robert Westman, Leah Whittington, Gareth Williams, Seth Williams, and Catherine Wilson.

I am especially grateful to Reid Barbour, Leonard Barkan, Anthony Grafton, Nigel Smith, and Jessica Wolfe, whose influence on my work has been profound. Stephen Campbell has been an angel from the beginning. Jim Porter lights up the void. I am thankful to Lauren Berlant for her rare friendship and for teaching me what it means to "show up." Julia Fish and Richard Rezac have been perpetual sources of inspiration in things both great and small. For their sustaining friendships, I want to thank Kevin Adams, J. K. Barrett, Adrienne Brown, Michael Burke, Corey Byrnes, Thom Cantey, Allan Christensen, Drew Daniel, Nicholas Elliott, Bryan Ewsichek, Harris Feinsod, Andy Ferguson, Andrea Gadberry, Alfredo Gadberry-Castillo, Andrew Gilson, Amber Gross, Rob Hardies, Brooke Holmes, Beth Johnston, Meredith Johnston, Emily Licht, Darin Mcanelly, Lisa Mignone, Molly Murray, Chris Nealon, Julia Otis, Dana Prescott, Philip Rand, David Ray, Zach Samalin, David Sartorius, Dash Shaw, Alan Stewart, Jean Strouse, Sonali Thakkar, Tristram Wolff, and Wes Yu.

The exceptional intelligence and generosity of my colleagues and students in English and comparative literature at the University of Maryland have shaped this book in more ways that I can count. I am grateful to Luka Arsenjuk, Amanda Bailey, Ralph Bauer, Kent Cartwright, Tita Chico, Kim Coles, Theresa Coletti, Oliver Gaycken, Matt Kirschenbaum, Ted Leinwand, Garth Libhart, Liz Papazian, Scott Trudell, and Edlie Wong. The late Marshall Grossman is still very much in mind and heart. I owe special thanks to Maud Casey, Sangeeta Ray, Kellie Robertson, and Orrin Wang. I have had the honor of coteaching two graduate seminars on materialism and ecopoetics with Josh Weiner, who has been a brilliant friend and interlocutor. I also want to thank Randy Petilos, the best of editors, Susan Karani, and everyone else at the University of Chicago Press. I am grateful to Beth Johnston and Amberle Sherman for their editorial acumen and to Marian Rogers for her attention to the manuscript in copyediting.

The research and writing of this book were framed by two institutions without which it could not have been written: the National Humanities Center and the New York Public Library's Cullman Center for Scholars and Writers. Writing about Leonardo with a view of the sea in Bogliasco—and the storms I experienced there—fundamentally changed my understanding of Leonardo's disasters; I thank the Bogliasco Foundation for that precious time. A year in Rome and the community of people I met there continue to feed the soul. I am thankful, as always, to the Museum of Jurassic Technology.

Learned audiences at the American University, University of Chicago, Columbia University, Harvard University, New York University, the University of Pittsburgh, Princeton University, the University of California's Santa Cruz and Los Angeles campuses, and the University of Massachuetts, Amherst, have contributed to this book in significant ways. The publication of this book was made possible in part by the Barr Ferree Foundation Fund for Publications, Department of Art and Archaeology, Princeton University.

For their unfailing love and support, I thank my family: Lyndsay, Patrick, Gabby, and Ellie Adesso; Maria and Lou Passannante; Len, Matt, and Dan Simon, Candy Carroll, and Danielle Williams.

This book is dedicated to my husband, best friend, and collaborator, David Carroll Simon, who makes everything better.

*

Sections of this book have been previously published as "On Catastrophic Materialism," in MLQ 78, no. 4 (2017): 443–64, and "Making 'Anything of Anything' in the Age of Shakespeare," in ELH 83, no. 4 (2016): 989–1008. A short excerpt from "Reading for Pleasure: Disaster and Digression in the First Renaissance Commentary on Lucretius," from *Dynamic Reading: Studies in the Reception of Epicureanism*, ed. Brooke Holmes and W. H. Shearin (Oxford: Oxford University Press, 2012), 89–112, appears here in altered form.

BIBLIOGRAPHY

PRIMARY WORKS

Alberti, Leon Battista. *Momus*. Translated by Sarah Knight and edited by Virginia Brown. Cambridge, MA: Harvard University Press, 2003.

———. *Musca*. In *Apologhi ed elogi*, edited by Rosario Contarino, 173–85. Genoa: Costa & Nolan, 1984.

Albertus Magnus. *Book of Minerals* [*De mineralibus*]. Translated by Dorothy Wyckoff. Oxford: Clarendon Press, 1967.

———. *Liber de causis proprietatum elementorum*. Translated by Irven M. Resnick. Milwaukee: Marquette University Press, 2010.

———. *On Animals: A Medieval Summa Zoologica*. Translated by Kenneth F. Mitchell Jr. and Irven Michael Resnick. 2 vols. Baltimore: Johns Hopkins University Press, 1999.

———. *Opera omnia*. Edited by Auguste Borgnet. 38 vols. Paris: Louis Vivès, 1890–99.

———. *Opus philosophie naturalis*. Brescia, 1490; Venice, 1496.

Anon. *Eikon e piste. Or, the faithfull pourtraicture of a loyall subject, in vindication of Eikon basilike. Otherwise intituled, the pourtraicture of His Sacred Majestie, in his solitudes & sufferings. In answer to an insolent book, intituled Eikon alethine: whereby occasion is taken, to handle all the controverted points relating to these times.* London, 1649.

Anton, Robert. *The Philosophers Satyrs*. London, 1616.

Aquinas, Thomas. *Basic Writings of St. Thomas Aquinas*. Edited by Anton C. Pegis. 2 vols. New York: Random House, 1945.

Arezzo, Ristoro d'. *Della composizione del mondo*. Milan: G. Daeli e Comp. Editori, 1864.

Aristotle. *Fragmenta Selecta*. Edited by W. D. Ross. Oxford: Clarendon Press, 1955.

———. *Metaphysics*. Translated by Hugh Tredennick. 2 vols. Cambridge, MA: Harvard University Press, 1933–35.

————. *Meteorologica*. Translated by H. D. P. Lee. Cambridge, MA: Harvard University Press, 1952.

————. *On Sophistical Refutations*. Translated by E. S. Forester and D. J. Furley. Cambridge, MA: Harvard University Press, 1955.

————. *On the Soul*. Translated by W. S. Hett. Cambridge, MA: Harvard University Press, 1957.

————. *Physica: Translatio Vetus*. Edited by Fernand Bossier and Josef Brams. Aristoteles Latinus VII/1.2. New York: Brill, 1990.

————. *Physics*. Translated by P. H. Wicksteed and F. M. Cornford. 2 vols. Cambridge, MA: Harvard University Press, 1957.

Ascoli, Cecco d'. *The Bitter Age*. Translated by Diane Murphy. Ascoli Piceno: Capponi editore, 2015.

Augustine. *Confessions*. Translated by William Watts. 2 vols. Cambridge, MA: Harvard University Press, 1988.

————. *Epistulae*. In *Corpus scriptorum ecclesiasticorum Latinorum*, edited by A. Goldbacher, vols. 34/1–2, 44, 57, 58. Vienna: Tempsky, 1895–1923.

————. *Sermons on Various Subjects, 341-400*. Translated by Edmund Hill, OP. Edited by John E. Rotelle, OSA. Hyde Park, NY: New City Press, 1995.

Bacon, Francis. *The New Atlantis*. London, 1626.

————. *The New Organon*. Translated by Lisa Jardine and Michael Silverthorne. Cambridge: Cambridge University Press, 2000.

————. *Novum Organum*. Edited by G. W. Kitchin. Oxford: Clarendon Press, 1855.

————. *The wisedome of the ancients, written in Latine by the Right Honourable Sir Francis Bacon Knight, Baron of Verulam, and Lord Chancelor or England. Done into English by Sir Arthur Gorges Knight*. London, 1619.

————. *Works*. Edited by James Spedding, Robert Leslie Ellis, and Douglas Denon Heath. 15 vols. Boston: Houghton, Mifflin, 1900.

Barruel, Abbé Augustin. *Memoirs, Illustrating the History of Jacobinism*. Translated by Robert Clifford. 4 vols. New York, 1799.

Baxter, Richard. *The reasons of the Christian religion*. London, 1667.

Beckett, Samuel. *Murphy*. New York: Grove Press, 2011.

————. *Three Novels: Molloy; Malone Dies; The Unnamable*. New York: Grove Press, 1965.

Beltrami, Luca, ed. *Documenti e memorie riguardanti la vita e le opere di Leonardo da Vinci in ordine cronologico*. Milan: Fratelli Treves, 1919.

Bembo, Pietro. *Lyric Poetry, Etna*. Translated by Mary P. Chatfield. Cambridge, MA: Harvard University Press, 2005.

Beroaldo, Filippo. *Annotationes Centum*. Edited by L. A. Ciapponi. Binghamton, NY: Medieval and Renaissance Texts and Studies, 1995.

————. *Commentarii in Propertium*. Bologna, 1487.

Bilson, Thomas. *The suruey of Christs sufferings for mans redemption and of his descent to Hades or Hel for our deliuerance.* London, 1604.

Boethius. *Consolation of Philosophy.* With the English translation of I.T (1609); revised by H. F. Stewart. Cambridge, MA: Harvard University Press, 1968.

Boulanger, Nicolas Antoine. *Oeuvres.* 8 vols. Paris: Jean Servières, 1792.

Boyle, Robert. *The Christian virtuoso shewing that by being addicted to experimental philosophy, a man is rather assisted than indisposed to be a good Christian.* London, 1690.

———. *New Experiments Physico-Mechanicall, Touching the Spring of the Air, and its Effects.* London, 1660.

Boys, John. *An exposition of the dominical epistles and gospels used in our English liturgie throughout the whole yeare together with a reason why the church did chuse the same.* London, 1610.

Brahe, Tycho. *Astronomiae instauratae progymnasmata.* 2 vols. Prague, 1602–3.

———. *De nova et nullius aevi memoria prius visa stella, iam pridem anno à nato Christo 1572, mense Nouembri primum conspecta, contemplatio mathematica.* Copenhagen, 1573.

Braun, Georg, and Frans Hogenberg. *Civitates Orbis Terrarum.* 6 vols. Cologne, 1572–1617.

Bruno, Giordano. *De l'infinito, universo e mondi.* London, 1584.

———. *The Expulsion of the Triumphant Beast.* Translated by Arthur D. Imerti. Lincoln: University of Nebraska Press, 1964.

Burton, Robert. *The Anatomy of Melancholy.* Edited by Thomas C. Faulkner, Nicolas K. Kiessling, and Rhonda L. Blair. Commentary by J. B. Bamborough and Martin Dodsworth. 6 vols. Oxford: Clarendon Press, 1989.

Calfhill, James. *An aunsvvere to the Treatise of the crosse wherin ye shal see by the plaine and vndoubted word of God, the vanities of men disproued.* London, 1565.

Calvin, John. *Opera omnia.* 9 vols. Amsterdam, 1667.

———. *Tracts Relating to the Reformation.* Translated by Henry Beveridge. 3 vols. Edinburgh: Calvin Translation Society, 1844–51.

Carleton, George. *Astrologomania: the madnesse of astrologers. Or An examination of Sir Christopher Heydons booke, intituled A defence of iudiciarie astrologie. Written neere vpon twenty yeares ago.* Oxford, 1624.

Cavendish, Margaret. *The Blazing World and Other Writings.* Edited by Kate Lilley. New York: Penguin Classics, 1994.

———. *Poems, and Fancies.* London, 1653.

Chambers, John. *A Treatise against Judicial Astrologie.* London, 1601.

Charleton, Walter. *Physiologia Epicuro-Gassendo-Charltoniana, or, A fabrick of science natural, upon the hypothesis of atoms founded by Epicurus repaired by Petrus Gassendus.* London, 1654.

Charron, Pierre. *Of wisdome.* Translated by Samson Lennard. London, 1608.

Cicero. *Academica*, in *De natura deorum; Academica*. Translated by H. Rackham. Cambridge, MA: Harvard University Press, 1967.

————. *De natura deorum*, in *De natura deorum; Academica*. Translated by H. Rackham. Cambridge, MA: Harvard University Press, 1967.

————. *De oratore*. Translated by Harris Rackham. 2 vols. Cambridge, MA: Harvard University Press, 1942.

————. *Letters to Friends*. Translated by D. R. Shackleton Bailey. 2 vols. Cambridge, MA: Harvard University Press, 2001.

————. *On Divination*. In *On Old Age; On Friendship; On Divination*, translated by W. A. Falconer. Cambridge, MA: Harvard University Press, 1923.

————. *Scipio's Dream*. In Macrobius, *Commentary on the Dream of Scipio*, translated and edited by William Harris Stahl, 67–78. New York: Columbia University Press, 1952.

Coleridge, Samuel Taylor. *Collected Letters*. Edited by Earl Leslie Griggs. 6 vols. Oxford: Clarendon Press, 1956–71.

Cooper, Thomas. *Thesaurus Linguae Romanae et Britannicae*. London, 1578.

Copernicus, Nicolaus. *On the Revolutions of Heavenly Spheres*. Translated by Charles Glenn Wallis. New York: Prometheus Books, 1995.

Descartes, René. *The Philosophical Writings of Descartes*. Translated by John Cottingham, Robert Stoothoff, and Dugald Murdoch. Vols. 1 and 2. Cambridge: Cambridge University Press, 1985.

Diderot, Denis, ed. *Encyclopédie ou Dictionnaire raisonné des sciences, des arts et des métiers*. 17 vols. Paris: Briasson et al., 1751–72.

Diels, Hermann, and Walther Kranz, eds. and trans. *Die Fragmente der Vorsokratiker*. 9th ed. 3 vols. Berlin: Weidmann, 1959–60.

Digges, Leonard. *A geometrical practise, named Pantometria diuided into three bookes, longimetra, planimetra, and stereometria, containing rules manifolde for mensuration of all lines, superficies and solides: with sundry straunge conclusions both by instrument and without, and also by perspectiue glasses, to set forth the true description or exact plat of an whole region: framed by Leonard Digges gentleman, lately finished by Thomas Digges his sonne. Who hathe also thereunto adioyned a mathematicall treatise of the fiue regulare Platonicall bodies, and their Metamorphosis or transformation into fiue other equilater vniforme solides Geometricall, of his owne inuention, hitherto not mentioned of by any geometricians*. London, 1571.

————. *A prognostication euerlastinge of right good effecte fruitfully augmented by the auctour, contayning plaine, briefe, pleasaunt, chosen rules to iudge the weather by the sunne, moone, starres, comets, rainebow, thunder, cloudes, with other extraordinary tokens, not omitting the aspects of planets, vvith a briefe iudgement for euer, of plenty, lacke, sickenes, dearth, vvarres &c. opening also many naturall causes vvorthy to be knovven. To these and other now at the last, are ioyned diuers generall, plea-*

saunt tables, vvith manye compendious rules, easye to be had in memory, manifolde vvayes profitable to al men of vnderstanding. Published by Leonard Digges Gentleman. Lately corrected and augmented by Thomas Digges his sonne. London, 1576.

Digges, Thomas. *Alae seu scalae mathematicae, quibus visibilium remotissima coelorum theatra conscendi et planetarum omnium itinera nouis et inauditis methodis explorari, tum huius portentosi syderis in mundi boreali plaga insolito fulgore coruscantis, distantia et magnitudo immensa, situsque protinus tremendus indagari, Deique stupendum ostentum, terricolis expositum cognosci liquidissime possit.* London, 1573.

———. Letter of Thomas Digges to Lord Burghley, December 11, 1572. Public Record Office, SP12/90/12.

———. *A Perfit Description of the Caelestiall Orbes, according to the most ancient doctrine of the Pythagoreans, lately revived by Copernicus and by Geometricall Demonstrations approved.* Appended to Leonard Digges, *A prognostication euerlastinge.* London, 1576.

Dio Chrysostom. *On Homer.* In *Dio Chrysostom*, vol. 4, translated by H. Lamar Crosby. Cambridge, MA: Harvard University Press, 1946.

Diogenes Laertius. *Lives of Eminent Philosophers.* Translated by R. D. Hicks. 2 vols. Cambridge, MA: Harvard University Press, 1950.

Donatus, Aelius. "On Comedy." In *Classical and Medieval Literary Criticism: Translations and Interpretations*, edited by Alexander Preminger, O. B. Hardison, and Kevin Kerrane, 305–9. New York: Frederick Ungar, 1974.

Donne, John. *The Courtier's Library: Or Catalogus Librorum Aulicorum incomparabilium et non vendibilium.* Translated and edited by Evelyn Mary Simpson. London: Nonesuch Press, 1930.

———. *Devotions upon Emergent Occasions.* London, 1624.

———. *Devotions upon Emergent Occasions.* Edited by Anthony Raspa. Oxford: Oxford University Press, 1987.

———. *Pseudo-martyr. Wherein out of certaine propositions and gradations, this conclusion is euicted. That those which are of the Romane religion in this kingdome, may and ought to take the Oath of allegiance.* London, 1610.

———. *The Variorum Edition of the Poetry of John Donne: The "Anniversaries" and the Epicedes and Obsequies*, edited by Gary A. Stringer. 8 vols. Bloomington: Indiana University Press, 1995.

Dyer, Edward. *The Prayse of Nothing.* London, 1585.

Eisenstein, Sergei. *Beyond the Stars: The Memoirs of Sergei Eisenstein.* Translated by William Powell. Edited by Richard Taylor. London: BFI Publishing, 1995.

———. *The Film Sense.* New York: Harcourt, Brace, 1947.

———. *Nonindifferent Nature: Film and the Structure of Things.* Translated by Herbert Marshall. Cambridge: Cambridge University Press, 1987.

Erasmus, Desiderius. *Adages Ii1 to Iv100*. Vol. 31 of *The Collected Works of Erasmus*. Translated by Margaret Mann Phillips. Edited by Roger Aubrey Baskerville Mynors. Toronto: University of Toronto Press, 1982.

Eusebius. *Eusebii Pamphili Chronici canones*. Edited by John Knight Fotheringham. London: Humphrey Milford, 1923.

Evelyn, John. *Diary and Correspondence*. Edited by William Bray. 4 vols. London: Henry Colburn, 1850.

Ficino, Marsilio. *Platonic Theology*. Translated and edited by Michael J. B. Allen and James Hankins. 6 vols. Cambridge, MA: Harvard University Press, 2001–6.

———. *Three Books on Life*. Translated and edited by Carol V. Kaske and John R. Clark. Binghamton, NY: Medieval and Renaissance Texts and Studies, 1989.

Freeman, Kathleen, trans. and ed. *Ancilla to the Pre-Socratic Philosophers: A Complete Translation of the Fragments in Diels, Fragmente der Vorsokratiker*. Cambridge, MA: Harvard University Press, 1983.

Freud, Sigmund. *Leonardo da Vinci and a Memory of His Childhood*. Translated by Alan Tyson. Edited by James Strachey. New York: W. W. Norton, 1964.

Frischlin, Nicodemus. *Consideratio novae stellae, quae mense Novembri, anno salutis MDLXXII in Signo Cassiopeae populis Septentrionalibus longè apparuit*. Tübingen, 1573.

Glanvill, Joseph. *Essays on several important subjects in philosophy and religion*. London, 1676.

———. *The vanity of dogmatizing, or, Confidence in opinions manifested in a discourse of the shortness and uncertainty of our knowledge, and its causes: with some reflexions on peripateticism, and an apology for philosophy*. London, 1661.

Hall, Joseph. *Occasional Meditations*. London, 1631.

Harsnett, Samuel. *A declaration of egregious popish impostures to with-draw the harts of her Maiesties subiects from their allegeance, and from the truth of Christian religion professed in England, vnder the pretence of casting out deuils*. London, 1603.

Harvey, Gabriel, and Edmund Spenser. *Three Proper and Wittie Familiar Letters*. London, 1580.

Harvey, John. *A discoursive probleme concerning prophesies*. London, 1588.

Harvey, Richard. *An astrological discourse upon the great and notable conjunction of the two superiour planets, Saturne & Iupiter, which shall happen the 28 day of April, 1583*. London, 1583.

Herschel, William. *Über den Bau des Himmels*. Translated by George Michael Sommer. Königsberg: Nicolovius, 1791.

Hippocrates. *Breaths*. In *Hippocrates*, vol. 2, translated by W. H. S. Jones. Cambridge, MA: Harvard University Press, 1923.

Holbach, Paul Henry Thiry, Baron d'. *Le Christianisme dévoilé, ou examen des principes et des effets de la religion chrétienne*. Paris, 1761.

Homer. *Odyssey*. Translated by A. T. Murray. Revised by George E. Dimock. 2 vols. Cambridge, MA: Harvard University Press, 1919.

Hooke, Robert. "Ansr to Dr Wallis & Ways to find ye Meridian. Read to ye RS Apr. 27. 1687." Royal Society archives Cl.P. xx.75.

———. *Lectiones Cutlerianae, Or a Collection of Lectures: Physical, mechanical, Geographical & Astronomical, Made Before the Royal Society on Several Occasions*. London, 1679.

———. *Micrographia, or, Some physiological descriptions of minute bodies made by magnifying glasses with observations and inquiries thereupon*. London, 1665.

———. *The Posthumous Works of Robert Hooke*. Edited by Richard Waller. London, 1705.

Howard, Henry, Earl of Northampton. *A defensatiue against the poyson of supposed prophesies*. London, 1583.

Hume, David. *An Enquiry Concerning Human Understanding*. Edited by Tom L. Beauchamp. Oxford: Oxford University Press, 1999.

———. *History of England from the Invasion of Julius Caesar to the Revolution in 1688*. 8 vols. Edinburgh and London, 1754–62.

———. *Letters of David Hume*. Edited by J. Y. T. Greig. 2 vols. Oxford: Clarendon Press, 1932.

Isidore of Seville. *The Etymologies*. Translated and edited by Stephen A. Barney, W. J. Lewis, J. A. Beach, and Oliver Berghof. Cambridge: Cambridge University Press, 2006.

James, William. *Writings, 1902–1910*. New York: Library of America, 1987.

Jerome. *Opera omnia*. In *Patrologiae cursus completus: Series Latina*, vols. 22–30, edited by Jacques-Paul Migne. Paris, 1845–89.

Kant, Immanuel. *Anthropology from a Pragmatic Point of View*. Translated and edited by Robert B. Louden. Cambridge: Cambridge University Press, 2006.

———. *Correspondence*. Translated and edited by Arnulf Zweig. Cambridge: Cambridge University Press, 1999.

———. *Critique of Judgment*. Translated by James Creed Meredith. Revised and edited by Nicholas Walker. Oxford: Oxford University Press, 2007.

———. *Critique of the Power of Judgment*. Translated by Paul Guyer and Eric Matthews. Edited by Paul Guyer. Cambridge: Cambridge University Press, 2000.

———. *Critique of Pure Reason*. Translated by Paul Guyer and Allen W. Wood. Cambridge: Cambridge University Press, 1998.

———. *Dreams of a Spirit-Seer Elucidated by Dreams of Metaphysics*. In *Theoreti-*

cal Philosophy, 1755-1770, translated and edited by David Walford and Ralf Meerbote, 301–60. Cambridge: Cambridge University Press, 1992.

———. "The End of All Things." In *Religion and Rational Theology*, translated and edited by Allen Wood and George di Giovanni, 217–31. Cambridge: Cambridge University Press, 1998.

———. *Immanuel Kants Schriften*. Ausgabe der königlich preussischen Akademie der Wissenschaften. Berlin: W. de Gruyter, 1902–.

———. *Kant's Cosmogony: As in His Essay on the Retardation of the Earth, and in His Natural History and Theory of the Heavens: With Introduction, Appendices, and a Portrait of Thomas Wright of Durham*. Translated and edited by W. Hastie. Glasgow: James Maclehose and Sons, 1900.

———. *Metaphysical Foundations of Natural Science*. Translated and edited by Michael Friedman. Cambridge: Cambridge University Press, 2004.

———. *Natural Science*. Translated by Lewis White Beck, Jeffrey B. Edwards, Olaf Reinhardt, Martin Schönfeld, and Eric Watkins. Edited by Eric Watkins. Cambridge: Cambridge University Press, 2012.

———. *Observations on the Feeling of the Beautiful and the Sublime and Other Writings*. Translated and edited by Patrick Frierson and Paul Guyer. Cambridge: Cambridge University Press, 2011.

———. *Only Possible Argument in Support of a Demonstration of the Existence of God*. In *Theoretical Philosophy, 1755-1770*, translated and edited by David Walford and Ralf Meerbote, 107–202. Cambridge: Cambridge University Press, 1992.

———. "On the Power of the Mind to Master Its Morbid Feelings by Sheer Resolution." In *Religion and Rational Theology*, translated and edited by Allen Wood and George di Giovanni, 313–27. Cambridge: Cambridge University Press, 1998.

———. "On a Recently Prominent Tone of Superiority in Philosophy." In *Theoretical Philosophy after 1781*, translated by Gary Hatfield, Michael Friedman, Henry Allison, and Peter Heath and edited by Henry Allison and Peter Heath, 425–46. Cambridge: Cambridge University Press, 2002.

———. *Philosophical Correspondence, 1759-1799*. Translated and edited by Arnulf Zweig. Chicago: University of Chicago Press, 1967.

———. *Universal Natural History*. In *Natural Science*, translated by Lewis White Beck, Jeffrey B. Edwards, Olaf Reinhardt, Martin Schönfeld, and Eric Watkins. Edited by Eric Watkins, 182–308. Cambridge: Cambridge University Press, 2012.

Kepler, Johannes. *Gesammelte Werke*. Edited by Walther von Dyck, Max Caspar, et al. 24 vols. Munich: C. H. Beck, 1937–.

Kircher, Athanasius. *The vulcano's, or, Burning and fire-vomiting mountains, famous in the world, with their remarkables collected for the most part out of Kircher's Subterraneous world, and exposed to more general view in English.* London, 1669.

Kirk, G. S., J. E. Raven, and Malcom Schofield. *The Presocratic Philosophers: A Critical History with a Selection of Texts.* 2nd ed. Cambridge: Cambridge University Press, 1983.

Lactantius. *Opera omnia.* In *Corpus scriptorum ecclesiasticorum Latinorum,* vols. 19 and 27, edited by Samuel Brandt and Georg von Laubmann. Vienna: Tempsky, 1890–97.

———. *The Works of Lactantius.* In *The Ante-Nicene Christian Library,* vols. 21–22, translated by William Fletcher. Edinburgh: T&T Clark, 1871.

Laplace, Pierre-Simon. *Traite de mécanique céleste.* 5 vols. Paris, 1798–1825.

Lascaris, Janus. *Epigrammata et Graeca et Latina.* Basel, 1537.

Leonardo da Vinci. *Leonardo da Vinci's Notebooks: Arranged and Rendered into English with Introductions.* Edited by Edward MacCurdy. New York: George Braziller, 1955.

———. *Libro di pittura: Codice Urbinate lat. 1270 nella Biblioteca Apostolica Vaticana.* Edited by Carlo Pedretti. Critical transcription by Carlo Vecce. 2 vols. Florence: Giunti, 1995.

———. *Notebooks.* Selected by Irma A. Richter. Edited by Thereza Wells. Oxford: Oxford University Press, 2008.

———. *The Notebooks of Leonardo da Vinci.* Edited by Jean Paul Richter. 2 vols. New York: Dover, 1970.

———. *On Painting: A Lost Book (Libro A) Reassembled from the Codex Vaticanus Urbinas 1270 and from the Codex Leicester.* Edited by Carlo Pedretti. Berkeley: University of California Press, 1964.

———. *Treatise on Painting (Codex Urbinas Latinus 1270).* Translated by A. Philip MacMahon. Princeton: Princeton University Press, 1956.

Lomazzo, Giovanni Paolo. *Trattato dell'arte della pittura, scoltura et architettura.* Milan, 1585.

Long, A. A., and D. N. Sedley, eds. *The Hellenistic Philosophers.* Vol. 1, *Translations of the Principal Sources with Philosophical Commentary.* Cambridge: Cambridge University Press, 1987.

Lucretius. *De rerum natura.* Edited by Giambattista Pio. Bologna, 1511.

———. *De rerum natura.* Edited and translated by W. H. D. Rouse. Revised by M. F. Smith. Cambridge, MA: Harvard University Press, 1997.

Machiavelli, Niccolò. *Discourses on the First Decade of Titus Livius.* Translated by Ninian Hill Thomson. London: K. Paul, Trench, 1883.

———. *Lettere.* Edited by Franco Gaeta. Milan: Feltrinelli, 1961.

———. *The Prince.* Translated by James B. Atkinson. Indianapolis: Bobbs-Merrill, 2008.

Macrobius. *Commentary on the "Dream of Scipio."* Translated and edited by William Harris Stahl. New York: Columbia University Press, 1952.

Melanchthon, Philipp. *Opera omnia.* In *Corpus Reformatorum*, edited by C. G. Bretschneider. Vols. 1–28. Halle and Braunschweig: Schwetschke, 1834–60.

———. *Orations on Philosophy and Education.* Translated by Cristine Salazar. Edited by Sachiko Kusukawa. Cambridge: Cambridge University Press, 1999.

Mendelssohn, Moses. *Last Works.* Translated by Bruce Rosenstock. Urbana: University of Illinois Press, 2012.

Mirandola, Giovanni Pico della. *Disputationes adversus astrologiam divinatricem.* 1496. Edited by Eugenio Garin. Florence: Vallecchi, 1946.

Montaigne, Michel de. *The Complete Works of Montaigne.* Edited by Donald Frame. Stanford: Stanford University Press, 1958.

———. *Les essais.* Edited by P. Villey and Verdun L. Saulnier. Paris: Presses Universitaires de France, 1978.

More, Henry. *Democritus Platonissans.* Cambridge, 1646.

———. *The immortality of the soul, so farre forth as it is demonstrable from the knowledge of nature and the light of reason.* London, 1659.

———. *Tetractys anti-astrologica, or, The four chapters in the explanation of the grand mystery of holiness which contain a brief but solid confutation of judiciary astrology, with annotations upon each chapter.* London, 1681.

Nashe, Thomas. *The apologie of Pierce Pennilesse. Or, strange newes, of the intercepting certaine letters and a conuoy of verses, as they were going priuilie to victuall the Lowe Countries.* London, 1592.

Nicholas of Cusa. *Complete Philosophical and Theological Treatises.* Translated and edited by Jasper Hopkins. Minneapolis: Arthur J. Banning Press, 2001.

———. *Opera.* Paris, 1514.

Nifo, Agostino. *De falsa diluvii prognosticatione, quae ex conventu omnium planetarum, qui in Piscibus continget, anno 1524 divulgata est: libri tres.* Florence, 1520.

Ovid. *Amores.* In *Heroides and Amores*, translated by Grant Showerman. Revised by G. P. Goold. Cambridge, MA: Harvard University Press, 1914.

———. *Metamorphoses.* Translated by Frank Justus Miller. 2 vols. Cambridge, MA: Harvard University Press, 1976.

———. *Ovidio Metamorphoseos vulgare in prosa tradotto da Giovanni de' Bonsignori di Città di Castello.* Venice, 1497.

Palingenius. *The Zodiake of Life.* Translated by Barnaby Googe. London, 1565.

Parker, Samuel. *A free and impartial censure of the Platonick philosophie: being a letter written to his much honoured friend Mr. N. B.* Oxford, 1666.

Pascal, Blaise. *Pensées.* Translated and edited by Roger Ariew. Indianapolis: Hackett Publishing, 2004.

———. *Pensées et opuscules.* Edited by Léon Brunschvicg. Paris: Hachette, 1909.

Pigghe, Albert. *Astrologiae defensio*. Paris, 1519.

Plato. *Ion*. Translated by W. R. M. Lamb. Cambridge, MA: Harvard University Press, 1990.

———. *Phaedo*. Translated by Harold North Fowler. Cambridge, MA: Harvard University Press, 1933.

———. *Phaedrus*. Translated by Harold North Fowler. Cambridge, MA: Harvard University Press, 1914.

———. *Republic*. Translated by Chris Emlyn-Jones and William Preddy. 2 vols. Cambridge, MA: Harvard University Press, 2013.

———. *Sophist*. Translated by Harold North Fowler. Cambridge, MA: Harvard University Press, 1921.

Pliny. *Natural History*. Translated by H. Rackham. 10 vols. Cambridge, MA: Harvard University Press, 1940.

Poe, Edgar Allan. "Ligeia." In *The Fall of the House of Usher and Other Writings*, 62–78. New York: Penguin, 2003.

Pope, Alexander. *Aus dem Englischen übersetzter Versuch vom Menschen des Herrn Alexander Pope*. Translated by Barthold Heinrich Brockes. Hamburg, 1740.

Power, Henry. *Experimental philosophy, in three books containing new experiments microscopical, mercurial, magnetical: with some deductions, and probable hypotheses, raised from them, in avouchment and illustration of the now famous atomical hypothesis*. London, 1663.

———. "In Commendation of the Microscope" (1661). In Thomas Cowles, "Dr. Henry Power's Poem on the Microscope." *Isis* 21, no. 1 (1934): 71–80.

Pseudo-Virgil. *Aetna*. In *Minor Latin Poets*, vol. 1, translated by J. Wight Duff and Arnold M. Duff. Cambridge, MA: Harvard University Press, 1934.

Ptolemy. *Almagest*. Translated and annotated by Gerald J. Toomer. London: Duckworth, 1984.

Puttenham, George. *The Arte of English Poesie* (1589). In *Elizabethan Critical Essays*, edited by George Gregory Smith, 2:1–193. Oxford: Oxford University Press, 1904.

Rabelais, Francois. *Gargantua and Pantagruel*. Translated by M. A. Screech. New York: Penguin Classics, 2006.

———. *Pantagruel's prognostication certain, true, and infallible for the year everlasting . . . and now of late translated out of French by Democritus Pseudomantis*. London, 1660.

Rousseau, Jean-Jacques. *Oeuvres complètes*. Edited by Bernard Gagnebin and Marcel Raymond. 4 vols. Paris: Bibliothèque de la Pléiade, 1959–69.

Scala, Bartolomeo. *Essays and Dialogues*. Translated by Renée Neu Watkins. Cambridge, MA: Harvard University Press, 2008.

Seneca. *Natural Questions*. Translated by Harry M. Hine. Chicago: University of Chicago Press, 2010.

Servius Grammaticus. *In Vergilii carmina commentarii.* Edited by Georg Thilo and Hermann Hagen. Leipzig: B. G. Teubner, 1881.

Sextus Empiricus. *Against the Logicians.* Translated by R. G. Bury. Cambridge, MA: Harvard University Press, 1935.

———. *Outlines of Pyrrhonism.* Translated by R. G. Bury. Cambridge, MA: Harvard University Press, 1933.

Shakespeare, William. *The Norton Shakespeare.* Edited by Stephen Greenblatt, Walter Cohen, Jean E. Howard, and Katherine Eisaman Maus. 2nd ed. New York: W. W. Norton, 2008.

Smith, G. C. Moore, ed. *Gabriel Harvey's Marginalia.* Stratford-upon-Avon: Shakespeare Head Press, 1913.

Sprat, Thomas. *The history of the Royal-Society of London for the improving of natural knowledge.* London, 1667.

Statius. *Silvae.* Translated by J. H. Mozley. Cambridge, MA: Harvard University Press, 1955.

Steno, Nicolas. *The prodromus to a dissertation concerning solids naturally contained within solids laying a foundation for the rendering a rational accompt both of the frame and the several changes of the masse of the earth.* Translated by Henry Oldenburg. London, 1671.

Stöffler, Johannes, and Jacob Pflaum. *Almanach nova plurimis annis venturis inservientia.* Ulm, 1499.

Stubbes, Phillip. *The second part of the anatomie of abuses.* London, 1583.

Stuckenberg, John Henry Wilbrandt. *The Life of Immanuel Kant.* London: Macmillan, 1882.

Taylor, C. C. W. *The Atomists, Leucippus and Democritus: Fragments; a Text and Translation with Commentary.* Toronto: University of Toronto Press, 1999.

Virgil. *Eclogues; Georgics; Aeneid: Books 1-6.* Translated by H. Rushton Fairclough. Revised by G. P. Goold. Cambridge, MA: Harvard University Press, 1999.

Voltaire. *Le Micromégas.* London, 1752.

Waller, Richard. "The Life of Dr. Robert Hooke." In Hooke, *The Posthumous Works of Robert Hooke,* edited by Richard Waller, i–xxviii. London, 1705.

Walton, Izaak. *The lives of Dr. John Donne, Sir Henry Wotton, Mr. Richard Hooker, Mr. George Herbert.* London, 1670.

Weemes, John. *Exercitations divine; containing diverse questions and solutions for the right understanding of the Scriptures.* London, 1632.

Whiston, William. *The Astronomical Year: or, on account of the many remarkable celestial phenomena of the great year 1736.* London, 1737.

———. *A New Theory of the Earth.* London, 1696.

Wilkins, John. *A discourse concerning the beauty of providence in all the rugged passages of it: Very seasonable to quiet and support the heart in these times of publick confusion.* London, 1649.

———. *Of the principles and duties of natural religion: Two books.* London, 1675.

Woodward, John. *An essay toward a natural history of the earth and terrestrial bodies.* London, 1695.

SECONDARY WORKS

Ackerley, Chris. *Demented Particulars: The Annotated Murphy.* Oxford: Oxford University Press, 2010.

Aït-Touati, Frédérique. *Fictions of the Cosmos: Science and Literature in the Seventeenth Century.* Chicago: University of Chicago Press, 2011.

Allen, Don Cameron. *The Star-Crossed Renaissance: The Quarrel about Astrology and Its Influence in England.* Durham: Duke University Press, 1941.

Allen, Michael J. B. *The Platonism of Marsilio Ficino: A Study of His "Phaedrus" Commentary, Its Sources and Genesis.* Berkeley: University of California Press, 1984.

Altman, Joel. *The Improbability of Othello: Rhetorical Anthropology and Shakespearean Selfhood.* Chicago: University of Chicago Press, 2010.

Ammer, Christine, ed. *American Heritage Dictionary of Idioms.* New York: Houghton Mifflin Harcourt, 2013.

Anderson, Judith H. "Working Imagination in the Early Modern Period: Donne's Secular and Religious Lyrics and Shakespeare's Hamlet, Macbeth, and Leontes." In *Shakespeare and Donne: Generic Hybrids and the Cultural Imaginary,* edited by Judith H. Anderson and Jennifer C. Vaught, 185–219. New York: Fordham University Press, 2013.

Arendt, Hannah. *Lectures on Kant's Political Philosophy.* Edited by Ronald Beiner. Chicago: University of Chicago Press, 1982.

Aston, Margaret. "The Fiery Trigon Conjunction: An Elizabethan Astrological Prediction." *Isis* 61, no. 2 (1970): 158–87.

Aubenque, Pierre. "Kant et l'épicurisme." In *Actes du VIIIe Congrès de l'Association Guillaume Budé,* 293–303. Paris: Les Belles Lettres, 1969.

Azzolini, Monica. *The Duke and the Stars: Astrology and Politics in Renaissance Milan.* Cambridge, MA: Harvard University Press, 2013.

Bambach, Carmen C., ed. *Leonardo Da Vinci, Master Draftsman.* New York: Metropolitan Museum of New York, 2003.

Barbour, Reid. *English Epicures and Stoics: Ancient Legacies in Early Stuart Culture.* Amherst: University of Massachusetts Press, 1998.

Barkan, Leonard. "'Living sculptures': Ovid, Michelangelo, and *The Winter's Tale.*" ELH 48 (1981): 639–67.

————. *Michelangelo: A Life on Paper*. Princeton: Princeton University Press, 2010.

Baxandall, Michael. "Alberti's Cast of Mind." In *Words for Pictures: Seven Papers on Renaissance Art and Criticism*, 27–38. New Haven: Yale University Press, 2003.

Beretta, Marco. "Leonardo and Lucretius." *Rinascimento* 49 (2009): 341–72.

Berger, Harry, Jr. "The Ecology of the Mind: The Concept of Period Imagination—An Outline Sketch." *Centennial Review* 8, no. 4 (1964): 409–34.

Bignone, Ettore. *L'Aristotele perduto e la formazione filosofica di Epicuro*. 2 vols. Florence: La Nuova Italia, 1936.

Blumenberg, Hans. *The Genesis of the Copernican World*. Translated by Robert M. Wallace. Cambridge, MA: MIT Press, 1987.

————. *The Legitimacy of the Modern Age*. Translated by Robert M. Wallace. Cambridge, MA: MIT Press, 1999.

————. *Paradigms for a Metaphorology*. Translated by Robert Ian Savage. Ithaca: Cornell University Press, 2010.

————. *Schiffbruch mit Zuschauer: Paradigma einer Daseinsmetapher*. Frankfurt: Suhrkamp, 1979.

————. *Shipwreck with Spectator: Paradigm of a Metaphor for Existence*. Translated by Steven Rendall. Cambridge, MA: MIT Press, 1997.

Boner, Patrick J. "Kepler v. the Epicureans: Causality, Coincidence, and the Origins of the New Star of 1604." *Journal for the History of Astronomy* 38 (2007): 207–21.

Boyancé, Pierre. *Lucrèce et l'épicurisme*. Paris: Presses Universitaires de France, 1963.

Bramly, Serge. *Leonardo: The Artist and the Man*. New York: Penguin Books, 1995.

Brewster, David. *The Martyrs of Science: Or, the Lives of Galileo, Tycho Brahe, and Kepler*. London: John Murray, 1846.

Broecke, Steven Vanden. *The Limits of Influence: Pico, Louvain, and the Crisis of Renaissance Astrology*. Leiden: Brill, 2003.

Brown, Alison. *The Return of Lucretius to Renaissance Florence*. Cambridge, MA: Harvard University Press, 2010.

Buch, Robert. *The Pathos of the Real: On the Aesthetics of Violence in the Twentieth Century*. Baltimore: Johns Hopkins University Press, 2010.

Calvi, Gerolamo. *I manoscritti di Leonardo da Vinci, dal punto di vista cronologico storico e biografico*. Bologna: Zanichelli, 1925.

Campbell, Stephen J. "Giorgione's 'Tempest,' 'Studiolo' Culture, and the Renaissance Lucretius." *Renaissance Quarterly* 56, no. 2 (2003): 299–332.

Canfora, Luciano. *Vita di Lucrezio*. Palermo: Sellerio, 1993.

Capra, Fritjof. *Learning from Leonardo: Decoding the Notebooks of a Genius.* San Francisco: Berrett-Koehler, 2013.

Carey, John. *John Donne: Life, Mind, and Art.* Oxford: Oxford University Press, 1981.

Casella, Maria Teresa. "Il metodo dei commentatori umanistici esemplato sul Beroaldo." *Studi Medievali*, 3rd. ser., 16 (1975): 685–701.

Cass, Oren. "Problem with Climate Catastrophizing: The Case for Calm." *Foreign Affairs*, March 21, 2017. https://www.foreignaffairs.com/articles/2017-03-21/problem-climate-catastrophizing.

Cassin, Barbara, Emily Apter, Jacques Lezra, and Michael Woods, eds. *Dictionary of Untranslatables: A Philosophical Lexicon.* Princeton, NJ: Princeton University Press, 2014.

Cassirer, Ernst. *Kant's Life and Thought.* Translated by James Haden. New Haven: Yale University Press, 1981.

Castelli, Patrizia. "Leonardo, i due Pico e la critica alla divinazione." In *Leonardo e Pico: Analogie, contratti, confronti; Atti del Convegno di Mirandola (10 Maggio 2003)*, edited by Fabio Frosini, 131–72. Florence: Olschki, 2005.

Castner, C. J. "*De Rerum Natura* 5.101–103: Lucretius' Application of Empedoclean Language to Epicurean Doctrine." *Phoenix* 41 (1987): 40–49.

Cavell, Stanley. *Disowning Knowledge in Seven Plays of Shakespeare.* Cambridge: Cambridge University Press, 2003.

Clark, David L. "We 'Other Prussians': Bodies and Pleasures in De Quincey and Late Kant." *European Romantic Review* 14 (2003): 261–87.

Clark, Kenneth. *Leonardo da Vinci.* Introduced by Martin Kemp. London: Folio Society, 2005.

Clay, Diskin. *Lucretius and Epicurus.* Ithaca: Cornell University Press, 1983.

Coen, Deborah R. *The Earthquake Observers: Disaster Science from Lisbon to Richter.* Chicago: University of Chicago Press, 2013.

Coffin, Charles M. *John Donne and the New Philosophy.* New York, 1927.

Cohn, Samuel K., Jr. *Cultures of Plague: Medical Thought at the End of the Renaissance.* Oxford: Oxford University Press, 2010.

Coles, Kimberly Anne. "The Matter of Belief in John Donne's Holy Sonnets." *Renaissance Quarterly* 68, no. 3 (2015): 899–931.

Compagnon, Antoine. *Nous, Michel de Montaigne.* Paris: Editions du Seuil, 1980.

Conger, George Perrigo. *Theories of Macrocosms and Microcosms in the History of Philosophy.* New York: Columbia University Press, 1922.

Connor, Steven. *Fly.* London: Reaktion, 2006.

Conte, Gian Biago. *Genres and Readers: Lucretius, Love Elegy, Pliny's Encyclopedia.* Translated by Glenn W. Most. Foreword by Charles Segal. Baltimore: Johns Hopkins University Press, 1994.

Coolidge, John S. *The Pauline Renaissance in England: Puritanism and the Bible.* Oxford: Clarendon Press, 1970.

Courtenay, William J. "The Demise of Quodlibetal Literature." In *Theological Quodlibeta in the Middle Ages,* edited by Christopher Schabel, 2:693–700. Leiden: Brill, 2006–7.

Dal Prete, Ivano. "'Being the World Eternal . . .': The Age of the Earth in Renaissance Italy." *Isis* 105, no. 2 (2014): 292–317.

Daniel, Drew. *The Melancholy Assemblage: Affect and Epistemology in the English Renaissance.* New York: Fordham University Press, 2013.

———. "The Empedoclean Renaissance." In *The Return of Theory in Early Modern English Studies,* volume 2, edited by Paul Cefalu, Gary Kuchar, and Bryan Reynolds, 277–300. London: Palgrave Macmillan, 2014.

Daston, Lorraine, and Katherine Park. *Wonders and the Order of Nature, 1150–1750.* Cambridge: Zone Books, 1998.

Deleuze, Gilles. *The Logic of Sense.* Translated by Mark Lester with Charles Stivale. Edited by Constantin V. Boundas. New York: Columbia University Press, 1990.

Del Nero, Valerio. "Giovan Battista Pio fra grammatica e filosofia: dai primi scritti al commento lucreziano del 1511." In *Sapere e/è potere: Il caso Bolognese a confronto; Actes du colloque de Bologne, avril 1989,* vol. 1, *Forme e oggetti della disputa delle arti,* edited by L. Avellini, 243–57. Bologna: Istituto per la Storia di Bologna, 1990.

de Man, Paul. *Aesthetic Ideology.* Edited by Andrzej Warminski. Minneapolis: University of Minnesota Press, 1996.

Diehl, Huston. "'Doth Not the Stone Rebuke Me?': The Pauline Rebuke and Paulina's Lawful Magic in *The Winter's Tale.*" In *Shakespeare and the Cultures of Performance,* edited by Paul Yachnin and Patricia Badir, 69–82. Aldershot, UK: Ashgate, 2008.

Dionisotti, Carlo. "Giovan Battista Pio e Mario Equicola." In *Gli umanisti e il volgare fra Quattro e Cinquecento,* 78–110. Florence: Le Monnier, 1968.

Dobin, Howard. *Merlin's Disciples: Prophecy, Poetry, and Power in Renaissance England.* Stanford: Stanford University Press, 1990.

Doyle, Charles. "*Sed in Atomo, in Ictu Oculi*: A Proposed Origin for the *Atomus in Tempore.*" Paper presented at Imbas 2015.

Drake, Ellen T. *Restless Genius: Robert Hooke and His Earthly Thoughts.* Oxford: Oxford University Press, 1996.

Dupré, Sven. "William Bourne's Invention: Projecting a Telescope and Optical Speculation in Elizabethan England." In *The Origins of the Telescope,* edited by Albert Van Helden, Sven Dupré, Rob van Gent, and Huib Zuidervaart, 129–45. Amsterdam: KNAW Press, 2010.

Durantaye, Leland de la. *Beckett's Art of Mismaking*. Cambridge, MA: Harvard University Press, 2016.

Eden, Kathy. *The Renaissance Rediscovery of Intimacy*. Chicago: University of Chicago Press, 2012.

Eissler, K. R. *Leonardo da Vinci: Psychoanalytic Notes on the Enigma*. New York: International Universities Press, 1961.

Ellis, Albert. *Reason and Emotion in Psychotherapy*. New York: L. Stuart, 1962.

Elton, William R. *King Lear and the Gods*. 1966. Reprint. Lexington: University of Kentucky Press, 1988.

Empson, William. *Essays on Renaissance Literature*. Vol. 1, *Donne and the New Philosophy*. Edited by John Haffenden. Cambridge: Cambridge University Press, 1995.

Enterline, Lynn. "'You Speak a Language that I Understand Not': The Rhetoric of Animation in *The Winter's Tale*." *Shakespeare Quarterly* 48, no. 1 (1997): 17–44.

Eyles, Victor A. "The Influence of Nicolaus Steno on the Development of Geological Science in Britain." In *Nicolaus Steno and His Indice*, edited by Gustav Scherz, 167–88. Copenhagen: Munksgaard, 1958.

Farago, Claire. *Leonardo da Vinci's "Paragone": A Critical Interpretation with a New Edition of the Text in the Codex Urbinas*. Leiden: E. J. Brill, 1992.

———. "Wind and Weather in Leonardo da Vinci's Abridged Treatise on Painting." In *Wind und Wetter: De Ikonologie der Atmosphäre*, edited by Alessandro Nova and Tanja Michalesky, 9–37. Venice: Marsilio, 2009.

Fenves, Peter. *A Peculiar Fate: Metaphysics and World-History in Kant*. Ithaca: Cornell University Press, 1991.

Ferrarin, Alfredo. *The Powers of Pure Reason: Kant and the Idea of Cosmic Philosophy*. Chicago: University of Chicago Press, 2015.

Fletcher, John Edward. *A Study of the Life and Works of Athanasius Kircher, 'Germanus Incredibilis': With a Selection of His Unpublished Correspondence and an Annotated Translation of His Autobiography*. Leiden: Brill, 2011.

Fowler, Don. *Lucretius on Atomic Motion: A Commentary on "De Rerum Natura," Book Two, Lines 1–332*. Oxford: Oxford University Press, 2002.

Frank, Günter. "Melanchthon and the Tradition of Neoplatonism." In *Religious Confessions and the Sciences in the Sixteenth Century*, edited by J. Helm and A. Winkelmann, 3–18. Leiden: Brill, 2001.

French, Peter J. *John Dee: The World of the Elizabethan Magus*. New York: Routledge, 2013.

Friedrich, Hugo. *Montaigne*. Translated by Dawn Eng. Edited by Philippe Desan. Berkeley: University of California, Press, 1991.

Frye, Northrop. *Fables of Identity: Studies in Poetic Mythology*. New York: Harcourt, Brace and World, 1963.

————. "Recognition in *The Winter's Tale*." In *Essays on Shakespeare and Eliza-bethan Drama in Honor of Hardin Craig*, edited by Richard Hosley, 235–46. Columbia: University of Missouri Press, 1962.

Fulton, Elaine. "Acts of God: The Confessionalization of Disaster in Reforma-tion Europe." In *Historical Disasters in Context: Science, Religion, and Politics*, edited by Andrea Janku, Gerrit J. Schenk, and Franz Mauelshagen, 54–74. New York: Routledge, 2012.

Gaisser, Julia Haig. *The Fortunes of Apuleius and the "Golden Ass": A Study in Trans-mission and Reception*. Princeton: Princeton University Press, 2008.

Gal, Ofer. *Meanest Foundations and Nobler Superstructures: Hooke, Newton, and the 'Compounding of the Celestiall Motions of the Planetts'*. Dordrecht: Kluwer, 2002.

Gale, Monica. *Myth and Poetry in Lucretius*. Cambridge: Cambridge University Press, 1994.

Galluzzi, Paolo. "Leonardo da Vinci's Concept of 'Nature': 'More Cruel Step-mother than Mother.'" In *Aurora Torealis: Studies in the History of Science and Ideas in Honor of Tore Frängsmyr*, edited by Marco Beretta, Karl Grandin, and Svante Lindqvist, 13–29. Sagamore Beach, MA: Science History Pub-lications, 2008.

Gantner, Joseph. *Leonardos Visionen von der Sintflut und vom Untergang der Welt*. Bern: Francke Verlag, 1958.

Garrard, Greg. *Ecocriticism*. London: Routledge, 2004.

Gaukroger, Stephen. *The Emergence of a Scientific Culture: Science and the Shaping of Modernity, 1210-1685*. Oxford: Clarendon Press, 2006.

Geneva, Ann. *Astrology and the Seventeenth-Century Mind: William Lilly and the Language of the Stars*. Manchester: Manchester University Press, 1995.

Ghosh, Amitav. *The Great Derangement: Climate Change and the Unthinkable*. Chi-cago: University of Chicago Press, 2016.

Gilbert, Anthony. "'Unaccomodated man' and His Discontents in *King Lear*: Edmund the Bastard and Interrogative Puns." *Early Modern Literary Studies* 6, no. 2 (2000): 1–11.

Goddard, Charlotte. "Epicureanism and the Poetry of Lucretius in the Renais-sance." PhD diss., University of Cambridge, 1991.

Goddard, Harold C. *The Meaning of Shakespeare*. 2 vols. Chicago: University of Chicago Press, 1951.

Goetschel, Willi. *Constituting Critique: Kant's Writing as Critical Praxis*. Trans-lated by Eric Schwab. Durham, NC: Duke University Press, 1994.

Goldberg, Jonathan. *The Seeds of Things: Theorizing Sexuality and Materiality in Renaissance Representations*. New York: Fordham University Press, 2009.

————. "The Understanding of Sickness in Donne's *Devotions*." *Renaissance Quarterly* 24, no. 4 (1971): 507–17.

Goldstein, Amanda Jo. *Sweet Science: Romantic Materialism and the New Logic of Life*. Chicago: University of Chicago Press, 2017.

Gombrich, E. H. "The Form of Movement in Water and Air." In *Leonardo's Legacy*, edited by C. D. O'Malley, 171–204. Berkeley: University of California Press, 1969.

———. "Leonardo and the Magicians: Polemics and Rivalry." In *New Light on Old Masters*, 61–88. Oxford: Oxford University Press, 1986.

Goukowsky, M. "Du nouveau sur Léonard de Vinci: Leonard et Janus Lascaris." *Bibliothèque d'Humanisme et Renaissance* 19 (1957): 7–13.

Goulding, Robert. "Wings (or Stairs) to the Heavens: The Parallactic Treatises of John Dee and Thomas Digges." In *John Dee: Interdisciplinary Studies in English Renaissance Thought*, edited by Stephen Clucas. Dordrecht: Springer, 2006.

Graff, Gerald. *Professing Literature: An Institutional History*. Chicago: University of Chicago Press, 1989.

Granada, Miguel A. "Giordano Bruno y la eternidad del mundo." *Endoxa* 31 (2014): 349–72.

———. "Kepler and Bruno on the Infinity of the Universe and of Solar Systems." *Journal for the History of Astronomy* 39 (2008): 469–95.

———. "Michael Maestlin and the New Star of 1572." *Journal for the History of Astronomy* 38 (2007): 99–124.

———. "Thomas Digges, Giordano Bruno y el Desarrollo del Copernicanismo en Inglaterra." *Éndoxa* 4 (1994): 7–42.

———. "Tycho Brahe's Anti-Copernican Campaign: His Criticism of Michael Maestlin and Thomas Digges in the *Astronomiae instauratae progymnasmata*." In *Celestial Novelties on the Eve of the Scientific Revolution 1530–1630*, edited by Dario Tessicini and Patrick J. Boner, 185–207. Florence: Olschki, 2013.

Greenblatt, Stephen. *Shakespearean Negotiations: The Circulation of Social Energy in Renaissance England*. Berkeley: University of California Press, 1988.

———. *The Swerve: How the World Became Modern*. New York: Norton, 2011.

Grendler, Paul. *The Universities of the Italian Renaissance*. Baltimore: Johns Hopkins University Press, 2002.

Guibbory, Achsah. *Returning to John Donne*. New York: Routledge, 2015.

Guldentops, Guy. "The Sagacity of Bees: An Aristotelian Topos in Thirteenth-Century Philosophy." In *Aristotle's Animals in the Middle Ages and Renaissance*, edited by Carlos G. Steel, Guy Guldentops, and Pieter Beullens, 275–96. Leuven: Leuven University Press, 1999.

Guthrie, W. K. C. *A History of Greek Philosophy*. Vol. 2, *The Presocratic Tradition from Parmenides to Democritus*. Cambridge: Cambridge University Press, 1965.

Guyer, Paul. *Kant and the Experience of Freedom: Essays on Aesthetics and Morality.* Cambridge: Cambridge University Press, 1996.

Hagendahl, Harald. *Latin Fathers and the Classics: A Study on the Apologists, Jerome, and Other Christian Writers.* Stockholm: Almquist and Wiksell, 1958.

Hall, Bryan. "Kant on Newton, Genius, and Scientific Discovery." *Intellectual History Review* 24 (2014): 539–56.

Hamacher, Werner. *Premises: Essays on Philosophy and Literature from Kant to Celan.* Translated by Peter Fenves. Cambridge, MA: Harvard University Press, 1996.

Hamilton, John T. *Security: Politics, Humanity, and the Philology of Care.* Princeton: Princeton University Press, 2013.

Hampton, John. *Nicolas-Antoine Boulanger et la science de son temps.* Geneva: Librairie Droz, 1955.

Hampton, Timothy. *Writing from History: The Rhetoric of Exemplarity in Renaissance Literature.* Ithaca: Cornell University Press, 1990.

Hankins, James. "Monstrous Melancholy: Ficino and the Physiological Causes of Atheism." In *Laus Platonici Philosophi: Marsilio Ficino and His Influence,* edited by Stephen Clucas, Peter J. Forshaw, and Valery Rees, 25–44. Leiden: Brill, 2011.

Hardy, Matthew. "'Study the warm winds and the cold': Hippocrates and the Renaissance Villa." In *Aeolian Winds and the Spirit in Renaissance Architecture: Academia Eolia Revisited,* edited by Barbara Kenda, 48–69. New York: Routledge, 2006.

Harries, Karsten. "Descartes and the Labyrinth of the World." *International Journal of Philosophical Studies* 6, no. 3 (1998): 307–30.

Harris, Victor. *All Coherence Gone: A Study of the Seventeenth-Century Controversy over Disorder and Decay in the Universe.* Chicago: University of Chicago Press, 1949.

Harrison, Peter. *The Fall of Man and the Foundations of Science.* Cambridge: Cambridge University Press, 2007.

Harvey, Elizabeth D., and Timothy M. Harrison. "Embodied Resonances: Early Modern Science and Tropologies of Connection in Donne's Anniversaries." *ELH* 80 (2013): 981–1008.

Hellman, Clarisse Doris. *The Comet of 1577: Its Place in the History of Astronomy.* New York: Columbia University Press, 1944.

———. "The Gradual Abandonment of the Aristotelian Universe: A Preliminary Note on Some Sidelights." In *Mélanges Alexandre Koyré,* vol. 1, *L'aventure de la science,* edited by Bernard I. Cohen and René Taton, 283–93. Paris: Hermann, 1964.

Hettner, Hermann. *Geschichte der deutschen Literatur im Achtzehnten Jahrhundert.* Edited by George Witowski. 4 vols. Leipzig: P. List, 1928.

Hirsch, David A. Hedrich. "Donne's Atomies and Anatomies: Deconstructed Bodies and the Resurrection of Atomic Theory." *Studies in English Literature, 1500–1900* 31, no. 1 (1991): 69–94.

Holford-Strevens, Leofranc. "*Horror vacui* in Lucretian Biography." *Leeds International Classical Studies* 1, no. 1 (2002): 1–23.

Holmes, Brooke. "Michel Serres's Non-Modern Lucretius: Manifold Reason and the Temporality of Reception." In *Lucretius and Modernity*, edited by Jacques Lezra and Liza Blake, 21–37. New York: Palgrave, 2016.

Hooykaas, Reijer. "Thomas Digges' Puritanism." *Archives Internationales d'Histoire des Sciences*, 1955, 145–59.

Huet, Marie-Hélène. *The Culture of Disaster*. Chicago: University of Chicago Press, 2012.

Hume, Angela. "Imagining Ecopoetics: An Interview with Robert Hass, Brenda Hillman, Evelyn Reilly, and Jonathan Skinner." ISLE 19, no. 4 (2012): 751–66.

Iannucci, Amilcare A. "Saturn in Dante." In *Saturn: From Antiquity to the Renaissance*, edited by M. Ciavolella and A. A. Iannucci, 51–67. Ottawa: Dovehouse, 1992.

Jaspers, Karl. *Leonardo, Descartes, Max Weber: Three Essays*. New York: Routledge, 2013.

Jeanneret, Michel. *Perpetual Motion: Transforming Shapes in the Renaissance from da Vinci to Montaigne*. Translated by Nidra Poller. Baltimore: Johns Hopkins University Press, 2001.

Johnson, Barbara. *Persons and Things*. Cambridge, MA: Harvard University Press, 2008.

Johnson, Christopher D. *Hyperboles: The Rhetoric of Excess in Baroque Literature and Thought*. Cambridge, MA: Harvard University Press, 2010.

Johnson, Francis R. "Thomas Digges and the Infinity of the Universe." In *Theories of the Universe*, edited by Milton K. Munitz, 184–97. New York: Free Press, 1957.

Johnson, Francis R., and Sanford V. Larkey. "Thomas Digges, the Copernican System, and the Idea of the Infinity of the Universe in 1576." *Huntington Library Bulletin* 5 (1934): 69–117.

Johnson, Gregory R. "The Tree of Melancholy: Kant on Philosophy and Enthusiasm." In *Kant and the New Philosophy of Religion*, edited by Chris L. Firestone and Stephen R. Palmquist, 43–61. Bloomington: Indiana University Press, 2006.

Jones, Matthew L. *The Good Life in the Scientific Revolution: Descartes, Pascal, Leibniz, and the Cultivation of Virtue*. Chicago: University of Chicago Press, 2006.

Jorgensen, Paul A. "*Much Ado About Nothing.*" *Shakespeare Quarterly* 5, no. 3 (1954): 287–95.

Kail, P. J. E. "Efficient Causation in Hume." In *Efficient Causation: A History,* edited by Tad M. Schmaltz, 231–57. Oxford: Oxford University Press, 2014.

Keele, Kenneth D. *Leonardo da Vinci's Elements of the Science of Man.* New York: Academic Press, 1983.

Keller, Catherine. *Apocalypse Now and Then: A Feminist Guide to the End of the World.* Boston: Beacon Press, 1996.

Kemp, Martin. *Leonardo da Vinci: Experience, Experiment, and Design.* Princeton: Princeton University Press, 2006.

———. *Leonardo da Vinci: The Marvellous Works of Nature and Man.* Oxford: Oxford University Press, 2007.

———. "Leonardo da Vinci: Science and the Poetic Impulse." *Journal of the Royal Society of Arts* 133 (1985): 196–214.

Kibre, Pearl. "Hippocrates Latinus: Repertorium of Hippocratic Writings in the Latin Middle Ages (V)." *Traditio* 35 (1979): 273–302.

King, Margaret L. *The Death of the Child Valerio Marcello.* Chicago: University of Chicago Press, 1994.

Konstantinou, Lee. *Cool Characters: Irony and American Fiction.* Cambridge, MA: Harvard University Press, 2016.

Koyré, Alexandre. *From the Closed World to the Infinite Universe.* Baltimore: Johns Hopkins University Press, 1957.

Krautter, Konrad. *Philologische Methode und humanistische Existenz: Filippo Beroaldo und sein Kommentar zum "Goldenen Esel" des Apuleius.* Munich: Fink, 1971.

Kretzmann, Norman. "Syncategoremata, exponibilia, sophismata." In *The Cambridge History of Later Medieval Philosophy from the Rediscovery of Aristotle to the Disintegration of Scholasticism, 1100-1600,* edited by Norman Kretzmann, Anthony Kenny, and Jan Pinborg, 211–45. Cambridge: Cambridge University Press, 1982.

Kusukawa, Sachiko. *The Transformation of Natural Philosophy: The Case of Philip Melanchthon.* Cambridge: Cambridge University Press, 1995.

Kwakkelstein, Michael W. "The Lost Book on 'moti mentali.'" *Achademia Leonardi Vinci* 6 (1993): 56–69.

Lamberton, Robert D. *Homer the Theologian: Neoplatonist Allegorical Reading and the Growth of the Epic Tradition.* Berkeley: University of California Press, 1989.

Landau, Aaron. "'No Settled Senses of the World Can Match the Pleasure of That Madness': The Politics of Unreason in *The Winter's Tale.*" *Cahiers Élisabéthains* 64, no. 1 (2003): 29–42.

Lange, Friedrich. *The History of Materialism and Criticism of Its Present Importance.* Translated by Ernest Chester Thomas. 3 vols. Boston: Osgood, 1880.

Langer, Ulrich. *Divine and Poetic Freedom in the Renaissance: Nominalist Theology and Literature in France and Italy.* Princeton: Princeton University Press, 2014.

Langholf, Volker. "L'air (pneuma) et les maladies." In *La maladie et les maladies dans la collection hippocratique, Actes du VIe colloque international hippocratique,* edited by Paul Potter, Gilles Maloney, and Jacques Desautels, 339–59. Quebec: Les Éditions du Spinx, 1990.

Lee, Mi-Kyoung, *Epistemology after Protagoras.* Oxford: Oxford University Press, 2005.

Longo, Susanna Gambino. *Savoir de la nature et poésie des choses: Lucrèce et Epicure à la Renaissance italienne.* Paris: Honoré Champion, 2004.

Lorenz, Philip. *The Tears of Sovereignty: Perspectives of Power in Renaissance Drama.* New York: Fordham University Press, 2013.

Lupton, Julia Reinhard. *Afterlives of the Saints: Hagiography, Typology, and Renaissance Literature.* Palo Alto: Stanford University Press, 1996.

Lutz, Cora E. "Democritus and Heraclitus." *Classical Journal* 49, no. 7 (1954): 309–14.

Lyotard, Jean-François. *Lessons on the Analytic of the Sublime: Kant's "Critique of Judgment,"* [sections] *23–29.* Translated by Elizabeth Rottenberg. Palo Alto: Stanford University Press, 1994.

MacPhail, Eric. "Montaigne's New Epicureanism." *Montaigne Studies* 12 (2000): 94–104.

Maiorino, Giancarlo. *Leonardo da Vinci: The Daedalian Mythmaker.* University Park: Pennsylvania State University Press, 1992.

Makkreel, Rudolf A. *Imagination and Interpretation in Kant: The Hermeneutical Import of the "Critique of Judgment."* Chicago: University of Chicago Press, 1994.

Mann, Joel E. *Hippocrates, On the Art of Medicine.* Leiden: Brill, 2012.

Manuel, Frank E. *The Eighteenth Century Confronts the Gods.* Cambridge, MA: Harvard University Press, 1959.

Marsh, David. *Lucian and the Latins: Humor and Humanism in the Early Renaissance.* Ann Arbor: University of Michigan Press, 1992.

Martin, Craig. *Renaissance Meteorology: Pomponazzi to Descartes.* Baltimore: Johns Hopkins University Press, 2011.

Martin, L. C. "Shakespeare, Lucretius, and the Commonplaces." *Review of English Studies* 21 (1945): 176–82.

Masters, Roger D. *Fortune Is a River: Leonardo da Vinci and Niccolò Machiavelli's Magnificent Dream to Change the Course of Florentine History.* New York: Plume, 1999.

McKibben, Bill. *The End of Nature.* New York: Random House, 1989.

Meek, Richard. *Narrating the Visual in Shakespeare.* New York: Ashgate, 2009.

Meinel, Christoph. "Early Seventeenth-Century Atomism: Theory, Epistemology, and the Insufficiency of Experiment." *Isis* 79 (1988): 68–103.

Mensch, Jennifer. "Intuition and Nature in Kant and Goethe." *European Journal of Philosophy* 19, no. 3 (2009): 431–53.

Methuen, Charlotte. "The Role of the Heavens in the Thought of Philip Melanchthon." *Journal of the History of Ideas* 57, no. 3 (1996): 385–403.

Moffitt, J. F. "The Evidentia of Curling Waters and Whirling Winds: Leonardo's Ekphraseis of the Latin Weathermen." *Achademia Leonardi Vinci* 4 (1991): 11–33.

Morton, Timothy. *Hyperobjects: Philosophy and Ecology after the End of the World.* Minneapolis: University of Minnesota Press, 2013.

Muir, Kenneth. "Samuel Harsnett and *King Lear.*" *Review of English Studies* 2, no. 5 (1951): 11–21.

Müntz, Eugène. *Leonardo da Vinci: Artist, Thinker, and Man of Science.* 2 vols. London: Heinemann, 1898.

Naddaff, Gerard. "Allegory and the Origins of Philosophy." In *Logos and Muthos: Philosophical Essays in Greek Literature,* edited by William Wians, 99–132. Albany: SUNY Press, 2009.

Nanni, Romano. "Le 'disputationes' pichiane sull'astrologia e Leonardo." In *Leonardo e Pico: Analogie, contatti, confronti,* edited by Fabio Frosini, 53–98. Florence: Olschki, 2005.

Neiman, Susan. *Evil in Modern Thought: An Alternative History of Philosophy.* Princeton: Princeton University Press, 2002.

Nelson, Axel. *Die Hippokratische Schrift "Peri physon."* Uppsala: Almqvist & Wiksell, 1909.

Niccoli, Ottavia. *Prophecy and People in Renaissance Italy.* Translated by Lydia G. Cochrane. Princeton: Princeton University Press, 1990.

Nicholl, Charles. *Leonardo da Vinci: Flights of the Mind.* New York: Viking, 2004.

Nicolson, Marjorie Hope. *Mountain Gloom and Mountain Glory: The Development of the Aesthetics of the Infinite.* 1959. Reprint. Seattle: University of Washington Press, 1997.

Nightingale, Andrea. "Night-Vision: Epicurean Eschatology." *Arion: A Journal of Humanities and the Classics,* 3rd ser., 14, no. 3 (2007): 61–98.

Nisbet, Hugh Barr. "Lucretius in Eighteenth-Century Germany." *Modern Language Review* 81 (1986): 97–115.

Nixon, Rob. *Slow Violence and the Environmentalism of the Poor.* Cambridge, MA: Harvard University Press, 2011.

Nova, Alessandro. *The Book of the Wind: The Representation of the Invisible.* Montreal: McGill-Queen's University Press, 2011.

Novikoff, Alex J. *The Medieval Culture of Disputation: Pedagogy, Practice, and Performance.* Philadelphia: University of Pennsylvania Press, 2013.

Oldroyd, David R. "Geological Controversy in the Seventeenth Century: 'Hooke vs Wallis' and Its Aftermath." In *Robert Hooke: New Studies*, edited by Michael Hunter and Simon Schaffer, 207–34. Woodbridge: Boydell Press, 1989.

———. "Robert Hooke's Methodology of Science as Exemplified in His 'Discourse of Earthquakes.'" *British Journal for the History of Science* 6, no. 2 (1972): 109–30.

Palmer, Abram Smythe. *Folk-etymology; A Dictionary of Verbal Corruptions Or Words Perverted in Form Or Meaning, by False Derivation Or Mistaken Analogy.* New York: Henry Holt, 1890.

Palmer, Ada. *Reading Lucretius in the Renaissance.* Cambridge, MA: Harvard University Press, 2014.

Panofsky, Erwin. "Father Time." In *Studies in Iconology: Humanistic Themes in the Art of the Renaissance*, 69–93. New York: Harper Torchbook, 1939.

Parcell, William C. "Signs and Symbols in Kircher's *Mundus Subterraneus*." In *The Revolution in Geology from the Renaissance to the Enlightenment*, edited by Gary D. Rosenberg, 63–74. Boulder, CO: Geological Society of America, 2009.

Passannante, Gerard. "The Art of Reading Earthquakes: On Harvey's Wit, Ramus's Method, and the Renaissance of Lucretius." *Renaissance Quarterly* 61, no. 3 (2008): 792–832.

———. *The Lucretian Renaissance: Philology and the Afterlife of Tradition.* Chicago: University of Chicago Press, 2011.

Pedretti, Carlo. *The Drawings and Miscellaneous Papers of Leonardo da Vinci in the Collection of Her Majesty the Queen at Windsor Castle.* Vol. 1, *Landscapes, Plants, and Water Studies.* New York: Harcourt Brace Jovanovich, 1982.

———. *Leonardo: A Study in Chronology and Style.* Berkeley: University of California Press, 1973.

———, ed. *The Literary Works of Leonardo da Vinci, Compiled and Edited from the Original Manuscripts by Jean Paul Richter: Commentary.* 2 vols. Berkeley: University of California Press, 1977.

———. "The Sforza Sepulchre." *Gazette des Beaux-Arts* 89 (1977): 121–31.

Phillips, J. H. "Lucretius and the (Hippocratic) *On Breaths*: Addenda." In *Textes médicaux latins antiques*, edited by G. Sabbah, 83–85. Saint Étienne: L'Universitaire de Saint-Étienne, 198.

Picciotto, Joanna. *Labors of Innocence in Early Modern England.* Cambridge, MA: Harvard University Press, 2010.

Pironet, Fabienne. "Sophismata." In *The Stanford Encyclopedia of Philosophy*, edited by E. Zalta. https://plato.stanford.edu/entries/sophismata/.

Poggi, Davide. "Standing in Front of the Ocean: Kant and the Dangers of Knowledge." In *Kant and the Metaphors of Reason*, edited by Patricia Kauark-Leite, Giorgia Cecchinato, Virginia De Araujo Figueiredo, Margit Ruffing, and Alice Serra, 87–106. Hildesheim: Georg Olms, 2015.

Poole, William. *The World Makers: Scientists of the Restoration and the Search for the Origins of the Earth*. Oxford: Peter Lang, 2010.

Porter, James I. "Lucretius and the Poetics of Void." In *Le jardin romain: Epicurisme et poésie à Rome*, edited by Annick Monet, 197–226. Lille: Presses de l'Université Charles-de-Gaulle, 2003.

———. "Lucretius and the Sublime." In *The Cambridge Companion to Lucretius*, edited by Stuart Gillespie and Philip Hardie, 167–85. Cambridge: Cambridge University Press, 2007.

———. *The Sublime in Antiquity*. Cambridge: Cambridge University Press, 2016.

Premuda, Loris. "Motivi senecani in Leonardo." In *Leonardo nella scienza e nella tecnica*, edited by Carlo Maccagni, 235–44. Florence: Giunti Barbèra, 1975.

Pumfrey, Stephen. "'Your astronomers and ours differ exceedingly': The Controversy over the 'New Star' of 1572 in the Light of a Newly Discovered Text by Thomas Digges." *British Journal for the History of Science* 44, no. 1 (2011): 29–60.

Pye, Christopher. "Against Schmitt: Law, Aesthetics, and Absolutism in Shakespeare's *Winter's Tale*." *South Atlantic Quarterly* 108, no. 1 (2009): 197–217.

Raimondi, Ezio. "Il primo commento umanistico a Lucrezio." In *Tra latino e volgare: Per Carlo Dionisotti*, 2:641–74. Padua: Antenore, 1974.

Rappaport, Rhoda. "Hooke on Earthquakes: Lectures, Strategy, and Audience." *British Journal for the History of Science* 19 (1986): 129–46.

Ray, Gene. "Reading the Lisbon Earthquake: Adorno, Lyotard, and the Contemporary Sublime." *Yale Journal of Criticism* 17, no. 1 (2004): 1–18.

Reeve, M. D. "The Textual Tradition of *Aetna*, *Ciris*, and *Catalepton*." *Maia* 27 (1975): 231–47.

Reiche, Harald. "Myth and Magic in Cosmological Polemics: Plato, Aristotle, Lucretius." *Rheinisches Museum* 114 (1971): 296–329.

Reti, Ladislao. *The Library of Leonardo da Vinci*. Los Angeles: Castle Press for Elmer Belt and Jake Zeitlin, 1972.

Rideal, Rebecca. *1666: Plague, War, and Hellfire*. New York: St. Martin's Press, 2016.

Roberts, Julian, and Andrew G. Watson, eds. *John Dee's Library Catalogue*. London: Bibliographical Society, 1990.

Robertson, Kellie. "Medieval Materialism: A Manifesto." *Exemplaria* 22, no. 2 (2010): 99–118.

Rogers, Henry. "The Genius and Writings of Pascal." *Edinburgh Review* 85 (January 1847): 178–220.

Rosen, Alan. *Dislocating the End: Climax, Closure, and the Invention of Genre.* New York: Peter Lang, 2001.

Rosen, Edward. *The Naming of the Telescope.* New York: H. Schuman, 1947.

Rosenthal, Arthur. "Dürer's Dream of 1525." *Burlington Magazine* 69 (1936): 82–85.

Rossi, Paolo. *The Dark Abyss of Time: The History of the Earth and the History of Nations from Hooke to Vico.* Translated by Lydia G. Cochrane. Chicago: University of Chicago Press, 1984.

Rudwick, Martin J. S. *The Meaning of Fossils: Episodes in the History of Paleontology.* Chicago: University of Chicago Press, 2008.

Rugoff, Ralph. *The Eye of the Needle: The Unique World of Microminiatures of Hagop Sandaldjian.* West Covina, CA: Society for the Diffusion of Useful Information Press, 1996.

Sadrin, Paul. "Diderot et Nicolas-Antoine Boulanger." *Recherches sur Diderot et sur l'Encyclopédie* 4 (1988): 42–47.

Saxl, Fritz. "Veritas Filia Temporis." In *Philosophy and History: Essays Presented to Ernst Cassirer,* edited by Raymond Klibansky and H. J. Paton, 228–40. Oxford: Oxford University Press, 1936.

Schabel, Christopher, ed. *Theological Quodlibeta in the Middle Ages.* 2 vols. Leiden: Brill, 2006–7.

Schaffer, Simon. "The Phoenix of Nature: Fire and Evolutionary Cosmology in Wright and Kant." *Journal for the History of Astronomy* 9 (1978): 180–200.

Schenk, Gerrit Jasper, ed. *Historical Disaster Experiences: Towards a Comparative and Transcultural History of Disasters across Asia and Europe.* Dordrecht: Springer, 2017.

Schlutz, Alexander M. *Mind's World: Imagination and Subjectivity from Descartes to Romanticism.* Seattle: University of Washington Press, 2009.

Schönfeld, Martin. "Kant's Early Cosmology." In *A Companion to Kant,* edited by Graham Bird, 47–62. Oxford: Blackwell, 2006.

———. *The Philosophy of the Young Kant: The Precritical Project.* Oxford: Oxford University Press, 2000.

Schrijvers, P. H. "Seeing the Invisible: A Study of Lucretius' Use of Analogy in *De rerum natura.*" In *Oxford Readings in Lucretius,* edited by Monica Gale, 255–88. Oxford: Oxford University Press, 2007.

Schulman, Alex. *The Secular Contract: The Politics of Enlightenment.* New York: Continuum, 2011.

Schumacher, Joachim. "'Il non finito,' 'Nothing,' and 'Second Nature' in Joseph Gantner's *Leonardos Visionen.*" *Renaissance News* 12, no. 4 (1959): 243–50.

Scodel, Joshua. *Excess and the Mean in Early Modern English Literature*. Princeton: Princeton University Press, 2002.

Screech, Michael Andrew. *Rabelais*. London: Duckworth, 1979.

Sedgwick, Eve Kosofsky. *Touching Feeling: Affect, Pedagogy, Performativity*. Durham: Duke University Press, 2003.

Sedley, David. "Irony and the Vacuum in Pascal and Montaigne." In *Esprit généreux, esprit pantagruélicque: Essays by His Students in Honor of François Rigolot*, edited by Reiner Leushuis and Zahi Zalloua, 279–97. Geneva: Droz, 2008.

Serres, Michel. *The Birth of Physics*. Edited with an introduction by David Webb. Translated by Jack Hawkes. Manchester: Clinamen Press, 2000.

Shea, William R. "Filled with Wonder: Kant's Cosmological Essay, the *Universal Natural History and Theory of the Heavens*." In *Kant's Philosophy of Physical Science*, edited by Robert E. Butts, 95–124. Dordrecht: D. Reidel, 1986.

Shell, Susan Meld. *The Embodiment of Reason: Kant on Spirit, Generation, and Community*. Chicago: University of Chicago Press, 1996.

Simon, David Carroll. "The Anatomy of Schadenfreude; or, Montaigne's Laughter." *Critical Inquiry* 43, no. 2 (2017): 250–80.

———. *Light without Heat: The Observational Mood from Bacon to Milton*. Ithaca: Cornell University Press, 2018.

Smith, Hallett. "Leontes's Affectio." *Shakespeare Quarterly* 14, no. 2 (1963): 163–66.

Smith, Webster. "Observations on the Mona Lisa Landscape." *Art Bulletin* 67, no. 2 (1985): 183–99.

Somaini, Antonio. *Ejzenštejn: Il cinema, le arti, il montaggio*. Turin: Einaudi, 2011.

Sorensen, Lee, ed. "Joseph Gantner." In *Dictionary of Art Historians*. https://dictionaryofarthistorians.org/gantnerj.htm.

Stewart, Alan. *Shakespeare's Letters*. Oxford: Oxford University Press, 2008.

Stewart, Susan. *The Poet's Freedom*. Chicago: University of Chicago Press, 2011.

Stowell, Steven F. H. *The Spiritual Language of Art: Medieval Christian Themes in Writings on Art of the Italian Renaissance*. Leiden: E. J. Brill, 2014.

Targoff, Ramie. *John Donne: Body and Soul*. Chicago: University of Chicago Press, 2008.

Temkin, Owsei. *The Falling Sickness: A History of Epilepsy from the Greeks to the Beginnings of Modern Neurology*. Baltimore: Johns Hopkins University Press, 1994.

Thorndike, Lynn. *A History of Magic and Experimental Science*. 8 vols. New York: Columbia University Press, 1938–54.

———. "Some Thirteenth-Century Classics." *Speculum* 2, no. 4 (1927): 374–84.

Tiffany, Daniel. *Infidel Poetics: Riddles, Nightlife, Substance*. Chicago: University of Chicago Press, 2009.

————. *Toy Medium: Materialism and Modern Lyric*. Berkeley: University of California Press, 2000.

Tredwell, Katherine A. "The Melanchthon Circle's English Epicycle." *Centaurus*, 2006, 23–31.

Trevor, Douglas. *The Poetics of Melancholy in Early Modern England*. Cambridge: Cambridge University Press, 2009.

Turner, A. J. "Hooke's Theory of the Earth's Axial Displacement: Some Contemporary Opinion." *British Journal for the History of Science* 7, no. 2 (1974): 166–70.

Valéry, Paul. "Introduction to the Method of Leonardo da Vinci." In *The Collected Works of Paul Valéry*, vol. 8, *Leonardo, Poe, Mallarmé*, translated by Malcolm Cowley and James R. Lawler, 3–63. Princeton: Princeton University Press, 1972.

————. "Note and Digression." In *The Collected Works of Paul Valéry*, vol. 8, *Leonardo, Poe, Mallarmé*, translated by Malcolm Cowley and James R. Lawler, 64–109. Princeton: Princeton University Press, 1972.

Van Hulle, Dirk, and Mark Nixon. *Samuel Beckett's Library*. Cambridge: Cambridge University Press, 2013.

Vecce, Carlo. "Leonardo e il gioco." In *Passare il tempo: La letteratura del gioco e dell'intrattenimento dal XII al XVI secolo*, 1:269–312. Rome: Salerno Editrice, 1993.

Veldman, Robin Globus. "Narrating the Environmental Apocalypse: How Imagining the End Facilitates Moral Reasoning among Environmental Activists." *Ethics & the Environment* 17, no. 1 (2012): 1–23.

Viatte, Françoise. *'Della figura che va contro il vento': Il tema del soffio nell'opera di Leonardo da Vinci*. Florence: Giunti, 2006.

Vila, Anne C. *Suffering Scholars: Pathologies of the Intellectual in Enlightenment France*. Philadelphia: University of Pennsylvania Press, 2018.

Waldron, Jennifer. *Reformations of the Body: Idolatry, Sacrifice, and Early Modern Theater*. New York: Palgrave Macmillan, 2013.

Wang, Orrin N. C. *Romantic Sobriety: Sensation, Revolution, Commodification, History*. Baltimore: Johns Hopkins University Press, 2011.

Warburg, Aby. "Sandro Botticelli's *Birth of Venus* and *Spring*." In *The Renewal of Pagan Antiquity: Contributions to the Cultural History of the European Renaissance*, translated by David Britt, 89–156. Los Angeles: Getty, 1999.

Webster, Charles. *The Great Instauration: Science, Medicine, and Reform*. 2nd ed. Oxford: Peter Lang, 2002.

Weichenhan, Micahel. *"Ergo perit coelum . . .": Die Supernova des Jahres 1572 und die Überwindung der aristotelischen Kosmologie*. Stuttgart: Franz Steiner, 2004.

Weisheipl, James A., ed. *Albertus Magnus and the Sciences: Commemorative Essays, 1980*. Toronto: Pontifical Institute of Medieval Studies, 1980.

Weschler, Lawrence. *Mr. Wilson's Cabinet of Wonders: Pronged Ants, Horned Humans, Mice on Toast, and Other Marvels of Jurassic Technology*. New York: Vintage, 1995.

Westman, Robert. *The Copernican Question: Prognostication, Skepticism, and Celestial Order*. Berkeley: University of California Press, 2011.

Wilkinson, L. P. *The Georgics of Virgil: A Critical Survey*. Cambridge: Cambridge University Press, 1969.

Williams, Gareth. *The Cosmic Viewpoint: A Study of Seneca's "Natural Questions."* Oxford: Oxford University Press, 2012.

Wilson, Catherine. *The Invisible World: Early Modern Philosophy and the Invention of the Microscope*. Princeton: Princeton University Press, 1995.

———. "The Presence of Lucretius in Eighteenth-Century French and German Philosophy." In *Lucretius and Modernity: Epicurean Encounters across Time and Disciplines*, edited by Jacques Lezra and Liza Blake, 71–88. New York: Palgrave Macmillan, 2016.

———. "Visual Surface and Visual Symbol: The Microscope and the Occult in Early Modern Science." *Journal of the History of Ideas* 49, no. 1 (1988): 85–108.

Wimsatt, W. K., and Monroe Beardsley. *The Verbal Icon: Studies in the Meaning of Poetry*. Lexington: University Press of Kentucky, 1954.

Wind, Edgar. "Mathematics and Sensibility." *Listener* (London), May 1, 1952, 705–6.

Wolfe, Jessica. *Humanism, Machinery, and Renaissance Literature*. Cambridge: Cambridge University Press, 2004.

Yeo, Richard. *Notebooks, English Virtuosi, and Early Modern Science*. Chicago: University of Chicago Press, 2014.

Zambelli, Paola. "Many Ends for the World: Luca Gaurico Instigator of the Debate in Italy and Germany." In *"Astrologi hallucinati": Stars and the End of the World in Luther's Time*, edited by Paola Zambelli, 239–63. Berlin and New York: Walter de Gruyter, 1986.

INDEX

Note: References to figures are denoted by an "f" following the page number.

Acosta, José de, 172
affection, 139–40
Aït-Touati, Frédérique, 164n61
Alberti, Leon Battista, 28, 54; *Momus*
(1450) of, 45–46
Albertus Magnus, 35–36, 37n41, 63
Altman, Joel, 128n44
analogy, 5n12, 6–8, 24, 29, 45–49,
97, 100, 102, 107, 129, 205, 243;
ancient, 56–58, 61, 66; and astrology, 118; catastrophic, 29,
62, 65; cosmic force of, 78; of
Democritus, 45–46; domesticating, 12n34, 49; of Donne,
107–8, 113; of dust in sunlight,
6–7, 23, 60, 99–100, 110, 119n15,
165–66, 198, 217–18; Epicurean
style of, 198–99; instrument of,
228; intoxication of, 57; involuntariness of certain kinds of, 29; of
Leonardo, 34, 45, 47, 49, 54–63;
materialist, 6–7, 18, 23, 34, 45–49,
56–61, 66, 76–77, 99–100, 107,
119n15, 158, 165–66, 217; microcosm-macrocosm, 20, 45–46,
76, 107; reasoning by, 16n49; of
the sensible with the insensible,
24, 28; terrestrial, 213; of wind

and water, 29, 47n76, 48, 54–58,
60–61, 66
Anaxagoras, 17n53, 45, 97, 119–21,
124
Anderson, Judith, 139
animals, 42, 44, 53. *See also* insects
Anonymous: *Eikon Basilike* (1649) of,
169; *Eikon e piste* (1649) of, 169–70;
"Fürstellung des Erdbebens zu
Lissabon" (1756) of, 215f
Anton, Robert, 131–32
apocalypse, 30, 117; biblical, 4n9,
81n7, 103; doomsday rhetoric of,
50; enthusiasm of, 170; in poetry,
81n7, 111; signs of, 84. *See also*
catastrophe; disaster; eschatology;
prophecy
apostrophe, 139, 139n68
Aquinas, Thomas, 66n143
architecture, 58
Aristotle, 5, 7, 17n52, 121; commentators on, 36; on logical fallacies,
118n12; *Physics* of, 119; on volcanoes, 61n126
art: description of, 69; divinity of,
67
astrology, 30n10, 32n23, 37n44, 82,
88–89, 133–34, 182; atomism and,

astrology (*continued*)
118, 131–32; critique of, 32, 121n24, 130–31; defense of, 143; doomsday, 134–35; doubters of, 80, 88; excess of, 118, 121. *See also* astronomy; catastrophe; disaster; Harvey, John; Harvey, Richard; prognostication; prophecy; stars

astronomy, 88–91, 94, 102, 141–42, 175; Copernican, 175; debates in, 80; supernova in, 81–82, 89, 92–93, 177. *See also* astrology; comet; Digges, Thomas; earth; infinity; Kepler, Johannes; mathematics; science; stars

ataraxia, 2, 2n2, 8, 22, 210

atheism, 88–90, 161

atomism, 2–7, 2n5, 8n22, 13–19, 28, 45, 57, 89, 98–99, 105–7, 131–35, 156–60, 163, 175; and astrology, 131–32; classical, 60, 124, 142–43; Kant's engagement with the tradition of, 196–98, 231; material, 111–12; principles of, 69; shaky ground of, 199; temporal, 111–12. *See also* Epicureans; insects; Lucretius; materialism

Augustine, Saint, 66n143, 95n49, 110n100, 112

Bacon, Francis, 134, 154n20, 154n22, 162, 174n89, 179n103, 191; *Instauratio Magna* (1620) of, 189; method of, 176; middle way of, 155n25; *The New Organon* (1620) of, 154, 156; skepticism of, 155; *The Wisedome of the Ancients* (1619) of, 154–55; use of Democritus of, 98–100, 154–57, 169

Barkan, Leonard, 39n54, 146

Barruel, Abbé Augustin, 224n88

Baxandall, Michael, 28

Baxter, Richard, 178n98

Beardsley, Monroe, 79

Beckett, Samuel: *Malone Dies* (1951) of, 114; *Murphy* (1938) of, 115n5 before and after, 214–20, 234

Bembo, Pietro, 63

Berger, Harry, "The Ecology of the Mind" (1964) of, 240

Beroaldo, Filippo, 74, 75n167, 77n174

bestiary, medieval, 37

Bible, 43, 43n61, 52–53, 153; interpretation of the, 121. *See also* Christianity; eschatology

Bilson, Thomas, 120

Blumenberg, Hans, 8n23; *Paradigms for a Metaphorology* (1960) of, 11; *Shipwreck with Spectator* (1985) of, 11, 13

Boethius, 95n49; *Consolation of Philosophy* (ca. 524) of, 94

Bologna, 74. *See also* Italy

Boner, Patrick J., 101

Boulanger, Nicolas Antoine, 187, 188nn125–26, 191; *Antiquité dévoilée* (1766), 189–90; catastrophizing of, 191; *Christianisme dévoilé* (1761, published under the name of Boulanger), 188n125; Diderot on, 190–91

Boyle, Robert, 161, 179n101, 214n68; *The Christian Virtuoso* (1690) of, 164

Boys, John, 145–46

Brahe, Tycho, 81n7; criticisms of Digges of, 82n9

Bramante, Donato, 32, 45

Braun, Georg, 214; map of Lisbon of, 214n71

Bruno, Giordano, 97, 101, 122; *Ex-*

pulsion of the Triumphant Beast (1584) of, 81
Buch, Robert, 70n153
Burton, Robert, *The Anatomy of Melancholy* (1621) of, 102, 109

Calfhill, James, 120
Calvi, Gerolamo, 61n125
Calvin, John, 126. *See also* Reformation
Campbell, Stephen J., 65n142
Carey, John, 104n76
Carleton, George, 143
Cassirer, Ernst, 201n30, 234
catastrophe, 78, 87–88, 133, 140, 152; anthropology of, 188; atoms and, 2–7, 10–19, 89, 98–99, 195; dedramatization of, 12, 48–49; encounter with materialism as a, 4–5, 79–113; etymology of, 10; experience of, 172; feeling of, 13; history of, 171, 187; human cost of, 173; images of, 47, 57, 62, 150, 237; imagining of, 34, 41–42, 67, 237; and the inevitability of ideas, 197; of Kant, 192–235; mental, 241–42; modern usage of the term of, 87; natural, 241; potential, 148; scientific study of, 48, 54; sounds of, 62; spectator of, 13; sudden, 173; thoughts of, 75, 149, 199, 218; uses in drama of the term of, 10, 88, 132. *See also* apocalypse; catastrophizing; comet; disaster; earthquake; fire; flood; plague; tragedy; volcano
catastrophic materialism. *See* materialism
catastrophizing, 1–26, 69, 86, 115–16, 132, 136, 166, 176, 208; addictive structure of, 217, 234; affective

structure of, 193, 221–23, 227–28, 231; and climate change, 236–44; habits of, 243; history of, 12, 148, 237, 241–43; horror of, 199; lessons of, 103; materialist, 113, 195–203, 217, 228; response to, 98, 113, 148; and self-reflection, 4, 9, 242n13, 243; the specter of, 158. *See also* catastrophe; disaster; materialism
Cavell, Stanley, 19–20; *Disowning Knowledge in Seven Plays of Shakespeare* (2003) of, 144
Cavendish, Margaret, 12–14, 165; *Blazing World* (1666) of, 13; *Poems, and Fancies* (1653) of, 165
Cecil, William (Lord Burghley), 82
Chambers, Richard, 117n9
Charents, Yeghishe, 148
Charleton, Walter, 163–65
Charron, Pierre, *De la sagesse* (1601), 141
Christianity: cosmology and, 98; eschatology of, 23; origins of, 188. *See also* apocalypse; eschatology; God; Paul; providence
Cicero, 8, 17, 94n48, 174, 185, 203, 228n101; *Academica* of, 136–39, 155, 155n24
Clark, David L., 210–11, 211n63, 226n93, 235n123
Clark, Kenneth, 48, 71n161
climate change, 236–44. *See also* catastrophizing
clinamen (swerve), 10, 196–97. *See also* atomism; Epicurus; Lucretius
Coleridge, Samuel, 203
comedy, 13; of riddles, 34, 42. *See also* Democritus; drama; laughter; riddle; satire
comet, 81–83, 88; of Halley, 87
Conger, George Perrigo, 107

Conte, Gian Biago, 6, 13n37, 49
Cooper, Thomas, 132
Copernicus, Nicolaus, 83, 90, 93–96, 99–101, 140–41, 142nn76–77, 175
Cornutus, 123. *See also* Homer
Corsali, Andrea, 38
creatio ex nihilo, 146. *See also* Christianity; God; theology

d'Arezzo, Ristoro, 37n44
da Rosate, Ambrogio Varesi, 32. *See also* astrology
d'Ascoli, Cecco, 32–33; *Acerba* (1473) of, 44
Dati, Giuliano, *Del diluvio di Roma* (1496) of, 33
da Vinci, Leonardo, 23–24, 27–78, 31n18, 68n148, 149–50, 150n6, 165, 200, 242; Codex Arundel of, 149; Codex Atlanticus of, 40f; description of disaster by, 51–54, 65, 71n158, 72, 78; domesticating analogy in, 48–49; on the expression of emotions, 34n32; fantasy of flight in, 42; on fluid dynamics, 54–56; on geology, 62n129; on knowledge, 64–65; list of books of, 45n69; and Machiavelli, 68n148; materialism of, 28–29, 34, 65; microcosm-macrocosm analogy in, 45; on nature, 43n61, 54; notebooks of, 32, 45, 47, 50, 52n90, 53n91, 54, 59, 62, 242; on perpetual change, 61; perspectives of, 41, 65, 73, 242; riddles of, 30–39, 30n13, 34n35, 39n52, 41–43, 46–50; satire of, 33; study of laughter of, 34; vegetarianism of, 44; on water, 48
da Vinci, Leonardo, plates of: "A deluge" (pl. 1) of, 72; "A tempest" (pl. 2) of, 72; "A tempest" (pl. 3) of, 72; "A deluge" (pl. 4) of, 73; "A deluge" (pl. 5) of, 73. *See also* anatomy; art; prophecy; riddle; science
death, 110; Donne on, 103–4, 108–9; Epicureanism on, 77n173; of the father of Pio, 74; fear of, 2; in flood, 52, 66; Lucretius on, 143; Montaigne on, 105n80; of the mother of Pio, 75; of the teacher of Pio, 74; scene of, 76; world of, 97, 99
Dee, John, 90, 92, 93n42. *See also* astronomy
de Man, Paul, 231
Democritus, 15–17, 23, 45–46, 64, 97–99, 107, 115, 121, 124, 131, 153–55, 155n24, 169, 186, 203, 225; as a character in Alberti's dialogue, 46; laughter of, 45n67, 50, 51n86, 132; philosophy of, 137; pit/well of, 16–18, 64, 133, 149, 153, 154–55, 169, 182–83, 197, 217, 241; praise of, 156. *See also* atomism; materialism
De Quincey, Thomas, 210
Descartes, René, 182n109, 205; on astrology, 182; *Rules for the Direction of the Mind* (ca. 1628) of, 181–82
desire, faculty of, 192, 234–35
d'Holbach, Paul-Henri Thiry, 188n125
Diderot, Denis, 189–91; encyclopedia of, 190n132
Diehl, Huston, 145
Diels, Hermann, 15
Digges, Leonard, 89n30, 93n44, 96n50. *See also* Digges, Thomas
Digges, Thomas, 25, 80, 83n13, 81–98, 116, 177; the leap of imagination

of, 82–102, 199; *Alae* (1573) of, 82, 89, 95; *Perfit Description of the Cae-lestiall Orbes* (1576), of, 93–97, 140, 142nn76–77; on providence, 90; use of Melanchthon of, 83–92, 96, 98, 101. *See also* astrology; astronomy; Copernicus; infinity

Diogenes Laertius, 2n2, 3n7, 45n70, 64n137, 84n15

disaster, 13, 21, 28, 51–53, 69, 72, 75, 132, 207, 243; as an act of God, 152; before and after of, 214–20; environmental, 241; etymology of, 134–35; as an event of thought, 218; feeling of, 114; figure of, 78; force of, 59; idea of, 38–39, 239; of illness, 103; image of, 5, 58, 75, 80, 166, 221–22, 237, 239; iter-ability of, 206–7; local, 33; meta-phor of, 239; metaphysical, 187; meteorological, 52; natural, 130; Newtonian, 223; as a punishment from God, 41, 74; purgative func-tion of, 43n62; representation of, 215; scene of, 132; speculative, 1; of speech, 146; and the sublime, 192–235; vision of, 143. *See also* catastrophe; fire; flood; plague; storm; tragedy

disgust, 44. *See also* emotions

Dobin, Howard, 117n9

Donne, John, 25, 108n92, 111n103; catastrophic style of, 104; illness of, 113; imagination of, 80, 104; little earthquakes of, 102–13; ma-terialism of, 104, 113; melancholy of, 109; poetic freedom of, 111; use of atomistic imagery of, 107n85, 111–12

Donne, John, works of: *The Courtier's Library* (1604–11), 128; *Devotions*

upon Emergent Occasions (1624), 103, 107–8, 110, 113; "The First Anni-versary" (1611), 106; *Pseudo-martyr* (1610), 128n45; "A Valediction: Forbidding Mourning" (ca. 1611), 79–80, 111

Doyle, Charles, 112n106

Drake, Sir Francis, 172

Drake, Ellen T., 167n68, 173n86, 175n93, 180n106

drama, ancient, 10. *See also* comedy; tragedy

Drew, Daniel, 3n8, 109n94

Dürer, Albrecht, 72

Dyer, Edward, *The Prayse of Nothing* (1585) of, 135n58

earth, 85, 91, 97, 99, 140–42; age of the, 174; axial rotation of the, 184–85; history of the, 184, 187; interior spaces of the, 149, 166; variegated surface of the, 163–65. *See also* astronomy; geology; stars

earthquake, 12, 74, 81, 169–70, 172–73, 200, 214, 217n74; in antiquity, 4–5, 173; of the giant in Leonardo, 41–42; history of, 25, 74, 149, 176, 187; in Lisbon (1755), 20–21, 25, 193, 213–17, 215f, 216f, 218f, 219f, 233n117; and the microscope, 147–91; of the mind, 79–113; in San Francisco (1906), 41n56; of the "Valediction" of Donne, 79–80. *See also* catastrophe; disaster

Eisenstein, Sergei, 53–54; *Nonindif-ferent Nature: Film and the Structure of Things* (1948) of, 69–71; *The Film Sense* (1942) of, 51–52, 69

Eissler, K. R., 27n2

Ellis, Albert, 1n1

Elton, William, 132n51

emotions: excessive, 77–78; and feelings, 1, 13, 22, 50, 53, 73, 77, 114, 193n3. *See also* catastrophizing

Empedocles, 3n8, 155, 203

Empson, William, 111; "Donne the Space Man" of, 79–80

England, 117, 122, 173, 214. *See also* London

English Civil War, 169–70

Enterline, Lynn, 146

Epictetus, 1n1

Epicureans, 101, 104, 105n81, 125, 159, 182n109, 232; absurdities of the, 162; catastrophizing of the, 195–203, 228; impiety of the, 209; swerve of the, 196; theory of infinity of the, 174. *See also* atomism; Epicurus; Lucretius; materialism; philosophy

Epicurus, 1–12, 77, 85–92, 99, 121, 197, 203; materialism of, 12, 85–88, 112–13, 196; rejection of divination of, 84n15; wisdom compared to Delphic oracle of, 6. *See also* atomism; Epicureans; Lucretius; materialism; philosophy; pleasure

epistemology, 124; and the microscope, 149, 184–85; uncertainty in, 166. *See also* philosophy

Erasmus, 88, 132, 137n61; humanism of, 88. *See also* humanism

eschatology, 81, 91–92, 100. *See also* apocalypse; catastrophe; disaster; materialism

etymology, critique of, 131

Eustathius, 123. *See also* Homer

Evelyn, John, 150, 152, 152n12

experience: aesthetic, 223, 243; in empiricism, 21, 57–70, 80, 91–92, 100, 158, 179. *See also* sense perception; science

Farago, Claire, 66

Fenves, Peter, 6n13, 197, 200n27, 210n56

Ferrarin, Alfredo, 234

Ficino, Marsilio, 77n174, 109–10, 211; *Platonic Theology* (1482) of, 86–87. *See also* humanism; Neoplatonism; Plato

fire, of London (1666), 152, 167, 169, 214

flood, 33, 52, 56; Dürer's representation of, 72; global, 72; history of the, 188–89; Leonardo's representation of, 65–73; of Noah, 171, 206; prognostications of, 36, 46–47, 52. *See also* catastrophe; disaster; storm

Florence, 49n80. *See also* Italy

Fowler, Don, 112

France, 71, 125, 187, 216; Leonardo's time in, 58, 71

freedom, 13; idea of, 228–29; natural, 188

free will, 10. See also *clinamen* (swerve)

Freud, Sigmund, 59n120

Friedrich, Hugo, 105n80

Frischlin, Nicodemus, 81n7

Frye, Northrop, 138, 146

Galilei, Galileo, 95, 156n30. *See also* astronomy; science

Galluzzi, Paolo, 69

Gantner, Joseph, 27–28; *Leonardos Visionen* (1958) of, 27

Garrard, Greg, 237n3, 238

Gaurico, Luca, 30n10

Genischen, J. F., 220–21

geology, 62n129, 70, 149, 170, 187. *See also* earth

Ghosh, Amitav, 240–41

Giese, Johan Henricus, Tobacco box (lid embossed with scene showing Lisbon before and after earthquake of 1755), 219f

Gilbert, William, 99, 101. *See also* astronomy; mathematics

Glanvill, Joseph, 153–54; *The Vanity of Dogmatizing* (1661) of, 153n17, 154n19

God/gods: 28, 41, 67, 84, 85, 88–89, 91, 97, 152; and atomism, 112; desire to know, 208; Epicurean, 8–9; fear creates the, 73; hand of, 166; in the heavens, 81, 84; of Homer, 186, 191; idea of, 195; justice of, 5, 37, 42–43, 49; king of the, 81; knowledge of, 88–89; in Leonardo, 28, 41, 67, 72–73; men turn to the, 188; of nature, 89, 152–53; perspective of the, 186; and the poets, 38, 144–45, 199; preservation of, 110; providential order of, 90–91; at the resurrection, 111–12; secrets of the, 65, 155n27; Titans and Giants and, 5; violent challenge to the, 5; of wind, 72; works of, 21n62, 90–91, 94, 95n49, 96–97, 108, 139n70, 151n9, 152, 162–63, 166; wrath of, 52, 74. *See also* Christianity; justice; providence

Goddard, Harold C., 136n60

Goetschel, Willi, 213n68

Goldberg, Jonathan, 65n142

Goldstein, Amanda Jo, 3n8

Gombrich, E. H., 31, 39, 50

Googe, Barnaby, 96n52

Goulding, Robert, 90

Granada, Miguel A., 90

Greenblatt, Stephen, *The Swerve: How the World Became Modern* (2011) of, 2

Grendler, Paul, 50n83

Guibbory, Achsah, 113

Guyer, Paul, 232

Hall, Joseph, *Occasional Meditations* (1631) of, 165n64

Halley, Edmund, 87, 171n78

Hamacher, Werner, 20–21

Hamilton, John T., 67

Hampton, Timothy, 123n32

Harsnett, Samuel, 127; and Shakespeare, 127n41

Harvey, Gabriel, 96, 116, 117n8

Harvey, John, 117–18, 121, 129–32, 134. *See also* astrology

Harvey, Richard, 116–17. *See also* astrology

Heraclides of Pontus, 123. *See also* Homer

Heraclitus, 45, 124

Herschel, William, 221

Hillman, Brenda, 242n12

Hippocrates, 58

Hirsch, David A. Hedrich, 111, 112n108

history: and aesthetic consciousness, 234; of catastrophizing, 12, 148, 237, 241–43; of culture, 188; cycles of, 170, 174; of disasters, 170, 185; diversion of, 75n166; of earthquakes, 187; of the flood, 186; in fossils, 167–71, 175–76, 188; inner, 230; intellectual, 107; of inventions, 174; literary, 107; materialist, 9, 20; movement of, 106; narration of, 74; philosophical, 1, 21; of religion, 191; time and, 215

Homer: and ancient philosophy, 123; the *Iliad* of, 185–87; in a nutshell, 185–86; readers of, 118, 123; similes

Homer (*continued*)
of, 47n76, 186, 190; time before, 174
Hooke, Robert, 25, 53, 149, 159n40, 162–70, 179n103, 182n109, 183–89; "Ammonite fossils" (1705) of, 168f; childhood of, 167n68; on earthquakes, 167, 170, 172–73, 176, 180n105, 183, 187; on extinction, 173–74; on fossils, 167–71, 175–76, 178, 180, 184–87; on the history of scientific discovery, 175; *Micrographia* (1665) of, 159–60, 162, 166, 167n69, 171, 177, 179, 185n120; on science, 176–78, 187; on species of creatures, 174; and Steno, 180n105, 182n109; vibration theory of matter of, 159–60
Howard, Henry, 149–50
humanism, 73. *See also* Beroaldo, Filippo; Erasmus; Ficino, Marsilio; Pio, Giambattista
Hume, David, 201n29, 216–17; Democritus as an echo in, 217; *An Enquiry Concerning Human Understanding* (1748) of, 217n74; letters of, 217n74
hylozoism, 230

infinity, 98n61, 99–102, 113, 122, 199. *See also* astronomy; Bruno, Giordano; Digges, Thomas; Gilbert, William; mathematics
insects, 16, 36, 38, 156–58, 160n47, 162, 165, 199–200; riddles concerning, 39; sociable qualities of, 36n39, 37n42. *See also* atomism
interpretation, 20, 115, 118, 122–23, 126; strained, 126–27, 135–36, 146. See also *quidlibet ex quolibet*
irony, 37, 130, 204, 224, 233

Isidore of Seville, 7, 60, 64n137, 154n18
Italy, 74. *See also* Bologna; Florence; Milan; Venice

Jacobi, Friedrich Heinrich, 223
James of Venice, 119
James, William, 41n56
Jaspers, Karl, 54, 57
Jeanneret, Michel, 52
Jerome, Saint, 86n18, 111, 112n106
Johnson, Barbara, 139n68
Johnson, Christopher D., 14n42, 16n49
Johnson, Francis R., 95, 97
Jones, Matthew L., 14n38
Jorgensen, Paul A., 135n58
justice, 5, 49; of God, 42–43. *See also* God; providence

Kail, P. J. E., 217n73
Kant, Immanuel, 11, 21–23, 25, 194n6; *Anthropology from a Pragmatic Point of View* (1785) of, 21–22, 201, 208n52, 211, 226–27, 230, 235; catastrophes of, 192–235; catastrophizing in, 211–14, 217, 221–23, 227–28, 231; "Copernican revolution" of, 212; cosmogony of, 199, 223; *Critique of Pure Reason* (1781) of, 209, 228n103, 235; *Critique of the Power of Judgment* (1793) of, 192, 201, 228–29, 231–34; on dementia, 211; on Democritus, 202–3, 224–25; *Dreams of a Spirit Seer* (1766) of, 224; on earthquakes, 220, 233n117; on Eastern philosophy, 210; "The End of All Things" (1794) of, 210; Epicureanism and, 196–98, 200; on genius, 201–2; hypochondria of, 226–27; on the imagination,

213–14, 222, 226–27, 230, 233n117; Lucretius and, 195–96, 199, 211, 228; on materialism, 196–97; on melancholy, 226–27; *Metaphysical Foundations of Natural Science* (1786) of, 225n89, 231n108; on metaphysics, 230–31; on Newton, 197–98; notebook reflections of, 235n124; *The Only Possible Argument for the Existence of God* (1763) of, 229, 231; phoenix of nature in, 207, 222; "On the Power of the Mind to Master Its Morbid Feelings by Sheer Resolution" of, 225; on *Schwärmerei*, 223–24, 227; on the sublime, 193–214, 218, 220–34, 228–30, 230n107, 232–33; *Universal Natural History* (1755) of, 193–200, 202–14, 220–34, 227–29, 231; use of Pope of, 227–28

Keller, Catherine, 4n9, 236n2
Kemp, Martin, 53, 60
Kepler, Johannes, 100–102
Kircher, Athanasius, 150–52; *Mundus subterraneus* (1665) of, 150, 151f, 152n10, 172; poem of, 152; *The Vulcano's, Or, Burning and Fire-Vomiting Mountains* (1669) of, 151–52
Kitchin, G. W., 156n30
Kleist, Heinrich von, 20–21
Koyré, Alexandre, 97

Lactantius, 7–8, 99, 153n17
Lamberton, Robert D., 186
Landau, Aaron, 135
Lange, Friedrich Albert, 3n6
Laplace, Pierre-Simon, *Traité de mécanique céleste* (1798–1825) of, 203n36
Larkey, Sanford V., 95
Lascaris, Janus, 58

laughter: of Democritus, 46, 50, 131–32; nervous, 51; study by Leonardo of, 34. *See also* comedy; satire
Le Bas, Jacques Philippe: "Basilica de Santa Maria. Ruins of Lisbon as Appeared Immediately After the Earthquake and Fire of the 1st November 1755" of, 216f
Leibniz, Gottfried Wilhelm, 193, 230n108
Leeuwenhoek, Anton van, 159n40
Lomazzo, Giovanni Paolo, 34
London, 122n27, 164, 170, 180n106, 206. *See also* England
Longinus, 22
Lorenz, Philip, 140n71
Lovejoy, Arthur, 3n8
Lucian, 36n39
Lucretius, 1–16, 2n4, 48–49, 60, 74–77, 98, 105n83, 110, 121, 157–58, 175n93, 196–97, 202–4; *De rerum natura* of, 11, 12n34, 45n66, 56–62, 66, 87, 105, 125, 142–43, 179n103, 197, 200n26, 208, 211, 227–28; as the favorite poet of Kant, 195–96, 199, 211, 227; the life of, 86n18; the madness of, 86–87; melancholy of, 77, 86–87; volcanic eruptions in, 75–76. *See also* analogy; atomism; Epicureans; Epicurus
Lupton, Julia Reinhard, 139
Lyotard, Jean-François, 193

Machiavelli, Niccolò, 30, 43n62, 68; Leonardo and, 68n148
Maestlin, Michael, 81n7; 84. *See also* astrology; astronomy
Makkreel, Rudolf, 233n119
Martin, L. C., 115

Masini, Tommaso di Giovanni (Zoroastro), 32

materialism, 1–6, 9–12, 18–20, 23, 28–29, 69, 75–77, 81, 91, 96–100, 102–5, 119, 133–34, 166, 178, 195–99, 230, 237, 243; ancient, 15, 67, 163n55, 196, 210; anxieties about, 166; the Boyle-Descartes version of, 158–59; catastrophic, 4–12, 18, 21–25, 51, 80–81, 100, 107, 116, 149, 193, 199, 204, 211, 220, 234–35; disasters of, 23, 143, 220; in early modernity, 3; encounter of Kant with, 193–214; Epicurean, 12, 85–88, 113, 196; eschatology of, 2; history of, 3n6, 5, 9, 12, 191; metaphysics of, 225; in the Middle Ages, 57n112. *See also* analogy; Anaxagoras; atomism; catastrophe; Democritus; Epicurus; Lucretius; sense perception

mathematics, 83–84, 92, 197–98. *See also* astrology; astronomy; science

McKibben, Bill, 238

medicine: ancient, 16n47; art of, 86; Hippocratic, 58. *See also* science

Meek, Richard, 129n47

Meinel, Christoph, 158

melancholy: of Donne, 109; of Kant, 227–28; of Lucretius, 77, 86–87

Melanchthon, Philipp, 80, 83–92, 88n25, 89n28, 98, 101, 197; on astrology, 84, 132; ideas of providence of, 84–85, 88–91; Neoplatonism of, 87n21; response to Epicureanism of, 80, 84n16, 85–87, 91, 195; on Terence, 88; writings of, 96. *See also* astrology; Digges, Thomas; materialism; Reformation

Mendelssohn, Moses, 225

metaphysics, 50, 95; delusions of, 225; desire for, 93; Kant on, 230–31; of materialism, 225. *See also* philosophy

meteorology, Renaissance, 21

Methuen, Charlotte, 90

Metrodorus, 121

microscope, 14, 160, 186–88, 231; analogies and the, 164; the early days of the, 156–61, 167; the earthquake and the, 147–91; epistemology and the, 185; future of the, 163; ideal, 162. *See also* optics; science; sense perception

Milan, 32, 45, 49n80; astrology in, 32n23. *See also* Italy

Millar, Andrew, 217n74

Mirandola, Giovanni Pico della, 84. *See also* astrology; philosophy

Moffitt, John F., 56

Montaigne, Michel de: "Apology for Raymond Seybond" of, 122–25; on atoms, 105–6, 136, 174; "Of Diversion" of, 104–5; on epistemology, 124–25; "Of Experience" of, 137n61; habits of mind of, 122, 123n32, 242; on "Hoc est corpus meum," 125–26; on Homer, 123; on interpretation, 122–24; kidney stone of, 104–5; on materialism, 105, 174; "Of Prognostications" of, 122n28; response to Epicureanism of, 105n81, 125

More, Henry, 98n61, 121

Morton, Timothy, 237–39; *Hyperobjects* of, 239

Museum of Jurassic Technology, 147, 150n8

mythology, 4; of Daedalus, 42; of the Giants, 4–5; of the Titans, 4

Nashe, Thomas, 117n8
nature, 69, 71; book of, 161, 184;
extreme, 238; ideas of, 221–22;
images of, 221–22; impersonal,
41–42; infinite causes of, 59; laws
of, 194, 222; principles of, 194;
slow processes of, 173n87; spectacles of, 221–22; violence of, 207,
221–22. *See also* universe
Neoplatonism, 87n21, 94; Christian,
95n49. *See also* Ficino, Marsilio;
philosophy; Plato
Newton, Isaac, 193–99, 200–208,
230; laws of, 196–98, 200, 203,
207; mechanics of, 196–99; *Principia Mathematica* (1687) of, 201
Niccoli, Ottavia, 33
Nicholas of Cusa, 95n49, 98. *See also*
infinity; mathematics; philosophy
Nicolson, Marjorie Hope, 163n53
Nifo, Agostino, 30
Nightingale, Andrea, 2
Nixon, Mark, 114n2
Nova, Alessandro, 72

Oldenburg, Henry, 180n105
Oldroyd, David, 176
ontology, 20, 122; language of, 116;
question of, 131. *See also* metaphysics; philosophy
optics: devices of, 186. *See also*
microscope; science; telescope
Ovid, 52, 61, 146n89, 203; Leonardo's
interest in, 45n65, 52, 61; *Metamorphoses* of, 45n65, 146n89

Palingenius (Pier Angelo Manzolli),
The Zodiake of Life (1536) of, 96–
98
Paracelsus, 20n58
Parcell, William C., 151n9

Parker, Samuel, 121n25, 177–78
Pascal, Blaise, 13–17, 21, 111, 186–87,
230, 230n107
Passannante, Gerard, *The Lucretian
Renaissance* (2011) of, 3n8, 23
Paul, Saint, 111, 145–46. *See also*
Christianity
Pedretti, Carlo, 39n54, 45n68, 53,
55n102, 71
perspective, 41, 51, 73; anthropomorphic, 73. *See also* relativism;
representation
philosophy, 182; ancient, 25, 46,
123n33, 156; dogmatism in, 16, 122;
of Epicureanism, 104; experience
of, 22; history of, 21; materialist,
1–4, 121, 175–76; mechanical, 177–
78; natural, 154–55, 161, 163; peace
of mind as a benefit of, 2; pre-
Socratic, 45, 65; reinvention of,
83; and science, 237; speculations
of, 177. *See also* Albertus Magnus;
Anaxagoras; Aristotle; atomism;
Augustine; Cavendish, Margaret;
Democritus; Epicurus; free will;
hermeneutics; Kant, Immanuel;
Lucretius; materialism; metaphysics; ontology; Pascal, Blaise;
perspective; Plato; relativism;
scholasticism; Seneca; skepticism;
theology
physicotheology, 229–30
Picciotto, Joanna, 169n72
Pio, Giambattista, 29, 73–78; edition
of *De rerum natura* (1511) of, 74–78;
humanism of, 29, 73–78. *See also*
humanism
plague, 32, 44, 58, 66–67. *See also* disaster; catastrophe
Plato, 5, 83–84, 151n9, 202; account
of Atlantis of, 173–74; the *Phaedo*

Plato (*continued*)
of, 119n18; the *Republic* of, 9; the
Theaetetus of, 110. *See also* Ficino,
Marsilio; Neoplatonism
Platonism. *See* Neoplatonism
Pliny, *Natural History* of, 185, 188
Plutarch, 115, 123
Poe, Edgar Allan, "Ligeia" (1838) of,
133–34
poetry, 6, 38, 61, 67, 144, 152, 199,
201; of atoms, 158; encyclopedic,
96; historical context of, 79; of
Homer, 186; humorous, 45n69;
and madness, 86, 212; as a narcotic, 212; task of, 228
Poole, William, 174n88
Pope, Alexander, 199; *Essay on Man*
(1733/34) of, 228; German translation of, 228n102
Porter, James I., 17–18, 64n134,
143n79, 231; *The Sublime in Antiquity* (2015) of, 22, 239n8
Power, Henry: *Experimental Philosophy* (1663) of, 156–59, 165, 178–80;
poem on the microscope of, 157
Premuda, Loris, 48n80
prognostication: astrology and,
82; of astrologers, 29–30, 33; of
Digges, 81–102; figure of, 141; of
Leonardo, 30–51, 30n13, 34n35,
39n52; Nifo on, 30. *See also* astrology; Harvey, John; Harvey,
Richard; prophecy
prophecy, 6, 10, 29–51, 117n9, 146;
ambivalence of, 51; on bees, 44;
in the collapse of the present and
future, 73; doomsday, 36, 46, 100;
horror of, 48, 51–52; language of,
92; visual equivalent of, 73. *See
also* apocalypse; astrology; catas-

trophe; disaster; prognostication;
riddle
Protestantism. *See* Reformation
providence, 5, 84, 89–91, 152–53,
161–62, 170. *See also* Christianity;
God; justice
pseudo-Hippocrates, *On Breaths* of,
58
psychology, 1n1
Ptolemy, 94, 142, 142nn76–77. *See
also* astronomy; mathematics
punishment, 43
Purchas, Samuel, 172
Puttenham, George, 144–45
Pye, Christopher, 140n71
Pythagoreans, 83, 95n49, 101. *See also*
mathematics; philosophy

quidlibet ex quolibet, 116–29, 132–33,
135, 138, 141, 144, 146. *See also*
interpretation

Rabelais, François, 119n15, 123
Ray, Gene, 233n117
Reformation, 18, 30
relativism, 5–6; catastrophic, 51; perspectival, 41, 173; in poetry, 38;
temporal, 173. *See also* perspective;
philosophy
religion: fanaticism in, 223–24; wars
of, 126. *See also* theology
representation, 73; of the imagination in Kant, 192, 208; pictorial,
52. *See also* perspective
riddle, 31, 33–38, 41–44, 50–51;
laughter of the, 45; perspective
and the, 46, 49. *See also* comedy;
da Vinci, Leonardo; prophecy;
satire; science
Robertson, Kellie, 57n112

Roth, Johann Michael, "Lisbon
 before and after" (1756), 218f
Rousseau, Jean-Jacques, 189
Royal Society, 149–50, 153, 155n25,
 167, 171; collaboration in the,
 167n67; experiments of the, 156;
 lecture before the, 184, 188–89.
 See also science
Rugoff, Ralph, 147–48

Sacrobosco, Johannes de: *De sphaera*
 (ca. 1230), 88. *See also* astrology;
 astronomy; Melanchthon,
 Philipp
Sadrin, Paul, 190n132
Sandaldjian, Hagop, 147–48; "Eternal Symbol (Mount Ararat)" (ca.
 1986) of, 148f. *See also* Museum of
 Jurassic Technology
satire, 13, 30, 39; humanist, 36;
 prophetic, 33. *See also* comedy;
 prophecy; riddle
Scala, Bartolomeo, 77n173. *See also*
 humanism
Schenk, Gerrit Jasper, 10n27, 88n25
scholasticism, 50, 116; alternative to,
 155, 160; parody of, 50; tradition
 of, 120. *See also* philosophy
Schönfeld, Martin, 207n47, 220n75
Schrijvers, P. H., 8n21, 227n101
Schultz, Alexander M., 227n100
Schumacher, Joachim, 27
Schwärmerei, 223–24, 227
science, 6, 18, 25, 92, 95, 154–60,
 159n41; earth, 173; of flight, 55; inquiry of, 149; modern, 155; new,
 81; philosophy and, 237; revolution of, 149; of wind, 54–55. *See
 also* anatomy; astronomy; experience; geology; mathematics;

medicine; meteorology; optics;
 technology
Sedgwick, Eve Kosofsky, 104
Seneca, 1n1, 48–49, 65, 152n13,
 172n80; *Natural Questions* of,
 48n80, 59, 152n10, 155n27
sense perception, 3, 15; experience
 of, 51; knowledge from, 159; ladder of, 55, 57; limits of, 9, 157, 162,
 166; skepticism about, 9; threshold of, 162, 223, 241; uncertainty
 of what is beneath, 59. *See also* experience; materialism; microscope
Serres, Michel, 10n28
Servius Grammaticus, 38
Sextus Empiricus, 15n46, 17n53, 124.
 See also skepticism
Sforza, Ludovico, 53
Shakespeare, William, 114–46; astrology in, 130; nothing in, 126–
 33, 135n58, 137–38, 140; readings
 of, 25; tragedies of, 19–20, 114,
 144
Shakespeare, William, characters
 in the plays of: Desdemona, 128;
 Edgar, 128–29, 132–33; Edmund,
 128–32; Gloucester, 128–30; Hermione, 135, 140n71, 145–46; Iago,
 127–28; Lear, 132–33, 138; Leontes,
 134–41, 143, 145–46; Mamillius,
 136; Othello, 127–28, 134, 138, 143–
 44; Paulina, 138n64, 145–46
Shakespeare, William, plays of: *King
 Lear*, 114n2, 115n3, 127–33; *A Midsummer Night's Dream*, 145; *Much
 Ado About Nothing*, 127; *Othello*,
 127–28, 134; *Twelfth Night, or What
 You Will*, 127; *The Winter's Tale*,
 134, 138–41, 145
Shea, William, 200–201

Shell, Susan Meld, 205

Sibyl (Cumaean), leaves of the, 122, 128

Simon, David Carroll, 12n35, 45n67, 51n86

sin, 43; disaster as a punishment for, 43

skepticism, 2n5, 9, 18–20, 20n59, 74, 81, 136, 143–44, 154n18; abyss of, 17, 197; of Bacon, 155; of Democritus, 16–18, 124, 153–54, 197; of Diderot, 190; radical, 154

Solomon, 36

Somaini, Antonio, 70n153

space, time and, 204, 207, 241

Spanish Armada, 117. *See also* prophecy

Spenser, Edmund, 116n6

Spinoza, Baruch, 210, 223

Sprat, Thomas, *History of the Royal Society* (1667) of, 155–56

stars, 81–82, 84, 92–98, 93n42, 116, 130; the earth as one of the, 85, 99–100; ill, 81, 100; influence of the, 129; the mystery of the, 87; new, 90, 96–97, 102, 106; over-reading the, 134; scattering of, 90, 93; science of the, 89; sphere of the, 93–94. *See also* astrology; astronomy

Statius, 203

Steno, Nicolas, 180–83; Catholicism of, 183; on Democritus, 182–83; on fossils, 180–82

Stewart, Alan, 129n47

Stoics, 136–37

storm, 51–53, 56; damage in Genoa by a, 53; and earthquake, 20n58; experience of Lear of a, 132–33; experience of Leonardo of a, 41, 53, 71; as an image of material-ism, 28–78; navigation of birds in a, 56n106; representation in Leonardo of a, 51–73; representation in Lucretius of a, 74–78; violence of a, 53, 71. *See also* catastrophe; disaster; nature

Stowell, Steven F. H., 29

sublime, 22, 25; in art, 201n31; disaster and the, 192–235; Kant on the, 220–23, 222n81, 228–29, 231n107, 232–33

Swedenborg, Immanuel, 224, 224n88, 227; fanaticism of, 224

Targoff, Ramie, 104

technology: in the domination of the earth, 44; of flight, 42n58; of vision, 18, 159, 166, 169. *See also* science

telescope, 163, 186, 188. *See also* optics; science

Terence, commentary on, 88. *See also* catastrophe; Melanchthon, Philipp

theater, 145; creative potential of the, 146; Protestant, 145n87

theology, 120, 126. *See also* philosophy; religion

Thorndike, Lynn, 81n6

Tiffany, Daniel, 5n12, 35n35

time, 6, 47, 183, 185–86, 188–89; bending of, 173; and history, 214; indefinite, 174; point in, 198; progress of, 185; and space, 204, 207, 241

tragedy, 36. *See also* catastrophe; disaster; drama

Tredwell, Katherine A., 89

universe: destruction of the, 204; infinite, 2n5, 25, 80, 96, 140, 142,

207–8; justice of the, 43; man is like the, 107; materialist vision of the, 112, 186; Newtonian, 197, 208; orderliness of the, 90; psychic, 127; space of the, 49, 51, 75–77; spiritualist, 224n88; structure of the, 25, 99, 204. *See also* nature

Valéry, Paul, 24, 47, 57, 65n138
Van Hulle, Dirk, 114n2
Vasari, Giorgio, 28
Vecce, Carlo, 33, 44n63
Venice, 49n80. *See also* Italy
Verrocchio, Andrea del, 36
Virgil, 35, 37–38, 52, 123; readers of, 118
Visconti, Gasparo, 45
volcano, 151–53
von Knobloch, Charlotte, 224

Wackenfels, Johannes Matthias Wacker von, 101n67
Wallis, John, 171n78, 183–85

Walton, Izaak, 103. *See also* Donne, John
war, 44. *See also* catastrophe; disaster; English Civil War; religion
Warburg, Aby, 55n102, 70n153
Webster, Charles, 170
Weemes, John, 121
Westman, Robert, 82n7, 83n11, 93n44, 101n67
Whiston, William, 205–6
Wilkins, John, 161, 170
Wilkinson, L. P., 38–39
William of Heytesbury, *Regulae solvendi sophismata* (1481) of, 50n83
Wilson, Catherine, 158, 160, 196n15
Wimsatt, W. K., 79–80
Wind, Edgar, 71
Windsor Castle, 27
Woodward, John, 171n79
Wright, Thomas, *An Original Theory or New Hypothesis of the Universe* (1750) of, 194–95, 204, 207

zoology, 36. *See also* animals; science